Theodore Roosevelt Abroad

Previous Books by J. Lee Thompson

A Wider Patriotism: Alfred Milner and the British Empire (2007)

Forgotten Patriot: A Life of Alfred, Viscount Milner of St James' and Cape Town (2006)

Northcliffe: Press Baron in Politics, 1865–1922 (2000)

Politicians, the Press and Propaganda: Lord Northcliffe and the Great War, 1914–1919 (1999)

THEODORE ROOSEVELT ABROAD

NATURE, EMPIRE, AND THE JOURNEY OF AN AMERICAN PRESIDENT

J. LEE THOMPSON

THEODORE ROOSEVELT ABROAD
Copyright © J. Lee Thompson, 2010.

First published in 2010 by
PALGRAVE MACMILLAN®
in the United States—a division of St. Martin's Press LLC,
175 Fifth Avenue, New York, NY 10010.

Where this book is distributed in the UK, Europe and the rest of the world,
this is by Palgrave Macmillan, a division of Macmillan Publishers Limited,
registered in England, company number 785998, of Houndmills, Basingstoke,
Hampshire RG21 6XS.

Palgrave Macmillan is the global academic imprint of the above companies
and has companies and representatives throughout the world.

Palgrave® and Macmillan® are registered trademarks in the United States,
the United Kingdom, Europe and other countries.

ISBN: 978–0–230–10277–4

Library of Congress Cataloging-in-Publication Data

Thompson, J. Lee, 1951–
    Theodore Roosevelt abroad : nature, empire, and the journey of an
American president / by J. Lee Thompson.
        p. cm.
    Includes bibliographical references and index.
    ISBN 0–230–10277–8 (alk. paper)
    1. Roosevelt, Theodore, 1858–1919—Travel—Africa. 2. Roosevelt,
Theodore, 1858–1919—Travel—Europe. 3. Africa—Description and travel.
4. Europe—Description and travel. 5. Roosevelt, Theodore, 1858–1919—
Political and social views. 6. Nature conservation—Africa—History—20th
century. 7. Imperialism—History—20th century. 8. United States—Foreign
relations—1909–1913. 9. United States—Politics and government—
1909–1913. 10. Ex-presidents—United States—Biography. I. Title.
E757.T47 2010
973.91′1092—dc22   2009039961

A catalogue record of the book is available from the British Library.

Design by Newgen Imaging Systems (P) Ltd., Chennai, India.

First edition: April 2010

D 10 9 8 7 6 5 4 3 2

Printed in the United States of America.

To Raymond Ulrich

Contents

Preface and Acknowledgments

A century ago, the journalist John Callan O'Laughlin published *From the Jungle through Europe with Roosevelt* (1910). Outside TR's own *African Game Trails* that same year O'Laughlin's work has until now remained the only other separate book-length study to seriously chronicle even part of Roosevelt's fifteen-month post-presidential odyssey.[1] The reasons for this neglect are many. First, hunting has not been a popular subject for contemporary historians, who also have been in the main loath to admit the key role played by gentlemen hunters such as Roosevelt in the founding and preservation of the American conservation movement.[2] In such natural pursuits TR had a long history, back to his boyhood studies of birds and other wildlife in New York, further stimulated at Harvard and in his brief, yet formative, "Cowboy" period in the Dakotas.

The most dynamic president the United States has ever had, TR was also the first, and sadly only, environmentalist head of state. Roosevelt's most lasting domestic legacy as president came in the conservation of vast tracts of wilderness for the future use and enjoyment of the nation. When he left the presidency in 1909, TR was well aware that many African species were already endangered, and he was careful to mount what was considered at the time a cutting-edge scientific safari. Stories of bloody Rooseveltian carnage have abounded ever since, yet out of hundreds of African big game trophies, the number taken for his personal collection was tiny, with almost all of the specimens going to the Smithsonian and other collections, where they are still studied by scientists today.

Another reason TR's tour has been given relatively little attention is simply that it represents a calm between the relative storms of his preceding presidency and the soon to follow 1912 Bull Moose campaign. Roosevelt attempted to leave politics behind in 1909, and wanted to allow his anointed successor and friend William Howard Taft to plow his own furrow. However, even in Africa, he could not escape the fight that soon developed at home between President Taft, who had promised to carry on the "Roosevelt policies" unchanged, and a band of insurgent Republicans who picked up TR's fallen progressive banner. This work argues that the impetus to make the 1912 Bull Moose fight against Taft, which for all practical purposes handed the presidency to Woodrow Wilson, was firmly established before Roosevelt ever returned to America's shores in June 1910.

Another theme in the following has to do with Roosevelt's post-expansionist imperialism, or as he would have preferred to call it, "Democratic Nationalism." The great majority of his 1909–1910 journey was spent in Britain's African Empire, and then ended in its seat, London. This affords an opportunity for a comparative glimpse of American and British imperialism as it was in the period just before World War I. As president, Roosevelt charted a new imperial and great power course for America. He also believed deeply in the destiny of what he called the English-Speaking peoples as a positive and civilizing force in the world. He both laid the foundation and solidified Anglo-American amity in a threatening new century.

The final major thread followed in this book is the little noticed peace mission Roosevelt carried out in Europe in 1910, in speeches and unofficial diplomacy, most importantly with his doppelganger Wilhelm II, Emperor of the "quasi-autocratic" German Empire.[3] Both men practiced a personal brand of diplomacy and interacted with each other through crises in Venezuela, Morocco, and the Far East, before they ever met in 1910. TR was famous for his foreign policy creed, borrowed from a West African proverb: "Speak softly and carry a big stick; you will go far." Wilhelm's motto might have been: "Speak loudly; and you will scare ancient enemies into each other's arms"— for this is exactly what he did with England, France, and Russia in the years before World War I. Wilhelm and his brethren in Europe fully expected that Roosevelt would once again be president of the United States, as did he in his heart of hearts, whatever protestations he made at the time.

The following work reveals Roosevelt's post-presidential journey largely through his words, in his letters and speeches, which remain eloquent and compelling today, and in the words of those who wrote to and about him, without overwhelming authorial prodding and comment. Luckily for the historian and biographer, TR carried on an immense private and public correspondence. The great majority of Roosevelt's papers and diaries are in two locations: the Manuscript Division of the Library of Congress, Washington, and The Theodore Roosevelt Collection at the Houghton Library, Harvard. In addition to these, research for this work was undertaken at the Smithsonian Institution Archives; the Smithsonian Institution National Museum of Natural History; the Parliamentary Archives, London; The Courtauld Institute, London; the Churchill Archives Centre, Churchill College, Cambridge; and the Cambridge University Library. In addition to the various Roosevelt collections, the papers of numerous contemporaries were also consulted for this work, which has been based, in part, on evidence not previously published.

*   *   *

I must express my thanks to the following individuals and institutions who made materials available to me, gave assistance or permissions without which this study could not have been completed: Mr. Wallace Finley Dailey, Theodore Roosevelt Collection, Houghton Library, Harvard University; Jennifer Brathovde, The Library of Congress, Manuscripts Division; The Smithsonian Institution Archives; Dr. Hans-Dieter Sues, Associate Director for Research and Collections, Linda Gordon, James Dean, Smithsonian Institution National Museum of Natural History; The Clerk of the Records of the Parliamentary Archives, on behalf of the Beaverbrook Foundation; The Churchill Archives Centre, Churchill College, Cambridge; The British Library Board; The Courtauld Institute of Art; The National Army Museum; Fauna and Flora International; and the Syndics of the Cambridge University Library. If I have unwittingly infringed on the copyright of any persons or institutions, I hope they will accept my sincerest apologies and notify me of the oversight. This work was supported by a Lamar University Research Enhancement Grant and much of the research was carried out while I was a Visiting Fellow at Wolfson College, Cambridge University.

In addition I wish to thank professors R. J. Q. Adams, Thomas Kennedy, and William Lubenow, and Dr. Hans-Dieter Sues, who read all or parts of the manuscript and whose gentle and insightful comments have greatly enriched the work. Thanks are also due to my research assistant, Tom Caraway. Special appreciation once again goes to my wife Diane, who has with good humor for many years shared her husband with various historical figures. Finally, I wish to dedicate this book to Diane's father Raymond Ulrich, both for his role in providing such an exemplary wife, and for his own example of a life well-lived and full.

Prologue

The fog lifted at New York harbor on the morning of June 18, 1910, to reveal beautiful summer weather, just in time to grace the arrival of the S.S. *Kaiserin Auguste Victoria* on which Theodore Roosevelt returned from a fifteen-month post-presidential odyssey that an enraptured American public had followed as though it were a serial story. Pandemonium reigned on land and sea and "such a shout went up from the shore as to waken the stones" when TR showed himself on the bridge of the revenue cutter ferrying him to the pier. It was the welcome home of a conquering hero rather than a private citizen in a frock coat. The impresario Flo Ziegfield cabled for a "line to the people" for his annual review set to include "within the limits of a stage spectacle" Roosevelt's triumphant return, recreating the scene of mounted Rough Riders, West Point Cadets, and other celebrities on hand to acclaim the near-legendary world traveler. After being greeted by Mayor Gaynor, and making a brief speech at the Battery, TR received "one continuous heartfelt ovation" from the hundreds of thousands who crowded the red, white and blue decorated streets to gain a view of their "Teddy" in his carriage as he rode up Broadway and Fifth Avenue.[1]

Roosevelt's great adventure in Africa fulfilled a long-held dream for the hunter-naturalist aspect of his multifaceted character. However, besides big game rifles, TR also brought along his "bully pulpit" and accompanying ideals. While he shot lion and elephant and rhino through their East African possessions, Roosevelt could not refrain from also lecturing Britain's Liberal government on the proper methods of keeping up their lion's share of the "White Man's Burden" of Empire, returning the sentiment his friend Rudyard Kipling had urged on America a decade before during the Spanish-American War.[2]

Once his safari was done, TR extended his preachments to Europe in pursuit of another dream—world peace. Andrew Carnegie, whose peace ambassador Roosevelt became abroad, in particular with the

German Kaiser, gushed that never was there "such a chance for mortal man to immortalize himself," as was now available to the former president. Writing from Skibo Castle in Scotland, the world's richest man went on, "You have only to approach Britain with the League of Peace idea to be welcomed." No party in England could afford to reject "such an invitation as you will now be able to give them, with the American people behind you." After TR's meeting with Kaiser Wilhelm, if he did no more than to reveal to the world that Germany was "responsible for the present unbearable position. Much will have been gained." What pleased Carnegie was that "our country is now leader in the movement to abolish war as a means of settling disputes." He dreaded TR's "descent into party politics as inevitably lowering the position you have now attained." Smaller men, in his opinion, could "fight political questions."[3]

The major "political question" on practically everyone's mind that June was the attitude Roosevelt would take toward his chosen successor, William Howard Taft. Theodore had gone abroad in part so that his friend Will could chart his own presidential course without the appearance of interference. Everyone assumed, and Taft declared, that he would continue TR's policies. In this they all, Roosevelt first, were wrong. The African trip was a tonic for him, but leaving Taft to his own devices in the wilds of Washington proved a huge error with devastating political results including an acrimonious split between the two that fatally divided the party and led directly to the election of Woodrow Wilson and eight years of Democratic rule.

At the heart of the problems between the two old friends, one who felt betrayed and one who felt abandoned, was the course Taft pursued in conservation policy culminating in the firing of TR's man Gifford Pinchot from his post as Chief Forester of the United States. Not long after Roosevelt's return, Pinchot confided to him, "you and I agree about Taft. We both realize his weakness, his disloyalty to you, and his incapacity to understand or to lead the people." He went on "you are progressive—Taft is not, and never had been or will be except under orders." The country was as progressive as TR and, in Pinchot's estimation, "wholly irrespective of whether you are to be President again or not, it wants you to lead it where in any event it is bound to go." Renominating Taft would give the special interests control of the Republican party and "check the forward movement" which was the "central result of your work." Taft had deceived them all once. That was his fault. If he did it again it would be their fault. And if he should be renominated and elected, "what else can we expect?"[4]

So what follows is a tale of daring adventure, of international celebrity and, sadly, of friendship lost and political legacy transformed. But there is also a more private story of true love and family devotion—the love of Theodore and Edith Roosevelt, and the deep bonds of affection TR held for his children, particularly his son Kermit who came along on the safari. All these remarkable and fascinating aspects are revealed in the following account of Theodore Roosevelt's 1909–1910 journey—a story almost as multi-faceted as TR's own personality. And one never before as fully told.

Chapter 1

The Old Lion Departs

On March 1, 1909, three days before he passed along the presidency, and with it the safekeeping of his progressive policies, to his friend Will Taft, Theodore Roosevelt held a first and last luncheon at the White House for his loose "tennis cabinet" of friends and advisors. At this affair the core of Washington insiders who had actually done battle with TR on the dirt White House court were intermixed with honorary members—western wolf-hunters, "two-gun" men, and others who came to the capital for the occasion. So that the various elements would get to know one another the thirty-one men were seated irrespective of precedence and rank. The press had made a good deal of fun of this group of presidential "playmates" but had never known just how extensive it was or how important a role it held in the administrations. Roosevelt meant the gathering to be his only official recognition of their contributions.

Those present were, among the Washington tennis players, James Rudolph Garfield, son of the twentieth president, secretary of the interior and considered the leader of the group; Gifford Pinchot, the patrician Chief Forester of the United States; Jean Jules Jusserand, the dapper ambassador of France; and TR's close advisor Elihu Root, until recently secretary of state. The honorary members from the West and elsewhere included Luther "Yellowstone" Kelly, who Roosevelt had first met on the Little Missouri River and was now an Indian Agent in Arizona, the wolf-hunter "Catch 'Em Alive Jack" Abernathy, and the Dakotas Marshal Seth Bullock of Deadwood fame, who TR had known since the 1880s "cowboy" years. The president's military aide,

Captain Archie Butt, himself a member of the company, was frankly amazed by the contrasting crew of wolf catchers, fox hunters, and one or two men who had been arrested some time in the past for holding up trains.[1]

Near the end of the luncheon, when TR rose and called the meeting to order, the clatter of knives and forks promptly stopped. The President surveyed the men in the room and then delivered what amounted to a funeral oration for his administration, while praising each man in turn. He paid particularly glowing tributes to Garfield and Jusserand. The first, who was soon to be replaced at the interior department in the new administration, Roosevelt called "one of the most useful Cabinet members who ever sat at the Cabinet table." The president noted that Garfield, who was not a wealthy man, symbolized those who would leave government with him. He had answered TR's call seven years before to join the administration as a civil service commissioner. When the Bureau of Corporations was created in 1903 to combat big business combinations, Roosevelt had entrusted Garfield to head it, and then three years later he had taken over the Interior Department and, with Gifford Pinchot, led the fight for conservation. All of this was done at great personal sacrifice to Garfield's promising legal career. Turning to the diminutive, bearded Jusserand, his ally in heading off the threatening Moroccan crisis between France and Germany four years before, TR declared that there had never been such a relationship between an ambassador and a president, "they were friends and playmates—and the help, the courage which the ambassador had imparted to him at times could not be estimated."[2] Uncharacteristically, the loquacious little Frenchman, the acknowledged "vice-president" of the group, was unable to find the words to reply.

Marshal Bullock had been chosen to make a speech for the company and to present a bronze mountain lion to the president. He, however, was unable to say a word and instead began to tear away at the floral centerpiece on the table in front of him that hid the statue. Once it was uncovered, still speechless, he simply gestured at the lion. At this point Henry Stimson, the U.S. district attorney for the Southern District of New York and future secretary of state, rose and told the president that Bullock's inability to express his feelings was shared by all, that "no one loving a father could express that love he felt" and that the president, had "glorified each one by his friendship to that point when each man had been reborn in matters of principle, in character, and in mind." Pinchot then arranged for a Forest Service photographer to take a group portrait on the White House lawn.[3]

The lion was a particularly appropriate gift for Roosevelt, who departed three weeks later for an African safari, meant to be a final great adventure before he became too old for such things. In this endeavor one of the prime objectives was to stalk the much larger and dangerous African cousins of the American cougar. When asked by Beekman Winthrop, the assistant secretary of the treasury and a descendant of the first governor of Massachusetts, what he thought was the most dangerous animal he would face, Roosevelt did not hesitate to name the African lion. Other big game hunters feared the elephant and tiger, and the hippo, but from what TR had heard the lion was far more dangerous because it was the quickest and showed the most "alertness and agility."[4] It was a perfect totem animal for Roosevelt and amongst themselves TR's four sons called him the Old Lion.

Planning for the post-presidential odyssey began more than a year before Roosevelt departed on March 23, 1909. He had first envisioned a trip to Alaska, with its store of large carnivores. But at a late 1907 White House dinner Carl Akeley, a hunter-naturalist for the Field Museum in Chicago who had just returned from Africa, tipped the scales with a riveting tale of a cave on Juja Farm in British East Africa (later Kenya) from which sixteen lions emerged. TR had long been fascinated by the Dark Continent and had amassed an impressive library of African lore. After hearing Akeley, he turned to Illinois Congressman James Mann, seated next to him, and remarked that he wished he had those lions to turn loose on Congress. "B-but Mr. President," said Mann after some hesitation, "aren't you afraid they might make mistakes?" "Not if they stayed long enough," he replied, with a characteristic snap of his teeth and to general laughter round the table. "Alaska," he added, "would have to wait."[5] The safari represented a test of Roosevelt and his nineteen-year-old son Kermit against the most dangerous big game that nature, "red in tooth and claw" (and horn on this occasion), could offer. As a gift to his wife Edith for her indulgence of his big game adventure, the couple planned to follow the safari with a briefer tour of Europe, Africa's civilized antithesis. Originally this part of the trip was to be a quiet second honeymoon of sorts.

Edith Kermit Roosevelt was in many ways a perfect complement to Theodore. Much more clear-eyed and wary in her outlook, Edith's composed nature moderated his exuberance, in domestic and political matters.

She was a combination of advisor and loving companion.[6] Growing up in the same wealthy circle, "Teedie" and "Edie" had been childhood sweethearts; her best friend was his sister Corinne. But while away at Harvard he became enchanted by, and married, the beautiful Alice Lee, who took Edith's place, temporarily at least, in his heart. Alice's tragic death soon after the birth of their first child, which came within twelve hours of the passing of his beloved mother, led TR never to mention his first wife's name again. Not even to their daughter Alice who, while he recovered from the double blow in the Dakotas Badlands, was put into the care of Theodore's older sister Anna—called "Bamie" by family and friends.

Within two years, TR had rekindled his romance with Edith and they married in 1886 at St George's, Hanover Square, London. At the private ceremony Theodore wore fashionable orange gloves suggested by his best man, Cecil Spring Rice, a bright young British diplomat attached to the Washington embassy that he had met on the boat to Europe. Thereafter a life-long friend, "Springy," as he was called, is perhaps most famous for his only half-jesting comment about TR to *The Times* of London foreign correspondent Valentine Chirol, "You must always remember that the President is about six."[7] When they returned from their honeymoon in Europe, Edith insisted that her husband's daughter Alice live with them and over the following years they also had five children of their own: Theodore Jr., Kermit, Ethel, Archibald, and the youngest Quentin, a miniature TR who led the adventures of the "White House Gang" often joined by the children of Washington's leading citizens. Being older, "Princess" Alice, as she was dubbed by a press fascinated with the doings of the energetic First Family, developed her own highly independent spirit and idiosyncrasies, including smoking cigarettes on the roof of the White House and forming a "Race Suicide" club to lampoon what she considered one of her father's more ludicrous hobby horses. TR famously told his writer friend Owen Wister that he could run the country or control Alice but could not possibly do both. Her sister Ethel, more central to this story, was in many ways the flamboyant and glamorous Alice's opposite. Reliable, responsible, and solid, she wanted none of the limelight Alice sought out.

Of all the children Kermit was most like his father in prizing outdoor challenges, and in the dedication of his book detailing their expedition, *African Game Trails*, Roosevelt dubbed him "My Side-Partner in Our 'Great Adventure.'" Kermit recalled that his father had notified him in 1908 that, after he left the presidency, he planned to make a trip to Africa and "that if I wished to do so I could accompany him." There was no need to ask whether he wanted to go. At school Kermit's compositions "invariably took the form of some imaginary journey" across the Dark Continent. But his father made it his practice to speak to the children as if they were his contemporaries and never ordered or told them to follow a certain line. There would be a discussion and then they were left to draw their own conclusions. Roosevelt told Kermit that he was allowing himself a holiday at fifty, after a very busy life, and that if his son came along the holiday would be coming at the beginning of his career, so afterwards, he would have to be prepared to work "doubly hard to justify both him and myself for having taken it."[8]

To prepare, Roosevelt devoured as many books about African game and hunting as he could find, raiding among others the library of the American Museum of Natural History in New York, of which he was a trustee. These volumes included J. H. Patterson's chilling best-seller *The Man-Eaters of Tsavo*, Abel Chapman's *On Safari: Big Game Hunting in British East Africa with Studies in Bird Life*, Richard Lydekker's *Game Animals of Africa*, Major P. G. H. Powell-Cotton's *In Unknown Africa*, and Boyd Alexander's *From the Niger to the Nile*, to name the most prominent. In addition to reading about Africa, Roosevelt also got first hand information by interrogating as many experienced naturalists, hunters, and explorers as he could lure to the White House or the "family sanctuary," their home Sagamore Hill at Oyster Bay, Long Island, where they summered.[9] At one such luncheon meeting at Sagamore Hill, TR astounded the learned naturalists on hand with his detailed knowledge of African mammals: which seemed equal to any man in the room.[10] In March 1908, he began to direct serious enquiries to the hunters and explorers for practical advice about an African trip.

First among these was perhaps the most famous big game hunter of them all, Frederick Courteney Selous, a British-born African hunter-explorer who had published numerous books detailing his exploits.[11] Some have seen Selous as the model for Henry Rider Haggard's character Allan Quartermain, the hero of *King Solomon's Mines*, and many other adventure stories. Roosevelt himself had more than a little in common with his friend Rider Haggard's hero. A recent biographer has commented that TR was "the living antidote to the dawning twentieth century's problems: small like Allan Quartermain; energetic, virile, an attractive and boisterous personality; an explorer of wildernesses; a hunter, both of grizzlies in the American west and of lions in Africa; a fighter (when needed) both of men and the powers of darkness in high places; and, not least, a prolific writer."[12]

After Selous visited the White House in 1905, TR's praise of the hunter's vivid and detailed stories inspired him to produce *African Nature Notes and Reminiscences*, which he dedicated to Roosevelt, who in turn added a Foreword. In this he described Selous as "the last of the mighty hunters whose experiences lay in the greatest hunting ground which this world has seen since civilized man has appeared therein." However, Selous was "much more than a mere big-game hunter." He was "by instinct a keen field naturalist, an observer with a power of seeing and remembering what he has seen." And finally, he was a writer who possessed "to a very marked and unusual degree the power vividly and accurately to put on paper his observations." Such a combination of qualities was "rare indeed." The inevitable disappearance of big-game, TR went on, "before the onrush of the greedy, energetic, force-ful men, usually both unscrupulous and short-sighted, who make up the vanguard of civilization" should make all the more prized Selous's "life-histories of the great, splendid, terrible beasts whose lives add an immense majesty to the far off wilds."[13]

On March 20, 1908, Roosevelt wrote to Selous, "A year hence I shall stop being President, and while I can not be certain of what I shall do, it may be that I can afford to devote a year to a trip to Africa." His aim was to "visit the Pleistocene and the world 'as it lay in the sunshine unworn of the plow;' to see the great beasts whose like our forefathers saw when they lived in caves and smote one another with stone-headed axes." Noting the limitations caused by his age, weight and sedentary lifestyle of the past seven years, TR asked Selous for his recommendations about hunting grounds, outfitting a safari, what sort of guns and clothing would be required, and myriad other questions.[14] For the next year, Selous aided Roosevelt in planning every aspect of the trip, from logistics to location, weapons, equipment, and provisions. The president reported to Kermit, still at Groton, that he had begun his correspondence about the African trip although it was not yet possible to say for sure whether it would be possible. Selous had suggested they go by Mombasa in British East Africa because the Uganda-Nile regions were not healthy and they could get acclimated in a more salubrious climate. Moreover, they could almost immediately have "some hunting to the good," even if the Nile portion of the trip was not a success.[15]

As did Selous, Roosevelt considered himself a "Hunter-Naturalist."[16] Indeed, had the biological curriculum at Harvard been more field-oriented, TR's greatest achievements might well have come in the scientific rather than the political arena. Roosevelt and other gentlemen enthusiasts such as himself saw no contradiction whatsoever in passionately pursuing both hunting and conservation. To them the two went hand in hand. In 1887, he and George Bird Grinnell, the editor of *Forest and Stream*, took the first steps towards establishing the Boone and Crockett Club of sportsmen who were also big game hunters. Roosevelt was the first president of the organization, which became a powerful force for the preservation of the nation's natural resources and forests—in particular the nation's remaining wild places and large game animals such as the buffalo, elk, and moose against the predations of commercial hunters.[17] TR continued a close association with the Boone and Crockett Club, even after the Spanish-American War and William McKinley's assassination changed his career path forever and afforded him the opportunity to use, first the governorship of New York, and then the presidency and the federal government, to spread conservationist ideas from his powerful bully pulpit.

Strange as it may appear a century on, when hunting is considered murder or worse to much of the environmental community, Roosevelt was equally comfortable with non-hunting preservationists and they with him. Such friends included several of the founders of the modern American conservation movement, notably John Burroughs and John Muir.[18] While president he camped in Yosemite with Muir, founder of the Sierra Club, and in Yellowstone with Burroughs, with whom he shared a passion for birds, first developed as a boy when the future president catalogued and stuffed specimens for his own private home museum.[19] He also shared with Burroughs an abhorrence of "nature fakers," writers who tried to pass off tall tales of animals as factual accounts. While president he joined Burroughs in a scathing attack on the work of one such writer in particular, Reverend William J. Long, who would in return lead the criticism of the African expedition as simply another "game butchering" adventure by Roosevelt.[20]

In 1908 TR reported to the elderly, bewhiskered Burroughs, whom he affectionately called Oom (Dutch for uncle) John, the birds he and Edith spotted through their field glasses in the White House garden.

Some of these he was not familiar with and wished Burroughs had been on hand to identify. Burroughs did join his friend that May at "Pine Knot," the rustic presidential retreat in the Virginia countryside, where they "tramped and pottered about the fields and gazed with absorbed interest at all kinds of little insignificant birds."[21] About TR's ambitions to shoot lion and elephant in Africa, Burroughs commented, "I am sure you will bag at least one lion but I had rather the elephants would escape." He looked forward "with great expectations" for the natural history notes Roosevelt would bring back. Burroughs was more interested in birds than big game and wanted to know more about their songs than he had been able to learn from any of the African hunting books. If there were swallows, he wanted to know where they nested. He wondered if the grouse drummed, or called as in America. All of these things, TR promised to investigate.[22]

The same month Burroughs visited "Pine Knot," Roosevelt opened the White House Conservation Conference with an impassioned address titled "Conservation as a National Duty." The first such national gathering ever held in any country, the White House Conference has been described as both the "great showpiece" of TR's last year as president and "one of the great landmarks in conservation history."[23] Those invited included all the state and territorial governors, the Supreme Court justices, congressmen, international visitors, and leading authorities on the natural resources of the nation. Out of this meeting came, among other things, the unanimous approval by the governors of a declaration in support of conservation, the birth of thirty-six state conservation commissions and the creation of a National Conservation Commission which inventoried the nation's resources over the next year.

At the time Roosevelt called the gathering "unique of its kind" and told Kermit that in it "we have taken a long first step in awakening the American people to the need of the conservation of their natural resources," and the need to exercise the qualities which really distinguished the "civilized men from the savage, foresight, forethought." With congress set to adjourn, this meant he had been able to "end my very active work as President in a way worthwhile." It was the end of his "active work," he explained, because after the nomination for the next presidency attention must "properly be concentrated" upon the nominee rather than the man who is finishing his last eight months.[24] The man Roosevelt made sure his Republican party chose the next month was the Secretary of War, William Howard Taft. TR confided to another friend and "intellectual playmate," the British historian and statesman Sir George Otto Trevelyan, that he had to fight "tooth and nail" to head off a stampede for his own renomination. He could not be sure of Taft's election, but he believed "the chances" favored it. Roosevelt went on that, "always excepting Washington and Lincoln," he thought Taft would "rank with any other man who has ever been in the White House."[25]

The man TR meant to leave behind to lead the conservation crusade in the hoped-for Taft administration was Gifford Pinchot, the chief forester of the United States.[26] For the previous seven years, first as head of the Division of Forestry in the Agriculture Department, and then Chief of the new Forest Service after 1905, the handsome, wealthy and stylish Pinchot had led a righteous (some would say self-righteous) crusade as Roosevelt's "lightening rod" and point man on what would later be called environmental issues.[27] Among the first "scientific foresters," Pinchot was forced to travel to France for his training since no such programs existed in the United States. He returned convinced that "forestry is the art of using a forest without destroying it."[28] Pinchot credited TR (and himself) with formulating and laying before the American people and the world a utilitarian "Conservation idea—the greatest good for the greatest number for the longest time, the development and use of the earth and all its resources for the enduring good of men—both on a national and international scale."[29]

The president did not know anyone he would sooner choose to send to a danger point than Pinchot and just before he left the White House, he wrote to the chief forester, "I owe you a peculiar debt of obligation for a very large part of the achievement of this administration."[30] In conservation these included the establishment of the first Federal Wildlife Refuge, and the growth of the system to fifty bird sanctuaries before TR left office; the creation of a new system of National Monuments such as the Grand Canyon, totaling eighteen by 1909; the addition of 150 million acres of timberland to the Forest Reserves, called National Forests after 1907; the withdrawal of waterpower sites to safeguard the growing demand for electricity; doubling the number of national parks; and the creation of the Federal Reclamation Service dedicated to irrigation and reforestation.

By the time the White House Conservation Conference adjourned, the African trip was taking more definite shape. Roosevelt told Edward

North Buxton, another of his British safari advisors, that he and Kermit expected to depart by early April, confessing that this was on account of his desire to "be away for a year or a year and a quarter immediately following the installation of my successor." If he did not go, "all kinds of small disagreeable things" were sure to happen. Especially if his successor, as he hoped, was Taft, "whose policy and actions I should loudly be accused of trying to dictate if I stay at home."[31] Buxton was chairman of the Society for the Preservation of the Wild Fauna of the Empire, dubbed by its critics the "penitent butchers."[32] TR was an honorary member of the British society, few members of which ever gave up the pleasures of hunting completely, repented or apologized. Roosevelt planned to follow Buxton's advice and make trips from the Uganda Railway through British East Africa of one or two months at a time. He wanted to make these long enough to be sure to get into "good game country and out of the ordinary tourist infested region." TR told Buxton he did not want any butchery. To the contrary, he expected the "chief value of my trip to consist of the observations I was able to make upon the habits of the game, and to a lesser extent, of the birds, smaller animals and the like."[33]

In part to forestall charges by his enemies that the safari would be simply another "game-butchering" trip, Roosevelt's original private junket scheme was transformed into a full-fledged scientific expedition, under the auspices of the Smithsonian Institution in Washington. He proposed the idea in June 1908 to Charles D. Walcott, the Secretary of the Smithsonian, which included the United States National Museum, as an opportunity to build a fine African collection of "unique value." TR told Walcott that he was "not in the least a game butcher" and that his "real and main interest" in the expedition was as a "fauna naturalist."[34] Walcott, fearing he might lose the chance to the rival American Museum of Natural History in New York, agreed to provide naturalist/taxidermists and to pay for the preparation and transport of the specimens.[35] In the end the Smithsonian hired three naturalists, one to preserve the big game shot by Roosevelt and Kermit, and two others to capture and catalog the smaller animals. An elated TR notified Selous that most of the safari's specimens would now go to the National Museum. His house was rather small and he imagined it would be a while before Kermit had any house at all so they did not really care for many trophies "for our own private glorification." Roosevelt was "greatly interested in natural history" and should like to make a largely scientific collecting trip, and to try and "add my mite to field observations of the habitats and life of big game."[36]

Despite charges to the contrary, no taxpayer dollars were spent on the expedition. Walcott created a special fund of $30,000 by private subscription so that, as the president suggested, congress would not need to be involved.[37] Roosevelt paid for his and Kermit's expenses, while an impressive list of donors made up of wealthy friends, raised the rest.[38] Most generous in the end was Andrew Carnegie, the world's richest man since 1901 when he sold his steel holdings to J. P. Morgan. Though the robber baron and the trustbuster had pointed differences over the years, TR came to respect Carnegie's philanthropic work. He consulted Roosevelt about his big charities and TR felt that, whatever his motivation, the plutocrat was doing "tremendous work in the world." Not so much by what he gave, but by the way he gave it. The conditions placed on the gifts, such as requiring the various cities to contribute their share, had, in Roosevelt's opinion, "a splendid effect upon the communities which meet these conditions."[39]

World Peace was prominent among the many causes Carnegie supported and he enlisted TR, as a kindred spirit to Germany's Kaiser Wilhelm II, to aid in this quest. Carnegie seemed to find no contradiction in turning to these two figures whose public personas often reflected the glorification of war and military virtues. One authority on the peace movement has commented that Carnegie coupled "an extraordinarily sanguine disposition" with "a simplicity of mind that blurred the contradictory implications of specific ideas and actions."[40] In 1903 he donated $1,500,000, a huge sum at that time, to build a "Temple of Peace" at The Hague to house the sessions of the permanent court of arbitration, the most lasting creation of the First Hague Conference called by the Russian Czar in 1899 to discuss disarmament. And over the rest of his life, as Carnegie followed his "Gospel of Wealth" to give away ninety per cent of his fortune, he proved a generous donor to peace organizations in the United States and abroad. After a White House dinner during which he and TR discussed the African expedition, Carnegie reported to his friend and fellow peace devotee in the British cabinet, John Morley, that he had told the president that the "big game he should hunt" was the German Emperor, France, Russia, and "especially you big fellows in London." He went on that TR had "fixed upon a hunt how-ever first" and understandably wanted to get "out of harness for a while."[41]

Unlike Carnegie, Roosevelt was not a wealthy man. His own father, also called Theodore, had used up much of his fortune in philanthropic pursuits, including the founding of the American Museum of Natural History in New York. Consequently, the future president inherited only $125,000, still not an inconsiderable sum at the time. But he had little interest or skill in financial affairs and one fourth of his already dwindling capital was lost when his Dakotas cattle herd froze in a blizzard. Since their marriage Theodore and Edith had been forced to economize to make ends meet. In 1908, both to fill the family coffers and to pay his and Kermit's way in Africa and Europe, TR accepted $50,000 from *Scribner's Magazine* for a series of twelve articles detailing the safari, to be published in book form for an additional twenty per cent royalty. He turned down an offer of twice as much from *Collier's*, which he did not consider as "dignified and appropriate" a venue for his writing. To forestall competition, the three naturalists who joined the expedition had to agree that they would not write or speak of the safari until Roosevelt's articles and book were published.

To make a living on his return from Africa, TR arranged to join another journal with sympathetic views, *The Outlook*, as a contributing editor for $12,000 a year. This turned out to be a wise investment for the journal, the circulation of which boomed after the ex-president's association became known. He could have made four times as much at other magazines and eight times more in business. Money aside, Roosevelt told a British friend, John St Loe Strachey, editor of the similarly liberal London *Spectator*, that it was the character of the men at *The Outlook* that made it "the best instrument with which I can work." The agreement was simply that whatever he had to say he would say in its columns. After the presidency, TR told Strachey, the work open to him "best worth doing" was "fighting for political, social, and industrial reform," just as he had done over his twenty-eight years in politics. Roosevelt felt like he could still for some years "command a certain amount of attention from the American public," and before his influence totally vanished he wanted to use it "so far as possible to help onward certain movements for the betterment of our people." He strongly disagreed with Strachey's assertion that ex-presidents should be given pensions and some continuing official role. To TR, it would be "personally an unpleasant thing to be pensioned and given some honorary position." He emphatically did not desire to "clutch at the fringe of departing greatness." In his view there was "something rather attractive, something in the way of living up to a proper democratic ideal," in having a president go out of office as he planned, and become "absolutely and without reservation a private man, and do only honorable work he finds to do." His first work would be to go to Africa for the National Museum. At fifty, after having led a very sedentary life for ten years, he felt it was his "last chance for something in the nature of a great adventure."[42]

To ensure the success of his adventure, Roosevelt was not reluctant to use his presidential connections and prestige to open doors in Africa. Since most of the trip would be in British territory he had Whitelaw Reid, the U.S. ambassador to the Court of St James in London, contact British officials for the necessary permissions and licenses. The Colonial Secretary, Lord Crewe, arranged for preserves to be opened in British East Africa and Uganda, as did the Sudan's governor-general, Sir Reginald Wingate. Wingate also put a small government steamer at Roosevelt's disposal to navigate the tributaries of the Nile.

For the previous decade and more, Roosevelt had been an admirer of the British Empire and a proponent of cooperation and friendship between the two great English-speaking peoples, later dubbed the "Special Relationship."[43] Over that time, for strategic and other reasons that suited both nations, Anglo-American relations became more cordial, particularly from the brief Spanish-American War.[44] British support for the United States in the "Splendid Little War" reversed Roosevelt's previous opinion. He told one of his many British friends, Arthur Lee (later Lord Lee of Fareham), that the attitude of England "worked a complete revolution in my feelings and the attitude on the continent at that time opened my eyes to the other side of the question." Soon after the war, TR wrote to Lee, who had seen action with him in Cuba as British Military Attaché and was made an honorary Rough Rider, "I feel very strongly that the English-speaking peoples are now closer together than for a century and a quarter, and that every effort should be made to keep them together; for their interests are really fundamentally the same, and they are far more closely akin, not merely in blood, but in feeling and in principles, than either is akin to any other people in the world." "Our two peoples," Roosevelt told Lee, were "the only two really free great peoples."[45] After TR became president this new sentiment was further nourished by the reality that both the United States and Britain were isolated in the international community by their policies in the Philippines and South Africa where each was engaged until 1902 in similarly bloody guerilla wars against enemies who refused to lay down their arms and obey the rules of "civilized" warfare.

In July 1908, TR instructed Whitelaw Reid that he wanted permission to shoot in British territory only where people were sometimes allowed, not closed areas such as Yellowstone Park in the United States. It would also, he told Reid, "be a matter of pride with me to kill the minimum number absolutely needed." Roosevelt had already assured Sir Frederick Jackson, the acting governor of British East Africa and the prototype for another of Rider Haggard's heroes, Captain Good, that he did not want to be any trouble to the local officials and meant to travel quietly just as would Selous or Buxton. This would be difficult with the small army of 250 or so men finally assembled for the expedition. After Africa, TR told Reid, he meant to go to Europe for a few weeks, without meeting heads of state. He wanted to spend a few weeks in the hill towns of Northern Italy and country districts of France before spending ten days or so in England with friends.[46]

Based on reports Buxton and others had sent on conditions in Africa, TR carefully listed the game he hoped to bag. The desired animals of British East Africa were, in order of priority: lion, elephant, rhino, buffalo, giraffe, hippo, eland, sable, oryx, koodoo, wildebeest, hartebeest, warthog, zebra, waterbuck, Grant's gazelle, reedbuck, and topi. Roosevelt feared he would not get a lion or elephant, but told Buxton he would "try hard," and ought to get all the others except the rare sable and koodoo. If he was able to go to Larga in Uganda, Roosevelt wanted to make "a hard try for white rhino." He would accept "the certainty of fever and a good deal more for a chance."[47] As it happened, Roosevelt had to cross into Belgian territory for his opportunity in part because he wished to avoid the bad publicity Winston Churchill had stirred up the previous year when he took a rare white rhino in a British preserve.

Churchill had carried out his hunt while Parliamentary under-secretary for the colonies, officially on a tour of East Africa to inspect the Uganda Railway, which had opened the country to settlement. TR had been thrilled by Churchill's *Strand Magazine* account of his hunt, which was one reason he wanted a white rhino so badly. The two men first met in Albany in December 1900 when Vice President Elect Roosevelt was still governor of New York. The new Member of Parliament was on a speaking tour in support of the British cause in the Boer War, out of which he had become a hero with a daring escape from a Boer prison. Roosevelt may well have heard, possibly through his friend Selous, who was a Pro-Boer, the rumor that Churchill had broken his word to his captors that he would not take flight. For whatever reason, though interested by his talk of India, from their first meeting TR disliked the young man. This was perhaps simply on account of Churchill's self-important and arrogant nature, of which Roosevelt had further reports in Africa. Alice later noted that her father considered Churchill bad-mannered and she and many others have thought the antipathy simply a case of like repelling like. TR dispatched a courteous thank you note nevertheless for the copy Churchill forwarded of his book, *My African Journey.*[48]

Roosevelt accepted an invitation to begin his hunt in British East Africa on the ranch of Sir Albert Pease, a wealthy settler and former Member of Parliament who split his time between Africa and London. He reminded Pease that he was "absolutely out of condition" and, he was sorry to say, had "not only grown fat, but also a little gouty" to which he hoped safari work would be an antidote. But he would have to begin "with great moderation." TR weighed twice the 124 pounds he had measured as a Harvard freshman. His waist also had almost doubled to forty-seven inches and his neck measured nineteen. He was also made "rather nervous" by his prospective host's assurance that he and Kermit would have the opportunity to shoot Hartebeest while riding out to his ranch. Roosevelt replied that "we shall both be utterly out of practice and we shall certainly miss our first shots." Nonetheless, he confided to Pease that he really found it difficult to "devote full attention to my Presidential work at present, because I am looking forward so eagerly to my African trip!"[49]

While he eagerly anticipated the safari, Roosevelt dreaded the prospect of being followed into Africa by tourists, or worse still, a "horde of reporters." He had learned as president the difficulty of hunting with reporters who scared the game or got in the line of fire. To be sure he would be free of newspapermen, for at least the first leg of his journey, TR banned from his party all the journalists clamoring to accompany him. Further, before going he issued a statement that during the safari he would not open his mouth for print and therefore anything published would be "without authority and foundation."[50] To forestall the American press monster his presidency had done much to feed, Roosevelt appealed to, among others, Melville Stone, General Manager of the Associated Press. He told Stone that it would be a "wanton outrage" for the press association to send reporters to cover him once he was a private citizen. Further, it would be "inexpressibly distasteful" and of "no possible benefit to any human being, to have any newspaper try to report or exploit the trip."[51]

Roosevelt did not think English newspapermen would follow him as they were "rather decent in such matters." American reporters were another matter and TR meant to have the authorities intervene until he could "elude them in the wilds." If he could "get ahead of them once," they would never catch up. On the off chance they did, he told Archie Butt he might see on his expense account for the Smithsonian something like: "One hundred dollars for buying the means to rid myself of one *World* reporter; three hundred dollars expended in dispatching a reporter of the *American*; five hundred dollars for furnishing wine to cannibal chiefs with which to wash down a reporter of the New York *Evening Post*."[52]

Jokes of cannibals aside, the real dangers of the looming safari reminded Roosevelt of his own mortality. Many people urged him not to go to Africa as he might be killed by a wild beast or die of sleeping sickness or in a thousand other ways, but in his opinion it did not do to try to live too long. TR told Butt that he was ready to go at any time and that fear of death would not deter him from doing what he wished. He did not know what the future had in store, but was "ready to rest my case here," or, he added with a characteristic laugh and flash of his teeth by way of emphasis, "after I have had a little fling in Africa."[53] For luck, TR's pal John Sullivan, the former Heavyweight Boxing Champion, gave him a gold-mounted rabbit's foot, which Roosevelt put on his watch chain and took to Africa.[54] His own amateur boxing activities while president had cost him the sight of one eye, a considerable drawback for shooting big game.

Even with only one useful eye (which required powerful spectacles to remedy his nearsightedness), Roosevelt simply could not exist without reading and among the essentials packed carefully away for the journey were a number of non-hunting books. At night and on any moment of rest, at home or on whatever trail he followed, TR always kept a volume handy. Those he took to Africa were dubbed the "pigskin library" for the weather-proof binding put on the four-dozen trimmed down volumes. The portable collection was designed to fit into a single aluminum crate weighing fifty-five to sixty pounds, the standard load for one native bearer. His sister Corinne presented

TR with the custom fitted case, with waterproof canvas cover, and the bindings, as a parting gift. "I want you to think of me," she told him, "when you are reading in some little mosquito cage in far off Africa."[55]

Among the books chosen were many classics such as *The Iliad* and *The Odyssey*, the *Chanson de Roland*, Dante's *Inferno*, Milton's *Paradise Lost*, the *Nibelungenlied*, and the works of Shakespeare. TR told Butt that, though he did not like Shakespeare's "dramatic poetry," he could "get all of him in three pocket volumes" and there was a lot of "compressed thought" in the bard—as the "soldier takes the emergency ration, not for the quality, but for the largest amount of sustenance in the smallest space." Historical tomes such as his friend and naval mentor Alfred Thayer Mahan's *The Influence of Sea Power Upon History*, Macauley's *History of England* and Carlyle's *Frederick the Great* were balanced by the poetry of Keats, Longfellow, Tennyson, Poe and Emerson. The collection also included the fiction of Twain, Bret Harte, Dickens and Scott. The original pigskin library did not include a Bible, and Roosevelt saw that Kermit brought his. He also presumed that his mother would "conceal the book of Common Prayer somewhere among his underclothes."[56]

The many perils they would face in Africa led several people to suggest it would be better if Kermit did not go, but TR knew that it would "absolutely break Kermit's heart" if he left him behind.[57] Among those who had sent warnings, including a pamphlet on the dangers to the young of "sleeping sickness," was Cecil Spring Rice, who in 1908 was attached to the British Embassy in Stockholm. TR replied to his old friend that he "laughed until he cried" over the pamphlet and the explanation in his letter that it was "perfectly possible that I would not die of that, because, in the event of my not being previously eaten by a lion or crocodile, or killed by an infuriated elephant or buffalo, malarial fever or a tribe of enraged savages might take me off before the sleeping sickness got me!" He was bound to say, however, that the letter gave his wife "a keen and melancholy enjoyment, and she will now have the feeling that she is justified in a Roman-matron-like attitude of heroically bidding me go to my death when I sail in a well-equipped steamer for an entirely comfortable and mild little hunting trip."[58]

However her husband might jest, Theodore's constant talk of the trip, reading maps and jungle literature, took a toll on Edith. It was bad enough that her soul mate soon would be disappearing into the wilds of Africa for almost a year, but he was taking along Kermit, her favorite, as company. Archie Butt and others noticed, "some beautiful understanding" between the reed-thin young man and his mother. He always stood near her with his arm around her waist and he never came into a room that he did not go up and kiss her.[59] The prospect of a long separation and the dangers of a safari appeared "pretty hard on Mrs. R," however, she told Captain Butt that "even wild-animal hunting in Africa" had its compensations when she thought of her anxiety when her husband was "appearing in public, a target for every crank who comes to these shores."[60] Edith was made somewhat less "anxious" when her husband arranged for Major Edgar Mearns, of the Army Medical Corps, who had seen much tropical service, to go along as one of the Smithsonian naturalists.[61]

Dr. Mearns suggested they take along a "movie picture machine" offered cost free by Thomas Edison in return for the advertising rights, but Roosevelt vetoed the idea. He told Mearns it would only hamper them and would not be useful enough to make up for the "very undesirable" advertising of the expedition that would result.[62] Though he doubted the value of the Edison machine, TR believed that making a photographic record of the expedition was of central importance and in fact might be its most lasting and valuable legacy. By 1908 photographic safaris were not unknown and another of TR's British advisors, Sir Harry Johnston, told the press that, if he had his say, he would "present a telephoto camera instead of a rifle to the president and entreat him to take shots at long range with that. Everywhere we witness the destruction of animals and birds indigenous to their native soils, and I am for preserving them rather than destroying them. Africa is no exception and the big game there is slowly being exterminated."[63] The naturalists all brought cameras, but Kermit acted as the expedition's official photographer. TR advised his son to take a plain Kodak in addition to the cumbersome and elaborate "Chapman apparatus" with which he had been practicing. He thought a good plan was to take a great number of pictures and "hope that one in ten will turn out well." Then of those, "we will be able to pick enough that we want."[64] In the end Kermit used a Graphlex Naturalist's camera for most of his thousands of photographs that chronicled the journey.

Roosevelt had planned to oversee the expedition himself and protested that he did not want to feel as if he were on a "kind of Cook's tour party," but he finally listened to reason and took Selous's advice to hire the firm of Newland and Tarlton in Nairobi to manage the safari.[65] This freed TR to concentrate on the game. One of the partners, Leslie Tarlton, joined them as a hunter and sometimes companion to Kermit, while Theodore's official guide was R. J. Cuninghame, an old African hand whom Carl Akeley had hired two years before to teach him to hunt elephants. By August the final details of the trip had been decided. TR reported to a close friend, Senator Henry Cabot Lodge, that they would leave New York on March 23rd, going by Naples to Mombasa in British East Africa. By December 1909 he expected to reach the head-waters of the Nile and would leave Cairo near the end of March 1910. Almost all the trophies would go to the National Museum which, he went on, was a "great relief to Edith" who felt she would "have to move out of the house if I began to fill it a full of queer antelopes, stuffed elephants and the like."[66] TR hoped to run the safari as economically as possible and pared what he considered luxuries including pâté de fois gras, canned prawns and French plums, white tablecloths and fancy china crockery. He also slashed the liquor supply from a gross of whisky to three flasks—for medicinal purposes.[67] Despite incessant rumors of his drinking bouts, TR was in fact practically a teetotaler.

As it turned out, the champion of the prohibition movement in the United States, William Jennings Bryan, also happened to be Taft's Democratic opponent in the 1908 election campaign. TR was unsure if he could transfer his undoubted popularity to Taft, and conventional wisdom held that a financial panic during an administration, such as happened in 1907, meant the defeat of the party in power in the following election. Nevertheless, before leaving for Africa and Europe it was imperative to Roosevelt that his chosen successor be elected to carry on his policies. He wrote to Buxton on 25 September that he had gotten into the campaign "as hard as I know how" and for the next six weeks he supposed "even Africa will a little bit submerged in interest compared to the desirability of electing Taft."[68]

The president's close friend was a political novice, unused to the rough and tumble of campaigning. An Ohio native, Taft had studied at Yale and been a lawyer and judge in Cincinnati before becoming Solicitor-General of the United States in 1890. Ten years later Taft was made president of the Philippine Commission and in 1901 the first Civil governor of the islands. In 1904 he became secretary of war, and since then had in addition done yeoman service as TR's agent over-seeing the construction of the Panama Canal, while also acting in 1906 as provisional governor of Cuba. Roosevelt might have done better to keep Taft close in Washington for the education in politics his chosen successor badly needed, but never got. Among these skills, making speeches was never a Taft strong point, while his opponent in 1908 was one of the most famous orators in American history.

On the stump, Taft had been citing decision after decision that he had rendered. This TR told him simply to stop, for "the moment you begin to cite decisions people at once think it is impossible to understand and they cease trying to comprehend and promptly begin to nod." Instead, he coached Taft to view his audience as one "coming, not to see an etching, but a poster." He must, therefore, "have streaks of blue, yellow and red to catch the eye, and eliminate all fine lines and soft colors." Taft at first, Roosevelt recalled, thought him a "barbarian and a mountebank," but he was pleased to say by the end of the campaign that his chosen successor was "at last catching the attention of the crowd" and, he thought, holding it.[69]

While he gave Taft as much aid as he thought wise, TR crafted several speeches of his own for delivery in Europe. The first of these sprung from his inability to resist the intellectual prestige in an invitation from the chancellor of Oxford, George Nathaniel Curzon, Baron Curzon of Kedleston, to give the Romanes Lecture at the university in June 1910. The lecture also afforded an official reason to visit England. A delighted TR replied to Curzon, "surely no man was ever asked to do a pleasant thing in such a pleasant way as you have asked me!"[70] Roosevelt practiced the speech, which he wrote while having his portrait painted by Joseph De Camp, on Ambassador Jusserand and Archie Butt. He also sent a copy of the lecture, titled "Biological Analogies in History," to his friend Henry Fairfield Osborn, the president of the American Museum of Natural History in New York. Osborn recalled that it was "full of analogies between the extinct animal kingdom and the kingdoms and principalities in the human world." Several of these, that he felt "likely to bring on war between the United States and the governments referred to," he advised TR to omit.[71]

When news of the Romanes Lecture got out, a torrent of invitations followed. So as not to hurt French sensibilities, and his friend Jusserand, Roosevelt agreed to give a Paris address at the Sorbonne. Then, after the Kaiser sent an invitation, the University of Berlin was added to the progress. He first turned down an invitation from the Nobel Committee to make a belated address in Norway for the Peace

Prize he had been awarded for mediating the Russo-Japanese War. However, TR finally heeded the urgings of Carnegie and others and decided to accept.

All this swept away TR's original intention not to go near a European capital. He had declared that he would sooner give up the trip than let it be made into a "peripatetic show"; however, as he told his friend Henry White, the U.S. ambassador in Paris, though he would like to avoid seeing any sovereigns, he realized this might make him look "churlish." He wanted to travel as a private citizen and was no "hanger-on to shreds of departing greatness." Therefore, he wanted any introductions to be as informal as possible and, so that he could actually speak with the rulers, under no circumstance did he want any formal dinners or other entertainments. Roosevelt supposed that when he reached England, he would be "informally presented" to Edward VII, who had sent his best wishes for the safari across his possessions, but he feared this would hurt the feelings of the German Kaiser, with whom he had also had a pleasant correspondence and in whom he found much to admire.[72] In the end, accepting the Berlin address also meant accepting Wilhelm's invitation to "meet somewhere and get personally acquainted."[73]

Making allowances for Edward and Wilhelm opened the royal floodgates. TR's larger than life personality and reputation led other kings, great and small, to vie with each other to honor him. European royals, as far as they gave their attention to anything or anyone outside their own inbred society, looked upon him as an interesting curiosity, a prince who had succeeded an assassinated ruler and then been elected temporary king is his own right in 1904. Roosevelt had also made a warrior's name for himself as Colonel of the Rough Riders in the Spanish-American War, living out a martial fantasy from which twentieth-century monarchs were excluded. More recently he had, in light of the bloody Philippine experience, curbed his expansionist imperialism and turned peacemaker.[74] The same year he won the Nobel Prize, TR also helped to foster an agreement at the Algeciras Conference in Spain called to settle the differences between Germany and France over the Moroccan crisis, which had threatened the peace of Europe and the world.

Any looming threat to Roosevelt's domestic policies also appeared to be settled when, as he expected, Taft won the 1908 election. An elated TR sent a telegram to his friend in Cincinnati: "I need hardly say how heartily I congratulate you, and the country even more." He told Taft that the returns made it evident that he was "the only man who we could have nominated that could have been elected." He had won a "great personal victory, as well as great victory for the party, and all those who love you, who admire and believe in you, and are proud of your great and fine qualities must feel a thrill of exultation over the way in which the American people have shown their insight and character, their adherence to high principle."[75] In his thank you note for TR's letter of congratulations, Taft seemed to give equal credit to "you and my brother Charlie" for his election—a statement Roosevelt would not forget and a first, and at the time small, fissure between the two men.[76]

Another early rift developed over Taft's cabinet, chiefly on account of the dismissal of the activist and TR loyalist James Garfield from the Interior Department. Of course Roosevelt made it clear that the new president had the perfect right to nominate whomever he chose, even if it meant dismissing many worthy men. Taft nevertheless felt uncomfortable about the president's obvious disapproval. From the Canal Zone, on his last inspection tour as vice president, he confided to Roosevelt that he was "very much torn up in my feelings in respect to the cabinet and leaving out so many men for whom I have the highest respect." But the president-elect believed he was "doing right in making selections with a view to a somewhat different state of reforms" which TR had started and he must carry on. He knew he would be attacked for having more lawyers than he ought to have, among them the new Secretary of the Interior, Richard Achilles Ballinger. There was also the problem that many of the men he wanted had big business ties. Nevertheless, Taft explained to Roosevelt that he "wanted to get the best" and could not do so "without securing those who have had corporate employment."[77]

The famously rotund Taft had not been physically up to the strenuous activity required for membership in the "tennis cabinet" and played golf instead. During his term in office, TR's beloved dirt court was covered over by an addition to the White House, an act symbolic of the deterioration in relations between the two old friends. Taft did ride regularly which, Roosevelt quipped, was both "dangerous to him and cruel to the horse." He advised Archie Butt, who was one of the select few chosen to stay on in the new regime, that life in the White House would be strenuous enough for Taft and that he should not take much exercise, which did him no good at any rate. If TR were the president-elect, he would "content myself with the record I was able to make in the next four years or the next eight and then be content to die."[78] While making his own record, Taft was also pledged to guard with his political life Roosevelt's progressive achievements, of which conservation was most prominent.

The success of the May 1908 White House Conference had led TR to call a North American Conservation Conference which two weeks before he left office brought Canadian and Mexican representatives to the White House. The delegates agreed on a declaration of conservation principles and, caught up in the spirit of the event, urged that, "all nations should be invited to join together in conference on the subject of world resources, and their inventory, conservation and wise utilization."[79] A delighted Roosevelt instructed his secretary of state to send invitations to forty-five nations to attend such a global conference at a date to be determined in the future. TR envisioned the conclave being held at Carnegie's Peace Palace at The Hague, but without his guidance and energy the proposed conference was stillborn and it would be more than half a century before such an event truly took place.

Another of Roosevelt's passions was building American sea power, often in the face of stiff congressional opposition, to safeguard U.S. interests in a hostile world. He was therefore very gratified before he left office to be on hand to greet the return of the Great White Fleet from its triumphant fourteen month, 42,227 mile, circumnavigation of the globe.[80] This armada of sixteen white-painted ships, practically the entire Atlantic battleship fleet, remains the largest ever to complete such a voyage. Setting forth at the end of 1907, the first objective had been to reach the U.S. west coast. With the Panama Canal still almost seven years from completion, it took the ships considerable time to sail down the Atlantic coasts of North and South America, past the Straits of Magellan and into the Pacific, all along the way making good will calls before large and appreciative crowds. When the fleet arrived at San Francisco, 1 million lined the Golden Gate. Across the Pacific at Australia, half a million greeted the flotilla at Sydney, and hundreds of thousands elsewhere, including Japan. The ships had departed amidst much criticism and some fear of war with the Japanese, whose considerable national pride had been deeply insulted by discrimination against their countrymen in California. As it fell out, however, the cruise proved entirely peaceful and demonstrated to a doubting world the capabilities of the Atlantic-based American Navy.

The multitude of yachts and steamers also waiting in the rain at Hampton Roads on George Washington's birthday, February 22, sailed by whistling and shrieking until Roosevelt appeared on the deck of the 273-foot presidential yacht *Mayflower*, a refitted twelve-gun dispatch boat, and lifted his hat. When he caught sight of the Great White Fleet's "forest of masts and fighting tops" in the distance TR exclaimed: "Here they are. That is the answer to my critics. Another chapter is complete, and I could not ask a finer concluding scene to my administration." "Until some American fleet returns victorious from a great sea battle," Roosevelt exalted in a toast to the commander, Admiral Sperry, never would "there be another such homecoming."[81] Unfortunately the ships, soon painted gray for better camouflage, were rendered obsolete even before they sailed by the all-big-gun, turbine powered, *Dreadnought*-class battleship unveiled by England in 1906 and soon accepted by all the great powers, including the United States, as the new standard.

As it came to an end, Roosevelt reflected on his presidency in a letter to one of the British champions of Dreadnought construction, Arthur Lee. His old friend of Cuban days had entered parliament and become such a staunch supporter of the United States in the Commons that he was derided as the "Member for America." TR told Lee that he was finishing his presidency "with just the same stiff fighting" that had marked it since he took office but was nevertheless having a thoroughly good time. He had achieved a large proportion of what he set out to do and felt he had "measurably realized my ideals." TR supposed he should be melancholy on leaving and "taking his hands off the levers of the great machine," but the African trip represented the "realization of a golden dream" and he looked forward to it with such delight that, he told Lee, it was "quite impossible for me to regret even the Presidency." Regarding Taft, Roosevelt declared that he could not express the "measureless content" that came over him to think that the work in which he so much believed would be carried on by his successor.[82] Whatever he put in letters, TR must have had at least some doubts about Taft. Shortly before he left office, he confided to his faithful Secret Service bodyguard of seven years, Jimmy Malone, that he hoped he was "not mistaken; that my policies will be made into law; but I may have to come back in four years and enter the fight."[83]

Roosevelt invited Taft and his wife Nellie to spend the night before the inauguration at the White House to "save all the bother of moving in on Inauguration Day itself." He also did not plan, as was the custom, to drive back to the White House after the ceremony. This had always struck TR as "a peculiarly senseless performance on the part of the man who had been President and was no longer."[84] Though he made his general wishes very clear, Roosevelt took care not, unless asked, to give Taft specific instructions on policy, save in one area. On his last day as president, at the behest of an almost frantic Admiral Alfred Thayer Mahan, who feared that Congress would allow the Japanese to do to a divided U.S. fleet what they had to Russia's, TR wrote to Taft: "One closing legacy. Under no circumstances divide the Battle Fleet between the Atlantic and Pacific oceans prior to the opening of the Panama Canal."[85]

Taft took the presidential oath on March 4, 1909, at a ceremony moved indoors on account of blizzard conditions. But even before he took office there were rumblings of discontent among TR's friends in Washington about the developing state of affairs. Archie Butt, who stayed on as Taft's military aide, was concerned with new president's "amiability and doctrine of expediency." To him the incoming regime looked a bit like the old days of McKinley and he noted that the Ohio school of politics bred "a peculiar genius" and corruption always flourished under it. The government seemed already to be drifting into the control of Roosevelt's enemies. The old crowd, typified by rich Senators such as Aldrich, Wetmore and Depew, were already "licking their chops and looking forward to seven fat years after seven lean years just about to close."[86] The central problem Taft faced, in Captain Butt's estimation, was that for those seven previous years he had been "living on the steam" of Roosevelt, who had furnished the "high pressure" behind Taft's accomplishments. With TR out of the country, the president would have find his own fuel and "like a child, will have to learn to walk alone." He thought Taft up to the task, but also that it would be "a readjustment all the same."[87]

The former president, who had decided to style himself in private life simply "Colonel" Roosevelt for his rank in the Spanish-American War, returned to Sagamore Hill for three weeks of rest and final preparations for the African expedition. Many thousands of farewell letters poured in. Among them was a note from the naturalist John Muir, who was taking their mutual friend John Burroughs on a tour of the West.

He told Roosevelt that they had had a delightful time at the Petrified Forest and Grand Canyon and he looked forward to taking Burroughs through Yosemite, "recalling our glorious campaign of 1903." To Muir, somehow the whole country seemed "lonesome to me since you left Washington & are so soon to sail for Africa. Heaven bless you dear friend & bring you safely back home."[88] Burroughs assured TR that he was "bound to bag big game wherever you hunt" and hoped that he would be "as successful in the wilds of Africa as you have been in the wilds of American politics & make 'em all dance to the same lively tune."[89]

While her husband and Kermit saw to vaccinations, had their teeth "overhauled" for the trip, and practiced on the rifle range, Edith busied herself with preparations as well, packing nine extra pairs of spectacles, medicines and other essential items. Quentin and Archie were due home for Easter vacation, which gave her some solace. "If it were not for the children," Edith confessed, she would not have the "nervous strength to live through these endless months of separation from Father."[90] Having no wish to face the throng of well-wishers at the Hoboken pier of their ship, the S. S. *Hamburg*, Edith said her private farewells to the voyagers from the piazza of Sagamore Hill on the morning of 23 March 1909. She tried mightily to be perfectly calm and self-possessed, but Kermit felt her heart was almost broken.[91]

In private life, Mrs. Roosevelt told Butt she wanted her husband "to be the simplest American alive." The funniest thing to her was that, while he also wished to live a simple life and promised to do so, the trouble was that he had really forgotten how. She tried to think of his year in Africa and her own planned trip to her sister's house in Italy as having "the effect the forty years wandering had on the Jews." At the end of that time they would enter their home at Oyster Bay "as gladly and as meekly as ever the children of Israel entered the Promised Land."[92] It was an enchanting dream, but alas not to be.

Chapter 2

The Great Adventure Begins

It was wise of TR's staid and reserved wife to say her farewells at Sagamore Hill, for the scene at the Hoboken pier on the morning of March 23, 1909 was frantic. Roosevelt, however, was in his element. He dove into the rowdy crowd of three thousand and spent two hours shaking five hundred or so hands. Well-wishers knocked off his trademark black felt slouch hat and grasped at the gilt buttons of the Colonel's overcoat for souvenirs, while he called for the Rough Riders present to show themselves. He then navigated through the throng towards as many as he could make out. To add to the raucous atmosphere, a brass band of Italian immigrants alternated enthusiastic versions of the "Star Spangled Banner" and the Italian national anthem, in repayment for the aid Roosevelt had sent to Messina for the earthquake victims he would soon see in person. President Taft had Archie Butt hand deliver a farewell letter, a photograph, and a gift (that his aide had chosen for its usefulness), a small gold-mounted ruler that would be drawn out to a foot, or a third, or two-thirds, with a pencil at one end. On it was engraved, "Theodore Roosevelt from William Howard Taft, Good-Bye—Good Luck."[1] This was TR's own favorite expression on seeing anyone off. He promised Butt that he would read the letter as soon as they got under way.

At eleven Roosevelt's ship, the S.S. *Hamburg*, festooned with bunting and signal flags, sounded its final whistle and the tugs nudged it on its way down the Hudson, accompanied by a noisy flotilla of a hundred other vessels crammed to the gills with friends and sightseers. The owners of the German Hamburg-Amerika liner had offered TR free passage but he insisted on paying at least a nominal fare. The line was chosen in part because it offered lower rates than its British Cunard and White Star competitors, but it was also the only one that would carry ammunition, stowed in several of the venture's two hundred six by four foot luggage cases below decks.

As they departed Roosevelt, against all regulations, perched on the ship's bridge, waving his hat in farewell, his glasses glinting in the sunshine. Passing through the narrows, the *Hamburg* received a twenty-one-gun salute from Fort Hamilton. TR occupied Cabin 1, the former "Emperor William Suite," four rooms on the starboard side of the promenade deck the steamship line redecorated in red and green damask for the new occupant, with pictures of Lincoln and Washington on the walls in place of the Kaiser. Coincidentally, four years before, the *Hamburg* had taken Wilhelm to Tangier, where his landing began the Moroccan crisis that TR had taken a hand in settling.

Once at sea, Roosevelt had time to read the president's letter. After the salutation, "My Dear Theodore," Taft confessed, "if I followed my impulse I should say "My Dear Mr. President," as he could not overcome the habit. Further, when he was so addressed, he turned "to see whether or not you are at my elbow." He wished his friend "as great pleasure and as much usefulness as possible in the trip you are about to undertake."

Turning to politics, Taft told TR that there had already been many questions he would have liked to consult him on, but he had "forborne to interrupt your well-earned quiet." The Old Guard Republican congressional chiefs, Senator Nelson Aldrich and Speaker Joseph "Uncle Joe" Cannon, he reported, had promised to "stand by the party platform and follow my lead." Roosevelt had been able to hold his own against the powerful Cannon and Aldrich, who feared him and his popularity. Unfortunately, they did not hold the more amiable, and pliable, Taft in the same regard.

The platform had called for a "revision" of the tariff, which had been taken up by a special session of congress. At least in the eyes of the progressive wing, the Republican Party was pledged to lower tariff rates in the general interest. Taft warned Roosevelt that when he returned he would no doubt "find me very much under suspicion by our friends in the West" enraged by the hides and other raw materials put on the free list for the benefit of Eastern manufacturers at the expense of farmers and cattlemen. The previous December, many of these progressives had joined with Democrats in a failed attempt to limit "Uncle Joe's" power as speaker. Taft did not support them, explaining to Roosevelt that he was "not disposed to countenance an insurrection of thirty men against 180 outside the caucus." Since he did not have TR's prestige or popular support, Taft did not want to make a "capital error" at the beginning of his administration by alienating the good will of Cannon and those whose votes he would need to get legislation passed—a course Roosevelt himself had advised Taft to follow.

Also lacking the former president's "facility for educating the public" through the press, Taft feared a large part of the populous would feel as though he had "fallen away from your ideals"; but told TR, "you know me better." He assured his friend that he did "nothing in my work in the Executive Office without considering what you would do under similar circumstances." Taft could never forget that the power that he now exercised was a "voluntary transfer from you to me" and that he was under obligation "to see to it that your judgment in selecting me as your successor...shall be vindicated."[2] TR, who had made no serious attempt as president either to revise the tariff, or limit the powers of Cannon, replied to this plaintive cry that day with a brief cable: "Am deeply touched by your gift and even more by your letter. Greatly appreciate it. Everything will surely turn out right, old man."[3]

Roosevelt was not a good sailor and suffered from violent seasickness. Consequently, despite perfect weather and smooth seas, he spent much of the first few days aboard ship reading in his suite's sitting room. This inactivity only made him more "homesick" for his wife. An ocean voyage, he wrote to his sister Anna, was "always irksome" but the only thing to do was enjoy it as much as possible, which was "easy enough in the present instance." The people on the ship were mainly Americans and, once he had gained his sea legs, TR found many connections of common friends.[4]

Also aboard were the three Smithsonian naturalists who would do the big game taxidermy and the trapping and shooting of the smaller fauna and flora that would make up the vast majority of the collection sent back to the National Museum. The lesser specimens were the responsibility of Professor J. Alden Loring, an expert on small animals, and Major Edgar Mearns, who was not only a retired Army Surgeon as already noted, but also a bird expert who had acquired his zoological experience on duty in the Philippines and while attached to the Mexican Boundary Commission. The other naturalist, Dr. Edmund Heller, was responsible for preserving the big game Theodore and Kermit shot. He had trained in Alaska and the Galapagos Islands and had already made two trips to Africa as a naturalist for the Field Museum in Chicago. After Heller agreed to join the venture, TR wrote him at his post at the University of California, Berkeley, that he was "delighted you can come." There was not "a man in America" he was "more anxious to have with me."[5]

A week into the voyage they reached the Portuguese Azores, which the Colonel found "very interesting; so quaint and old-world." Kermit went ashore at Horta for a "snoop" and souvenir shopping while the three naturalists began shooting birds and gathering plants for the collection. On a second island, Punta Delgada, they visited Sao Miguel, a picturesque town of 25,000, where the streets, sidewalks, and houses were made of solid rock, painted white or pink. Major Mearns recorded that Roosevelt was in "fine fettle' and Kermit was "the real stuff." Leaving the island group they sailed by a snow-capped mountain that Mearns thought as beautiful as Fujiyama.[6]

At the Azores a gossip from the *Hamburg* spread the tale that Roosevelt had been attacked by a deranged man from steerage. This account soon made its way into the papers in New York to the horror of Edith, who for the last seven years had dreaded the assassination of her husband. A few days later, at scenic Gibraltar, Roosevelt told reporters that there had been no attack, but that a man, muttering in Italian, had approached him only to be quickly taken in charge by the crew. He had later gone down to steerage and shaken the hands of the Italian passengers to assure them there were no hard feelings. TR described Gibraltar's British governor, general Sir Frederick Forestier-Walker, as looking "as if he had walked out of Kipling." The general's "nice Kipling-like aides," showed the Colonel what there was to see and a pleasant niece gave him tea at the Governor's Palace.[7] This was a first example of the extraordinary courtesy Roosevelt was shown throughout the British Empire, in which he spent most of the next year.

The expedition members changed ship for British East Africa at Naples, where TR and Kermit were greeted by Emily Carow, Edith's maiden sister who lived in Italy, and by Lloyd Griscom, the U.S. ambassador. After a long and busy day ashore, amidst crowds of well wishers reminiscent of Hoboken, the travelers boarded the *Admiral*, another very comfortable German liner bound for Mombasa via the Suez Canal, the Egyptian lifeline to Britain's Empire. TR reported to his sister Corinne that among the "polyglot crowd aboard" there were "plenty of people with whom it is really pleasant to talk in English or in those variants of volapuk which with me pass for French or German."[8] Kermit made friends with all the young people who could speak English and some older than him as well. He had brought his mandolin along and organized a ship's musical, during the chorus of which his father drifted off to sleep.

To Roosevelt's delight Frederick Selous, bound for a safari of his own, was able to join him on this leg of the voyage. Along the way the two men held forth on deck chairs trading stories for the amusement of all and sundry. Selous shared the sort of hunting tales that had so impressed Roosevelt at the White House, while the Colonel spun stories of Cuba, but mainly of "his old pals in the West—John Willis, and Seth Bullock and 'Cold Turkey' and 'Hell Roaring Bill Jones' and the 'lunatic what hadn't his right senses'—not forgetting the Goblin Bear and the boom town reduced to desolation because 'hell-and-twenty Flying A cowpunchers had cut the court-house up into pants' "[9] All "two-gun" tales he would tell again to the delight of royals across Europe.

Another traveler on the *Admiral* was Francis Warrington Dawson, the United Press wire service chief at Paris and its European correspondent. He appeared at Naples with a letter of introduction from TR's friend Henry White and had other connections with Roosevelt's family.[10] Dawson made himself useful by helping the Colonel to repudiate a bogus and insulting interview published in the French press. The offending paper, *Le Journal*, consequently was denied serialization rights for TR's safari articles. This incident, and the false report of the attack on the *Hamburg*, convinced Roosevelt that it might be useful to head off such episodes in the future by filling the news vacuum with authorized bulletins. For this he enlisted Dawson and Robert W. Foran, an ex-Captain in the East African constabulary based in Nairobi, who represented the Associated Press Syndicate.

En route to Mombasa the *Admiral* made several stops, the first a sympathy call at earthquake and tidal wave ravaged Messina in Sicily, where 100,000 had died the previous December. At the time TR had immediately committed $500,000 in United States aid, and personally donated $500 to the Red Cross relief effort. He also diverted American supply ships from the Great White Fleet then at Suez to join the relief effort. Two American vessels and their crews were still on duty at

Messina when Roosevelt arrived at the heart-breaking scene, which he reported to his sister Anna, was "terrible beyond description." However, he went on that it was "enough to make one glow with pride to see how our little group of officers and men from the Navy were doing their work." They were so "cheerful, ready and absolutely efficient" and, in his estimation, by building hundreds of wooden huts for the survivors and in other relief efforts had "literally done more than the Italians themselves, or than all the other Europeans combined."[11] TR allowed Dawson to send off a dispatch to this effect for the press.

Back at Sagamore Hill, Edith and Ethel already missed the travelers dreadfully. Mrs. Roosevelt consoled herself with food, gaining fifteen pounds in the first two weeks of her husband's absence. She confessed to Alice that the "prospect of not seeing Father till next March is unsupportable." Ethel wrote to her brother that it was "horrid not having you and father with us on Easter." Her depression had not been helped at church where the sermon dwelt on mankind's having "gone to the bow-wows."[12] Meanwhile, at Port Said in Egypt, Roosevelt was received by the British and French canal officials, and was given a copy of Dumas's *Louves de Machecoul* to add to the "Pigskin Library" by the brother of his friend Ambassador Jusserand. Specimen collecting continued. Referring to the African trip they had taken as children thirty-eight year before, TR told Corinne that bird skins from Suez were "drying in my room at the moment, just as if we were once more on the Nile."[13] Another hunt was carried out at Aden en route so that by the time they reached Mombasa they already had 102 "nicely prepared" birds of three species and many shells and plants.[14]

On April 21, in a torrential downpour, the *Admiral* arrived at the picturesque and historic island city, with its white walls, pink fortress, and stately palms. British East Africa (after 1920 called Kenya) had only been a Protectorate since 1895 and the area was still a wilderness. White settlement in the more temperate highlands, where wheat, corn, and coffee could be grown, and cattle and ostrich raised commercially, had only begun a few years before with the completion of the Uganda Railway between Mombasa and the immense Lake Victoria Nyanza. In 1909 the ultimate success or failure of the colony, with its few thousand European settlers surrounded by several million tribal Africans, was still an open question. The geography, people, and conditions continually reminded TR of the American West thirty years before.

At Mombasa's Kilindi Harbor, Roosevelt was greeted by Acting Governor Sir Frederick Jackson, flanked by an honor guard of Royal Marines from the *HMS Pandora* anchored amidst native dhows and other vessels. Also on hand were the two hunters assigned to the safari, R. J. Cuninghame and Leslie Tarlton. The lean and heavily bearded Cuninghame was a Scotsman and a Cambridge man who had been, among other things, a whaler in the Arctic, a professional elephant hunter and collector of animals for the British Museum. Tarlton, also an accomplished hunter, was a red-headed, blue-eyed Australian who had fought in the Boer War and stayed on in Africa. The first night they were all given a dinner at the Mombasa Club, where TR met an interesting crowd of local merchants, planters and government officials. He was most intrigued, however, by a German settler on hand who had taken part in hunting down the famous man-eating lions of Tsavo that the Colonel had read of and now heard about at first hand. In his after dinner remarks, Roosevelt praised the civilizing influence of the British Empire in Africa and forecast peace in Europe where the naval rivalry between Britain and Germany, whose own slice of East Africa lay only sixty miles to the south, continued to ratchet up tensions. In his remarks Selous voiced the hope that TR might help bring about an understanding between the two nations when he visited their capitals the following spring.

The next afternoon the Colonel and his party boarded Governor Jackson's special train for the 275 mile rail trip inland from Mombasa up to the cooler climate of the hunting grounds, first crossing the seventeen hundred foot long Salisbury bridge to the mainland. To keep people from shooting game from the train, the British had declared the land along the railroad a huge preserve which the Colonel declared a "naturalist's wonderland." To better view the exotic wildlife, he and Selous stationed themselves on a special platform built onto the cowcatcher of the small locomotive, which TR noted proudly was an American wood-burning Baldwin. He was delighted literally to be passing through "a vast zoological garden." Kermit clambered up on the roof of his carriage to gain a better vantage point. They saw herds of giraffe, waterbuck, hartebeest, ostrich, impala and even a rhinoceros all of whom, TR wrote, were "in their sanctuary and they knew it."[15]

At the Kapiti Plains station the next day, TR and Kermit joined the waiting safari. The venture was one of the largest ever outfitted in those parts and the Colonel remarked that the camp, with its seventy-three tents arranged in neat rows, crowned by the large American flag flying in front of his own, looked as if "some small military expedition was about to start." Leslie Tarlton was waiting for them and called the company to order for TR's inspection. The scientific nature and ambitious goals of the safari meant that two hundred porters were needed to carry the necessary equipment and supplies, including four tons of salt to preserve the specimens prepared by the three Smithsonian naturalists. The porters, though mainly Swahili speaking Wakamba, were chosen from several different tribes to minimize the danger of mutiny. In any case, to keep order and meet any trouble, the expedition also included fifteen rifle-carrying askari guards, ex-soldiers dressed in red fez, blue blouse, and white knickerbockers.

Compared to the rough and ready camp life he knew on the Great Plains, Roosevelt found the accommodations almost too comfortable. His green canvas twelve by nine waterproof tent was equipped with mosquito netting and included a rear extension for a daily hot bath. To escape the ever-present ticks, scorpions and other bothersome creatures there was a ground canvas and a cot for him to sleep on. Kermit's tent was specially lined to do double duty as a darkroom for his photographs. TR had two tent boys to see to his needs, Ali, who knew some English, and Bill, who did not speak at all. In addition he had two gun bearers, Muhamed and Bakari. They carried his three big game rifles: a 30-caliber 1903 Springfield Sporter, a Model 1895 Winchester 405 and a 500/450 Holland & Holland royal grade double-barreled elephant gun donated by a group of English friends and admirers, led by Edward North Buxton.[16]

Roosevelt described the Holland & Holland, which had the presidential seal and his initials engraved in gold on the buttstock, as the "prettiest gun I ever saw, and the mechanism as beautiful as that of a watch."[17] Their own rifles, TR told Buxton, looked "coarse and cheap and clumsy beside it." He had only fired it a half a dozen times as the recoil was heavy and it "made my ears sing."[18] Buxton was in turn delighted that the Colonel found the gun "so much to your taste." He knew it to be effective and trusted it would "prove a good friend to you at interesting moments."[19] To complement this heavy weaponry, Roosevelt brought a customized Ansley H. Fox No. 12 shotgun for birds. This "beautiful bit of American workmanship" was also capable of being loaded with ball as back-up gun for lions. Kermit had his own Winchester 405, as well as a 30–40 Winchester, and for the biggest game a 450 Rigby double-barreled elephant gun. To find the game and study their habits TR carried a telescope given him on the *Admiral* by an Irish Hussar Captain going out to India. To weigh the game he brought an ingenious beam scale given to him by his friend Thompson Seton.

The Colonel also had two "saises," Hamisi and Simba, who looked after his horses, for which he brought his Whitman tree army saddle. He had made special arrangements for a selection of mounts to be on hand and chose two, a sorrel and a brown, which he dubbed Tranquility and Zebra-shape. The natives soon assigned Roosevelt a similarly descriptive name, "Bwana Tumbo" (Mr. Portly Man), while Kermit became "Bwana Mtoto" (Mr. His Father's Sprout).[20] In his account TR records another, more flattering, title for himself, "Bwana Makuba" (Great Master), and for Kermit "Bwana Merodadi" (the Dandy Master).[21]

Outfitted in khaki safari gear and sun-helmet, hob-nailed or rubber-soled boots depending on conditions, and with the nine extra pairs of eye glasses Edith had packed distributed throughout his gear for safe keeping, Roosevelt could now begin his personal quest to bag the five most dangerous African animals: elephant, rhinoceros, buffalo, leopard, and lion. The larger aim of the expedition was to collect family groups for museum display and research of all the major, and minor, species of interest they encountered. Before they were finished ten months later, this would amount to more than 11,000 mammals, birds, reptiles, amphibians, plants and even invertebrates. For big game, the rule established was that the expedition would shoot only what was needed for museum specimens or food. At night and on days of rest which also allowed the taxidermists to catch up, TR sat at his portable writing table scribbling installments on a special two carbon pad for the *Scribner's* magazine series published the next year as *African Game Trails: An Account of the African Wanderings of an American Hunter-Naturalist*. The two copies were dispatched in separate blue canvas envelopes to insure one made it to New York. He sent off the first article, titled "A Railroad Through the Pleistocene," on May 12.

As had been planned, after two days of preparation Roosevelt began his hunt on the way to Kitanga, the seven thousand acre ranch on the Athi River of Sir Alfred Pease, who had met the train at the Kapiti Plains station and, TR reported to his sister Anna, was a "perfect trump." Theodore, Kermit, Pease, and another settler, Clifford Hill, set forth with gun bearers, sais, and a few porters to carry the game, while the rest of the heavily laden safari followed behind. Nearby were herds of hartebeest, wildebeest, and Grant's and Thomson's gazelles. The last, called "tommies," the Colonel recorded, were "pretty, alert, little things" half the size of the American prong-buck. They had one "very marked characteristic:" their tails kept up an "incessant nervous twitching, never being still for more than a few seconds at a time" while their larger cousins hardly moved their tails at all. Roosevelt thought the Grants the most beautiful of the antelope he had seen, rather larger than a whitetail deer, with "singularly graceful carriage," and long lyre-shaped horns carried by the old bucks. His first recorded kill, for the table, was a tommy shot at one hundred and twenty-five yards.[22]

What TR really sought to collect on this first day, however, were a bull and cow wildebeest, a variety of the brindled gnu or blue wildebeest of South Africa. Their shaggy manes, heavy forequarters, and generally bovine look reminded him of a much less bulky version of the American bison. The hunt for the wary and tough animals was successful, but took several shots at long range, and a hard horseback pursuit of many miles, led by Kermit, to take down the tough old bull. The naturalist Roosevelt noted that both animals were covered with ticks. Around the eyes, "the loathsome creatures swarmed so as to make complete rims like spectacles." He was astonished that the game seemed to mind them so little. The biting flies appeared more of a bother, "and the maggots of the bot-flies in their nostrils must have been a sore torment. Nature is merciless indeed."[23] Such observations, along with contents of stomachs and other measurements, were duly recorded for almost every animal. TR sketched many of his kills in his 1909 diary; the simple but striking line drawings resembling nothing more than the Lascaux cave paintings brought into the modern world by the dotted bullet holes illustrating his marksmanship, or more often lack thereof, as he regularly bemoaned his poor aim.[24]

The party traveled sixteen miles further to the Kitanga Hills and Sir Alfred Pease's farm, where they would be guests for two weeks between hunting sorties. The veranda of the ranch house afforded lovely views of valley and forest, and in the evening they could see, "scores of miles away, the snowy summit of mighty Kilimanjaro turn crimson in the setting sun."[25] The ranch house was still a work in progress and TR endeared himself to Sir Alfred's wife, Helen, by comparing it to those he knew and loved in the American West. She found in him a "sympathetic heart united to courage, good sense, and intelligence" which amounted to a "streak of genius." She did not wonder that the American people loved him. To her husband Roosevelt was an exemplary guest, "simple in his habits & wants—always kind, genial, courteous & tactful." He was a great man who still knew how to "be a boy and enjoy things like a boy."[26] Pease was less laudatory concerning the impetuous Kermit, who gave his father a rather bad scare when he became separated from one of these early hunting parties and stayed out alone on horseback overnight. Only the first of many such unsettling episodes to come.

The area was in the second year of a drought and reminded TR of the cattle country he knew so well. There were even bushes the color and size of sagebrush, but covered with flowers like morning glories. He also noted the "infinite variety of birds, small and large, dull colored and of the most brilliant plumage." For the most part they "had no names at all or names that meant nothing to us."[27] True to his lifelong passion for birds, the many detailed and colorful descriptions of them in *African Game Trails* would make a notable separate volume of its own.

Pease was himself later the author of a classic study, *The Book of the Lion*, and endeavored to supply a number of the animals for Roosevelt, who placed the great cat first on his list of desired big game. While hunting from the Pease farm he soon was able to bag two, though disappointing, specimens. These were cubs the size of mastiffs, who dashed out of the bush and were shot before they could be identified. The Colonel would have preferred not to kill them, but he took no chances with lions, which both he and Selous considered the most dangerous African game. Some they spoke to thought the buffalo, rhino and elephant posed greater risks; however, wherever they traveled Theodore and Kermit took grim note of the graves of many more hunters, settlers and natives killed by lions than by any other creature. As additional reminders along the way, Major Mearns's medical skills would also be called upon numerous times to patch up freshly mauled settlers and natives. Such predations had led the British authorities to categorize lions (and leopards) as vermin, which could be taken in unlimited numbers without any license needed.

Their first efforts were disappointing, but finally, on another hunt, which included Lady Pease and her daughter Lavender, TR and Kermit were able to track down full-grown lion specimens, a female weighing

283 pounds and a male weighing 400. These Roosevelt took, with some help, dismounted at close range with his 405 Winchester, which he came to call his "medicine gun" for lions. He described the end of the male in a passage in *African Game Trails* representative of many others, that is colorful and lively, yet at the same time almost apologetic, in his respect for the prey:

> Right in front of me, thirty yards off, there appeared, from behind the bushs [*sic*] which had first screened him from my eyes, the tawny, galloping form of a big maneless lion. Crack! The Winchester spoke; and as the soft-nosed bullet ploughed forward through his flank the lion swerved so that I missed him with my second shot; but my third bullet went through the spine and forward into his chest. Down he came, sixty yards off, his hind quarters dragging, his head up, his ears back, his jaws open and lips drawn up in a prodigious snarl, as he endeavored to turn to face us. His back was broken. But of this we could not at the moment be sure, and if it had merely been grazed, he might have recovered, and then, even though dying, his charge might have done mischief. So Kermit, Sir Alfred, and I fired, almost together, into his chest. His head sank, and he died.[28]

The next day, after killing his first eland, the largest of the antelope, Roosevelt had his first opportunity at a rhinoceros, when a local Wakamba man came up to tell them one was on a hill nearby. The poor eyesight of the rhino allowed TR to walk within thirty yards of the giant beast, which he described as standing "like an uncouth statue, his hide black in the sunlight; he seemed what he was, a monster surviving over from the world's past." For the first time, the Colonel used the powerful Holland & Holland double-barreled rifle. After a first direct hit, the rhino nevertheless was able to get up and charge, and it took two more shots to bring it down, "ploughing up the ground" just thirteen paces from him. In a fashion that would be repeated many times over the next months, TR returned to the main camp to fetch a party of porters to skin and prepare the hides of his kills. One hundred men returned for the rhino and eland, which were within three quarters of a mile of each other. Heller soon complained of "rhinoceritis" (and later "hippopotamaiasis") when he and his crew of six skinners, all Wakamba with their incisors filed to sharp points, could not keep up with the efforts of the hunters. The rhino kill had put the porters in "high feather" and they chanted to an accompaniment of whistling and horn blowing as they all tramped through the moonlight back to the carcasses.[29]

A man of his times, Roosevelt had a patently Darwinistic, paternalistic and racist view of the Africans on the safari. He and Kermit became very fond of several of the men who served them, but never really thought of them as "men" at all. They were children to be taken care of and guided. It was the responsibility of the British to protect and to raise them up to civilized level, which they reckoned would take generations. In turn the Africans should be grateful for the benefits of British rule. Although he realized mistakes would be made, TR thought the natives he saw fortunate to be in the "care" of the British Empire, rather than one of the many less benign alternatives. Independence, given the imperial realities of the ongoing early-twentieth-century "Scramble for Africa," was not perceived as an alternative. Roosevelt told Sir Harry Johnston that he firmly believed in "granting to Negroes of all races the largest amount of self-government which they can exercise," but he had an "impatient contempt for the ridiculous theorists who wish to give to the utterly undeveloped races a degree of self-government which only the very highest have been able to exercise with advantage." To TR, an "even more noxious type" was the man who pandered to these theorists in the utopian treatment "of races that are far away, but promptly repudiates their theories when the application is sought nearer home."[30]

To a large extent "raising up" the Africans was left to missionaries who were often belittled, along with their converts, by travelers. Roosevelt, to the contrary, had seen what he considered the good work done with Native Americans and while he was in Africa he made sure to visit many missions. His first such stop was at the interdenominational American Station at Machakos, where he had lunch with the missionaries, whose work, he admitted had many difficulties and often offered "dishearteningly little reward." The Colonel himself attended either Episcopal or Dutch Reformed services, but praised the efforts of all denominations, Protestant or Catholic. He often said that all religion could be condensed into the eighth verse of the sixth chapter of the prophet Micah: "And what doth the Lord require of thee; but do justly, and to love mercy, and to walk humbly with thy God?" The order of the verse, first to do justly, and only then, to love mercy was important. In TR's view no parent, or missionary, should simply be gentle and merciful to their charges. Justice must be meted out first as his own father had done.[31]

While TR was staying with Pease, Selous and a neighbor, William Northrup McMillan, rode over for lunch. McMillan, a man of Taft-like proportions, was a wealthy American expatriate who had taken up the life of an English gentleman and split his time between East Africa and London. He and Selous reported many lions, including a rare black-maned male, near Juja Farm, McMillan's ranch in the Mua Hills. This alluring prospect led Roosevelt to relocate the safari's base to the McMillan house, which was so comfortable, with a library, drawing room and cool, shaded veranda, that he found it hard to "realize we far in the interior of Africa and almost on the equator." However, he was reminded by the abundant wildlife on the twenty thousand acre spread. Hartebeest, wildebeest, and zebras grazed in sight on the open plain, while hippopotami that lived in the nearby river raided the garden at night. He also noted the plumage and calls of the many exotic birds, among them for the first time the famous honey-guide which led men to rob the hives, and then waited to feast on the bee grubs.

In addition, McMillan and his wife Lucie kept a private menagerie of caged animals including a "fairly friendly" leopard, which allowed Mrs. McMillan to pet it, five lions, two of which were "anything but friendly," and three cheetahs which were continually taken out on leashes, although they "did not lead well." TR found them interesting, "aberrant" cats, standing very high like dogs, with non-retractable claws and faster than any hound or other animal over half a mile. The first time he heard one of their curious chirping calls he had been sure it was a bird and spent some time looking about before he realized it came from one of the cheetah.[32]

The National Zoological Park at Rock Creek in Washington had budgeted $5000 for the purchase of live animals by the expedition, but this was saved when McMillan instead donated most of Juja Farm's collection. He told Mearns that he was tired of having to shoot game for all the big cats, which constant practice also scared away the herds. The animals consequently packed up and dispatched consisted of the five lions and the leopard, one Grant's and one Thomson's gazelle, two cheetahs, a warthog, an eagle, a buzzard and a vulture. These exceeded the expectations of the Zoological Park and were particularly well suited as they were already accustomed to cages.[33] All but the lions were new to the park and only two animals failed to survive the arduous trip to Washington.

The day he arrived at Juja Farm, May 15, TR reported to Lodge that the first three weeks of hunting had so far had been very successful. They were in settled country and there had been no hardship. He had shot "neither well nor badly; having made a number of misses that he had no right to; but having killed most of the things that I specially desired to kill—the lions and rhino." He was rather pleased to find that the American rifles he brought, which everyone had warned him against, had done well. The British authorities had been most kind and "cordially approved of the tact of the people who had arranged my caravan, in providing a large American flag, with which I am solemnly marching through Africa."[34] Lodge had written Roosevelt of America's fascination with his journey, which the people followed in the daily news as if it was a serial story. Many of the papers had no love for TR but published the accounts anyway as the public demanded it. "They follow it all," he told his friend, "with the absorbed interest of a boy who reads 'Robinson Crusoe' for the first time." Lodge had known Roosevelt would be missed, but confessed he was "not prepared for the intensity of the popular interest in every movement you might make after you had left office."[35]

Lions would prove elusive at the McMillan ranch, but Theodore and Kermit had no shortage of other hunting. Included in the Colonel's bag were water-buck and impala. The first he described as a "stately antelope, with long, coarse gray hair and fine carriage of the head and neck." Despite the name he did not find it prone to going in the water, but it did live near streams and lakes. The impala, often found with the water-buck, were joined with the Grant's in his mind as among the most handsome of all antelope. About the size of white-tailed deer, the impala's "beautiful annulated horns" made a single spiral, and their coat was like satin with its contrasting shades of red and white. They also had the most graceful movements of any animal he knew, and when frightened it was extraordinary to see them "bounding clear over the tops of tall bushes, with a peculiar bird-like motion and light-ness." Once again, on close examination, the specimens they took were infested with ticks.[36]

Juja Farm was bounded by three rivers: the Athi, Nairobi, and Rewero, all of which contained hippopotami and crocodiles. Roosevelt was particularly keen to get the first, but while on the lookout for a specimen came across instead an aggressive old female rhino, which he had no choice but to shoot after it charged within forty yards.

Though they tried mightily to avoid repetitions of this incident, over the course of the safari several other rhino met similar unfortunate ends. Under such circumstances, TR wrote, it was not to be expected that men would take "many chances when face to face with a creature whose actions are threatening and whose intentions it is absolutely impossible to divine." In fact, he did not see how the rhino could be permanently safeguarded, except in very out of the way places or game preserves. Otherwise, its "stupidity, curiosity, and truculence" made up a "combination of qualities which inevitably tend to insure its destruction."[37] That afternoon, Roosevelt also shot his first hippopotamus in a deep pool, but it submerged and he did not know whether he had killed it until the body surfaced the next day and was pulled to shore. All this he very briefly reported to Dawson at Nairobi for publication, on the condition that he share the information with his press colleagues there, including Captain Foran, Ambrose Lambert of the *New York Sun* services, and Vaughan Evans of the London *Daily Mail*. Many more such brief bulletins would follow at intervals of ten days to two weeks.

At Juja Farm TR was also able to finish four more articles for *Scribner's*. Though he had plenty to write about for publication, it was not always easy to do so in the field, and he told his sister Corinne that he really did not know how he had done it. In fact, sometimes when he came in early from a hunt he point blank refused to write at all but spent an hour or so with a book from the "Pigskin Library" which, he assured his sister, had been "the utmost comfort and pleasure." Fond though he was of hunting and the wilderness, he could not thoroughly enjoy either if he were not able, from time to time, "to turn to my books."[38]

While Mearns and Loring went on a collecting trip down the Nairobi River, TR and Kermit visited Kamiti Ranch, between the Kamiti and Rewero Rivers. This was the home of Herbert Heatley, and at twenty thousand acres the largest dairy cattle farm in East Africa. The cattle and the climate led Roosevelt to compare what he saw to Wisconsin. The similarities, however, did not include the African buffalo or the completely un-Wisconsin-like papyrus swamps along the Kamiti in which he hunted them. There the papyrus grew to a height of twenty feet and the green stalks were so thick that in many places it was impossible to see more than six feet ahead. Once inside, in hip deep mud and water following the channels made by the hundred or so buffalo in the herd, TR lost all sense of direction.

Considered by some to be the most dangerous of all the game, Roosevelt described the buffalo as "an enormously powerful beast with, in this country, a coat of black hair which becomes thin in the old bulls, and massive horns which rise into great bosses at the base." Sometimes in old age these bosses met "so as to cover the forehead with a frontlet of horn." The buffalo on Heatley's farm had been relatively unmolested by hunters, but were still wary. Fortunately for TR, Kermit, and Cuninghame, they found the herd on an island outside the swamp and were lucky to take four animals. An elated Colonel invited the two pressmen, Dawson and Foran, up from Nairobi, to stay a few days at his camp. He told Foran, "bring your blankets, we'll put you up." That morning, he reported, "Kermit and I killed three buffalo bulls." In the afternoon, they got a wounded bull "in the edge of the papyrus & finished him off."[39]

At the end of May the two parties rejoined at Nairobi, the capital of British East Africa. TR and Kermit stayed at Government House with Acting Governor Jackson, who was also one of the leading experts on East African birds and spent many hours helping Mearns to identify and arrange his specimens for the National Museum. At the same time Heller packed eighty-six large animals, almost all shot by Roosevelt. He reported to Walcott's assistant in Washington that at the pace they were going, they would be able to "fill every nook and cranny of the museum with large mammals." Also that Mearns and Loring were "gleefully engaged in securing the small animals and had shown no tendencies to become big game hunters."[40] While the naturalists prepared the first shipment for the Smithsonian, the local notables feted TR and Kermit. The British at Nairobi, as those across the Empire, tried to recreate the comforts and rituals of society at home, down to meals and gardens. At one dinner the menu included hors d'oeuvres, bouillon, lobster sauce mayonnaise, chicken aspic and jardinière, roast duck, roast lamb, peas, cauliflower, roast potatoes, ice cream, and asparagus béchamel.

Though most outsiders, including Warrington Dawson, found it a hideous place full of tin huts, TR was quite taken with Nairobi and its houses, standing on their own, and usually "bowered in trees, with vines shading the verandas and pretty flower gardens round about." It was in his estimation a "very attractive town, and most interesting with its large native quarter and its Indian colony." One of the streets was made up entirely of Indian shops and bazaars.[41] Since he had arrived at

Mombasa, busy Indian merchants had been prominent wherever there had been settlements, and Indian agents also manned many of the rail stations along the way.

Almost unanimously the settlers with whom Roosevelt stayed, or otherwise conversed, saw the Indian population already on the ground and any further Asian immigration as a threat to making British East Africa, as they put it, a "White Man's Country." Their dream was to create in Africa another white dominion, a miniature New Zealand or Australia, and to this notion they found TR sympathetic, at least to the discouragement of any further Indian settlement in the highlands where they would "come into rivalry with whites."[42] Indian immigration was one of the issues the Colonel was exhorted to take up on the settler's behalf once he reached England. They also complained of Winston Churchill who, not quite two years before, had made a tour of British East Africa to inspect the newly opened railway to Uganda. The then Parliamentary Under-Secretary at the Colonial Office had seen army service in India, the "Jewel in the Crown" of Britain's Empire, and to him East Africa was a backwater which was not paying its own way and consequently a drain on thin British resources.

Arrogant as ever, Churchill spent much of his time hunting from his private rail car, where iced buckets of champagne awaited him at the day's end. He looked down upon the settlers and, once he got home, declared himself sympathetic to Indian immigration.[43] The people TR met had "hoped much" from Churchill's visit, but, as he told his British friend Sir George Otto Trevelyan, "for various reasons most of them had disliked him when he passed through the country, and felt that his speeches and writings when he returned showed that he either had not really grasped the situation or else did not care to do them justice."[44] These writings included *My African Journey*, in which Churchill derided the settler's cry for a "White Man's Country" as a "White Man's Dream," and praised the industriousness of his Asian rival "the brown man," who, he pointed out, had been in East Africa long before the British.[45]

The safari's next destination was the Sotik, a huge limestone plain on the Protectorate's border with German East Africa, where over the following month they found the best shooting, and collecting generally, of the whole trip. Taking the railroad from Nairobi to Kijabe, on June 5 they began a sixty-five mile trek across the desert to the Guaso Nyero River. This slow journey through "the Thirst," with a line of two hundred porters on foot trailing behind the horses and with four huge, white sail-topped, ox-wagons along to carry their water supply, was perhaps most like a scene from Rider Haggard's *King Solomon's Mines* than any other episode in Africa. Along the way they encountered the cattle, sheep and donkey herds of the tall, dignified, and friendly Masai, whom TR described as "herdsmen by profession and warriors by preference, with their great spears and ox-hide shields." The Masai reflected the "ethnic whirlpool" of the area. Some were of the "seemingly pure negro type"; others like "ebony Nilotic Arabs." Still others he found strikingly like "the engravings on the tombs, temples, and palaces of ancient Egypt; they might have been soldiers in the armies of Thothmes or Ramses."[46]

For a few days there were no comfortable tents at night and TR and Kermit slept on the ground in their army overcoats with their saddles as pillows. In the evenings round the campfire they traded stories. Cuninghame and Tarlton spoke of elephant hunting in the Congo, and adventures with lion and buffalo. Mearns described his long hikes and fierce fighting in the hot Philippine forests, including a shocking story of a night spent collecting Moro heads for the Smithsonian. Loring and Heller told of hunting and collecting in Alaska, the Rockies, and along the Mexican border. Always, TR recorded, "our talk came back to strange experiences with birds and beasts, both great and small, and to the ways of the great game." The naturalists trapped and shot a wealth of birds and mammals including "very spry and active" meercats, "things akin to a small mongoose" which lived out on the open plains as did prairie dogs and looked like "pocket-pins when they stood up on end to survey us." However, TR and Kermit were not completely without mercy when it came to collecting specimens. They found a "wee hedgehog, with much white about it," that would cuddle up in the Colonel's hand "snuffing busily with his funny little nose." They did not have the heart to turn the "friendly little fellow" over to the tender mercies of the naturalists and so released him.[47]

At the Guaso Nyero, Mearns and Loring stayed in the vicinity of the camp collecting small game, including many varieties of poisonous snakes, while Heller accompanied TR and Kermit farther south. Once again their intention was to collect family groups of all the major species. Over the next five weeks the hunters bagged various antelope, including eland and their first topi, closely related to the hartebeest and wildebeest. The topi could be distinguished at long distance by their darker color. The wildebeest was the "least normal and most grotesque and odd-looking of the three," and his "idiosyncrasies of temper" were also the most marked. The hartebeest came next with his "high withers, long face and queerly shaped horns." The topi's power of leaping was great. TR had seen one "when frightened bound clear over a companion, and immediately afterward over a high ant-hill."[48] Besides antelope, the party also shot lion, cheetah, zebra, rhinoceros, hyena, and giraffe. To Roosevelt the last, which were such big targets they could be shot at three hundred yards, were particularly interesting. He wanted a large bull, two cows and a young one for the Smithsonian and found to his surprise that the young were the shyest and most suspicious. It was the adults who exhibited a "tameness bordering on stupidity."[49] He was able to bag his group while Kermit, whose shoulder was sore from a fall from his horse, devoted himself to taking shots with his camera.

TR enjoyed the time the safari gave him with his son very much, however, he continued to fret for Kermit's safety. He confided to Ethel that her brother was the most pleasant of companions "when he is where he can't get in a scrape," but also a constant source of worry owing to his "being very daring, and without proper judgment—as to what he is, and what he is not, able to do." He was very hardy, a good rider and carried himself admirably in danger, but did not know his own limitations and that at nineteen he still had much to learn. TR was very proud of Kermit and "devotedly attached to him," but told his daughter, "Heavens, how glad I shall be to get him out of Africa!"[50]

After more than two weeks in the Sotik, Roosevelt reported to his sister Anna that "certainly life in this particular wilderness is delightful." The nights were so cool as to make warm blankets a necessity, although they had to be careful of the sun at noon. The multitude of game made it a hunter's paradise, so no wonder he enjoyed it so. Their game bag so far included over a hundred animals from rhino to giraffe to dikdik, a "tiny antelope no bigger than a hare." TR had not looked at a newspaper since he left home and had already sent six chapters to Scribner's but had no idea whether they were good or not.[51] In the same vein Theodore told his sister Corinne that he was happy to say he knew "nothing whatever of politics at home" and hoped to keep "in that same blessed state of ignorance" until he returned the next June. Then he would take up political work again, "probably not in any direct partisan sense," but chiefly in the pages of the *Outlook* on matters such as the "conservation of natural resources, the control of big corporations, and how to deal with socialism and the like."[52]

Roosevelt's contention that he knew "nothing whatever of politics at home" was a bit of an exaggeration. Though he did not have newspapers at hand he did receive reports, though irregularly and a month or so after they were written, from family and friends, notably his wife and Henry Cabot Lodge.[53] The last, who supported the Massachusetts manufacturing interests in the senate, had already written about the ongoing congressional fight over tariff revision, a major economic issue in these years and also a political minefield that TR had sidestepped while in office. He had told the muckraking journalist Ray Stannard Baker that he was "not deeply interested" in hard economic problems such as banking and the tariff; "my problems are moral problems, and my teaching has been plain morality."[54] Taft was left behind to referee the ensuing congressional free for all over the tariff bill, which split the Republican party between an Old Guard "standpatter" protectionist faction and the insurgent progressive wing which supported downward revision. The president was pledged to the latter; however, following his own conservative inclinations, Taft drifted into the standpatter camp. He felt abandoned by TR, who almost certainly would have steadied his course. Before too long, disillusionment with Taft in the congressional tariff battle led one senator to comment that as a consequence "it may not be so wild a prophecy to say that the next President will be an African." This reference to TR brought down the house.[55]

As fate would have it, Taft was further isolated in May 1909 by the stroke which incapacitated his wife Nellie. She, along with TR, had pushed him into the presidency and was a close confidant and advisor. The seriousness of her condition was kept from the press and consequently Edith Roosevelt only sent consolations the next month, assuring Taft that she would have written sooner had she known the truth of Nellie's illness which she had only learned from Captain Butt's recent visit to Sagamore Hill. Edith also told Taft, who had had no contact with her husband since his departure, that her letters from Africa were full of accounts of good hunting and that "Theodore feels that already the trip has been immensely successful, beyond all his hopes."[56] Hearing news of TR's African triumphs, while he was alone in Washington beset by beasts of another sort, cannot have been pleasant for the president.

Though Roosevelt did not write directly, he did ask their mutual friend Elihu Root, his former secretary of state who had taken a New York seat in the senate, to give his warm regards to Taft, whom he had heard from Lodge was "doing excellently." Of course, TR went on, "Fixing up a Tariff" was much more important than his present occupation, but "not nearly so alluring." Taft was bound to have "his little problems and worries" as president, but that simply was to be expected and things would be all right. TR also confided to Root his worries over the finances of the expedition, which had proved much more expensive than envisioned and after only two months had already used up much of its original funding. Unless Walcott at the Smithsonian could arrange more, the naturalists, who had been doing really remarkable work, would have to go home that summer. He and Kermit would have to finish the trip "on a hunter basis—which would be a pity" for he did not think a chance like this would ever occur again.[57] To keep the naturalists on board, in the end Roosevelt was forced himself to send a plea to Andrew Carnegie, who supplied a further $20,000. In return he would expect a grateful TR to use his influence in Europe to further the millionaire's dreams of international arbitration, disarmament and a league of peace.

From the parched Sotik, the party marched north four days to the lush shores of Lake Naivasha, where hippopotamus was again the prey. They camped near Saigo Soi Ranch, the home of the Attenborough brothers, who provided a steam launch, and big heavy rowboat to use in the hunt. Once again tall green papyrus groves fringed the lagoons, which were covered by water lilies, bearing purple or pink flowers. Across the lilies ran richly colored birds called "lily-trotters" with toes so long and slender the lily pads supported then without sinking. In the lagoons there were also a number of hippo that bellowed and roared at night when they came ashore to feed. On land TR found them "astonishingly quick in their movements for such shapeless-looking, short-legged things." In the water they were also unexpectedly quick, particularly in the shallows where they could "gallop very fast on the bottom under water." After several frustrating days in the launch and rowboat, Roosevelt finally shot a hippo on shore which, in its attempt to get back into deep water, charged the boat "with jaws open bent on mischief." Kermit snapped photos while his father stopped the hippo with a brain shot.[58]

At Lake Naivasha the Colonel received the upsetting news of the dismissal from the Paris embassy of his friend Henry White, a mere three months after Roosevelt had assured White that Taft would keep him in place. Now an embarrassed TR confided to his friend in Paris that the "last thing he wanted to do was criticize his successor," but he wanted him to know that "everything I could do for you was done," not out of his affection for White, "but because as I told Taft I regard you as without exception the very best man in our diplomatic service." Though he had not made a personal request of Taft, he had told him that there were "certain men whose qualifications were of so high an order that I felt I ought to dwell on them and that conspicuous among these was yourself." Taft had told TR and Lodge that he meant to keep White, but he added, ominously for the future, that of course, it was "not a promise any more than my statement that I would not run again for President was not a promise."[59]

More lighthearted news came from Jusserand, to whom Roosevelt had reported that he was as usual having a grand time. The French Ambassador replied that had seen various reports over the previous four months, but doubted the veracity of most of them, and was delighted to hear from TR "direct." Now he knew the "truth of it; all is as it should be, and you are having, 'The Time of Your Life,' just as you had it at the White House, Oyster Bay, Cuba, North Dakota, etc." For the Colonel's amusement, the Frenchman enclosed a newspaper cartoon which showed TR in pith helmet writing on a "Mombasa Souvenir Postcard" addressed to the U.S. Senate, Washington, DC, with the message: "Every time I shoot something I think of you." Jusserand told his friend to continue, "but not too long and mind the mosquitoes." And if the Smithsonian did not have enough room for all his "Rhinos and Hippos" he enclosed another drawing by Clifford Berryman (whose 1902 TR cartoon had inspired the Teddy Bear), which showed a parade of fashionable ladies wearing elephant, rhino and antelope heads, lion muffs and antelope stoles, outside a shop. In its window a sign declared "Latest importations from our agent in East Africa" and another in front of a male lion head stated: "This superb specimen killed by Bwana Tumbo (T.R.)."[60]

Among the many requests sent to Roosevelt from home was one for the permission needed to trademark a "Bwana Tumbo: Hunting in Africa" children's game, but youngsters needed no official rules to take themselves off into the woods pretending to be intrepid hunters in mock safaris of their own. This trend gave fodder to one critic, Dr. William J. Long, whose "nature faker" writings TR had attacked mercilessly while he was president. In a *New York Times* article, Long declared that the "worst feature in the whole bloody business" was not the "killing of few hundred wild animals in Africa," but the "brutalizing influence" which TR's reports of this from Africa had on thousands of American boys. While tramping through some woods only the previous week, Long claimed to have come across "half a dozen little fellows," the oldest calling himself "Bwana Tumbo," who were "shooting everything in sight, killing birds at a time when every dead mother meant a nest full of young birds slowly starving to death." How could he convince them that their work was "inhuman," Long asked, when "the great American hero" was "occupied at this time with the same detestable business?" And why should they not also "be heroic and make a few fine shots" since "faunal naturalists and other game butchers have killed off all our buffaloes?"[61]

All the interest at home, good and bad, led TR to call for action from his editor at *Scribner's*, Robert Bridges. Roosevelt instructed Bridges that he ought to publish the two additional chapters he had sent from Lake Naivasha as articles as soon as possible. Further, his trip had attracted, not only the avid attention of the country, but also the competition. He had been told that no less than eight books were in preparation on hunting and traveling in British East Africa and scheduled to be published by the beginning of the following year. The object, of course, was to "forestall our book." Therefore, to get the first article out by October or November would be "from every standpoint advisable." TR also told Bridges that he thought Kermit had done very well with the photographs and "from the zoological standpoint they are the most important of all" and they ought to use "quite a number of them."[62] The *Scribner's* articles began running in the October 1909 issue and finished the following September, just before the book was published.

On Lake Naivasha searching for a bull hippo to complete the group, chance took the Colonel's rowboat smack into a school of hippo which bumped the bottom several times in their panic to flee after Roosevelt opened fire. The first jar caused them all to sit down. They were struck again, and, he recorded:

> the shallow muddy water boiled, as the huge beasts, above and below the surface, scattered every which way. Their eyes starting the two rowers began to back water out of the dangerous neighborhood, while I shot an animal whose head appeared on my left, as it made off with frantic haste. I took it for granted that the hippo at which I had first

fired...had escaped. This one disappeared as usual, and I had not the slightest idea whether or not I had killed it. I had small opportunity to ponder the subject, for twenty feet away the water bubbled and a huge head shot out facing me, the jaws wide open. There was no time to guess at its intentions, and I fired on the instant. Down went the head, and I felt the boat quiver as the hippo passed underneath...a head burst up twenty yards off, with a lily-pad plastered over one eye, giving the hippo and absurd resemblance to a discomfited prize fighter, and then disappeared with great agitation.[63]

Within an hour four dead hippos appeared on the surface, a big bull and three big cows.

This unwanted carnage occurred simultaneously with an onset of the fever Roosevelt had been subject to since his days in Cuba and the combination sent him into a depression such as Warrington Dawson, who was at the base camp, had not seen. A distraught TR told Dawson that he greatly regretted the hippo incident but had been forced by circumstances to fire into the herd, never dreaming he would kill so many. He went on, "I don't know what to do about it. We shall have to let the papers know. And this is *not* a game-slaughtering expedition."[64] The Colonel was painfully aware of the articles being published at home alleging just such butchery. A week earlier he had written to Captain Foran, who had been lion hunting himself, about the proper response. Before he sent anything TR wanted to discuss the matter, but he told Foran that he thought all that was necessary to say was that "not an animal has been shot except for food or to be preserved for the National Museum, and that as a matter of fact almost all have been thus preserved."[65] As it fell out, the press response to the incident on Lake Navaisha did not prove as violent as feared and within a few days Roosevelt had rebounded, both from the fever and his depression.

In Nairobi for a refit, and to ship the second lot of specimens, TR again enjoyed the considerable hospitality of the McMillans, this time at their house, Chiromo, "with its broad, vine-shaded veranda, running round all four sides, and its garden, fragrant and brilliant with innumerable flowers."[66] The mail waiting at Nairobi included a letter from Lodge, who passed along a comment of their mutual friend Elihu Root, now occupying the New York senate seat previously held by "Boss" Thomas Platt who in 1900 had maneuvered the troublesome TR out of the governor's chair into the vice presidency. About one of the newspaper dispatches on the hunt, Root jibed: "Of course

Theodore shot three lions with one bullet and Kermit shot one lion with three bullets."[67] Roosevelt instructed Lodge to tell Root that he did not "at all like his hardened skepticism about the lions" and if this sort of thing continued he would have to "lead an insurrection" to put Tom Platt back in Root's New York seat when his "term expires—if as I anticipate the worthy Platt at that period still continues to exist in a condition of wicked and malevolent mummification."[68]

Back on safari Roosevelt wrote to his friend Spring Rice, "Here I am, way out in the desert with nobody but the hunter Cuninghame—a trump—and the funny grasshopper-like blacks." Sometimes, he went on, "I have shot well, sometimes badly; and I am now an old man, and wholly unable to make exertions which once I should not have regarded as exertions at all." But still on the whole he felt he had done pretty well, and from the scientific standpoint the trip would be of value as no such collection of complete skins of big game had ever been sent out of Africa by any one expedition. TR looked forward to seeing Spring Rice in England and talking to him about what he had seen in "your African colonies." He greatly liked and admired "your officials, and your settlers seem to me in all essentials just like our westerners." It was in fact difficult for him to remember that he was "not a fellow countrymen of theirs"; and they certainly acted as if they thought he was "an especial friend and champion who sympathized and believed in them." TR concluded by telling Spring Rice that he was "dreadfully homesick for Mrs. Roosevelt. Catch me ever leaving her for a year again, if I can help it."[69] While he lived out his dream of Africa Edith, equally homesick for Theodore, had struck out on an expedition of her own to Europe.

Chapter 3

A Lion Roars in East Africa

While Theodore stalked British East Africa with Kermit, Edith took three of the children, Ethel, Archie, and Quentin, on an expedition of their own to Europe. They sailed on the S. S. *Crete* and she brought along $10,000 to finance a five months "endless sightseeing tour," for the children's education.[1] The voyagers arrived on July 12, 1909 at Genoa where Edith's maiden sister, Emily Carow, awaited them. By nightfall they were all ensconced seventy miles away at Emily's tiny house, Villa Magna Quies (Villa of Great Quiet), outside Porto Maurizio. Though small, the villa in the Ligurian Hills featured breathtaking views of olive groves and the Mediterranean. For a few restful weeks the children rode bicycles and took daily French, Italian, and Latin lessons at the nearby Franciscan monastery. Edith ignored the journalists who snapped their pictures while they strolled on the pebbly beach or the donkey trails, protected by a Secret Service Agent. At the end of July, Ethel and Archie embarked for a tour of Provence with the U.S. ambassador to Italy, Lloyd Griscom, and his wife. On Edith's forty-eighth birthday, August 6, she and Quentin explored the *Palais Des Papes* and saw a play at the amphitheatre at Orange before traveling to Lyons to be reunited with Ethel and Archie. Edith confided to her aunt Lizzie that she was beginning to feel "a little more confident in my powers of looking out for myself."[2]

A week later the family was back together in a Paris apartment in the Rue Gabriel. Over the next month they carried out an intensive campaign of museums, palaces, and cathedrals from their Paris base. Their friend Henry Adams, who summered there and had written an important book on French cathedrals, joined them for sightseeing. He complained of playing "dancing bear to Mrs. Roosevelt," but in fact the curmudgeonly Adams admired her and enjoyed his time with the children. He was particularly fond of Quentin and on Ethel's eighteenth birthday gave her a party at the ornate *Le Petit Palais* on the Left Bank, built for the 1900 Paris Universal Exhibition. Her father was happy to hear (some weeks later) that the party had been such a success and that Ethel's mother had become a real "pretty miss dimples" when she thought of his struggles with "my one chicken" Kermit. TR reported to Ethel that the "one chicken" was off on "his own hook now" with a "haggard deputy hen" in the shape of Tarlton, but he was much less anxious than he had been about the risks. His chief concern at present was that Kermit, because he was so keen and active, did not understand that TR had to take the first chance at the game, "because a large part of the value to the museum vanishes if I do not shoot it myself." Kermit could not bear to think the trip would ever end while TR looked forward to the last of March and being reunited at Khartoum with his wife and daughter.[3]

On September 11, to return to their schoolwork, Archie and Quentin took ship home accompanied by an adult chaperone, Ward Theron. That day Edith confided to Spring Rice that "for the last six months my life has been made up of partings which seemed more or less inevitable." She reported that Warrington Dawson had come to Paris from Africa with "many tales of the hunters." There was nothing left to them now but "white rhino and a few rare species with unheard of names." She did rather dread the long trip through the less healthy climate of Uganda, but knew that precautions would be taken. Dawson had reported that TR was in perfect health and that Kermit was "absolutely tireless." Of the whole safari of 200 there was no one who could keep up with him. She asked Spring Rice if he remembered "what a frail little midget" Kermit was as a boy, "with a great iron brace on his leg." Edith told Spring Rice to write to her and not to mind saying things about sleeping sickness as she knew "all about it" and did not need to "pretend to you that I think Africa is a Paradise, in any case it is less dangerous to life than the White House!"[4]

The departure of the boys left Edith and Ethel free to visit Switzerland, Milan, Verona, Venice, Padua, and Turin before returning to Porto Maurizio on 8 October. Later in the month they added Florence, Siena, and Rome to their itinerary. At the last, in the early hours of November 6, Edith was awakened by news of "a terrible rumor" circulating that Theodore had been killed in Africa. Only at five that afternoon did a cable finally arrive from TR's friends in Nairobi confirming that the report was false. An immensely relieved Edith nevertheless told their friend Spring Rice that the fright, "took something out of me which can't come back until I see him."[5] When he learned of his wife's distress over the false report, Roosevelt moved up his arrival in Khartoum by two weeks, to mid-March. On November 12, 1909, Edith and Ethel sailed for New York.

The same day, from their camp on the 'Nzoi River, near Mount Elgon in British East Africa, TR poured out his heart to Edith in one of the few love letters she attached enough importance to not to later destroy in an attempt to protect their privacy. "Oh sweetest of all sweet girls," he wrote, "last night I dreamed that I was with you, and that our separation was but a dream; and when I awoke it was almost too hard to bear. Well, one must pay for everything. You have made a real happiness in my life; and so it is natural and right that I should constantly [be] more and more lonely without you." He went on, "Darling, I love you so. In a little over four months I shall see you, now."

Of his present situation, Roosevelt explained that the 'Nzoi, a rapid muddy river with crocodiles and hippos in it, was one of the streams that made up the headwaters of the Nile. Its banks were fringed with strange trees, and the surrounding country was covered with grass so high as to make it hopeless to look for lions. But they had killed many antelope of kinds new to them, and whose names would mean little to her—bohor, sing sing, oribi, lelwel, kob. It seemed to be a healthy country for men but half their horses had died and they might have to go on to the railway by foot. He worried whether his *Scribner's* articles had been well received but hoped at least "you have liked them" and confessed that it had been "a very real resource to have them to do." He reassured her that he never would have taken the safari as "merely a pleasure trip, a mere hunting trip." He signed the letter "Your Own Lover."[6]

Over the previous months, TR had been busy himself. At Nairobi on August 3, 1909, before an audience of two hundred settlers and officials, he gave the first of many public preachments to follow over the next ten months on a variety of topics, ranging from his view of Britain's imperial mission to world peace, taking to the wider world the "bully pulpit" he had made famous at home. The Colonel told his Nairobi audience that he had come on a pleasure trip and any ex-president or ex-statesman who desired "an antidote for the pleasures or troubles of the past," would do well to "have recourse to lion shooting" for then they would live "in the immediate present." Without detracting from the lion, hunting buffalo in a papyrus swamp was also "unrivalled for distracting the attention of the mind from the past." In addition to being "the most attractive playground in the world," Roosevelt believed the country had a great agricultural and industrial future. From the first time he stood on the Kapiti Plains, conditions in British East Africa struck him as similar to those he knew in the American West years earlier and, though times were hard at present, he believed that eventually the same wealth that came West during the last quarter century would come to the protectorate.

Men of means and business should be encouraged, but in TR's view for the colony to prosper most newcomers must settle on the land, and be of the right type, farmers, and ranchers from "tough fighting stock" like those who had gone to the Rocky Mountains and Great Plains thirty years before. Such settlement was now possible because of the Uganda Railroad. The construction of this he compared to the Panama Canal and railways in the American West, both built for future needs and not in terms of whether they would pay or not. He had not the "slightest sympathy" with those at home in the Liberal government who expected an immediate return. Not many people outside of Africa realized that this was one of the few regions in the world fit for new white settlement and that the protectorate was in fact "a real white man's country." He had been told that white children could not prosper, but had seen them "as sturdy as anyone could wish to see" and as "healthy as any in America or the British Isles."

Up to this point, TR had been preaching to the choir and his comments roundly applauded, but he warned his audience that he was now going to speak "at the risk of not receiving so much sympathy." In making this a "white man's country," Roosevelt asked them to remember that "not only the laws of righteousness but your own real and ultimate self-interest demand that the black man be treated with justice, that he be safeguarded in his rights and helped upward, not pressed downward." However, he had no patience with "sentimentalists," who he believed did more damage than did brutality. In his view, the native tribes were "hopelessly incompetent to better themselves or to utilize this country to advantage, without white leadership and direction."

Neither did he have any patience for those at home who "prate of self-government" for people who have "not governed themselves and never could." The white population must "occupy a position of unquestioned mastery and leadership," but with a "deep sense of all the responsibility which it entails." This was why Roosevelt believed in helping the missionary, of whatever creed, who labored "sincerely, disinterestedly, and with practical good sense in his fieldwork." He judged men by their conduct, not by creed or origin.

In the difficult task of building this new nation, TR told his audience, "you are entitled to the heartiest support and encouragement" from the "men who stay at home." Responding to those who had asked for his aid on this front, he went on that he meant to "speak frankly" when he reached London. The Colonel concluded with an exhortation to "stand by each other" and to remember that "time spent in back biting" was wasted, and to "work heartily together" so that they would soon "turn this region into a real and prosperous white man's country." As the rest of the speech, this peroration was greeted with prolonged and loud applause.[7]

Roosevelt really liked the men he met in British East Africa and he found all the officials to be "most kind." He commented to Lodge that the day was past when an American was regarded as a poor relation and "if we remain self-reliant and powerful it will never return." TR was interested to see how extensive American influence was and in how many directions it was felt. For example among the novels in the houses no English ones were more common than those of the American authors Edward Noyes Westcott and Winston Churchill, adding, "I mean of course our Winston Churchill, Winston Churchill the gentleman." Their hunter Tarlton, an Australian, was fond of books and among his favorites were Longfellow, Bret Harte, and Mark Twain, and he felt towards the United States "just about as he feels towards England—if anything more warmly."[8] He told Lodge that half the people he met looked as though they had walked out of the pages of Kipling, but they greatly resented his saying so as they looked upon Kipling "much as Californians look upon Bret Harte."[9]

Two days after the Colonel's Nairobi speech, the congressional insurgents who had waved TR's progressive banner in the tariff fight finally lost their battle as Taft signed into law the Payne-Aldrich Tariff. The measure in fact changed things little overall, but it was seen as an upward revision and this perception ruled the day, to the detriment of

Taft's political future. Archie Butt, however, reported to his old chief on the tariff, in his opinion the only important matter that had come up since Roosevelt left, that he would be pleased to learn that Taft had "whipped the old-timers" such as Aldrich and Cannon. Though not pleased with the bill, the president had got "certain fundamentals incorporated in it" which he felt made the measure "one he could sign." Butt also reported that he had been playing golf, a game he had never liked, with Taft and was beginning to suspect it had "charms of which I have been ignorant." In their old White House days he had "corns on my right hand from tennis." Now his right hand was as "delicate as that of a girl," while there were corns on his left hand, "the change of hands showing the change of administrations."[10]

Roosevelt departed Nairobi August 8 for a month's elephant hunting at Mount Kenya and beyond. Decades of ivory hunting had driven the herds to more and more remote areas and led the British to extend protections from extermination. No cows were allowed to be shot except by special license for museums and no bulls with ivory weighing less than thirty pounds. In Roosevelt's opinion, too much praise could not be given the "government and the individuals who had brought about this happy result" as it would be "a veritable and most tragic calamity if the lordly elephant, the giant among existing four-footed creatures, should be permitted to vanish from the face of the earth."[11] Wherever he had gone, no other animal, not even the lion, was so widely spoken of and respected as the great pachyderm. "Not only to hunters," TR wrote, "but to naturalists, and to all people who possess any curiosity about wild creatures and the wild life of nature" the elephant was the "most interesting of all." This was because of the unrivalled combination of its "huge bulk, its singular form, the value of its ivory, its great intelligence—in which it is only matched, if at all, by the highest apes, and possibly by one or two of the highest carnivora—and its varied habits." In line of descent and physical formation the elephant stood by itself, "wholly apart from all the other great land beasts, and differing from them even more widely than they differ from each other."[12]

Rejoining Mearns and Loring at Lake Naivasha, the party trekked sixty miles northeast through Kikuyu country across the high plains of the Aberdare range to Neri in the foothills of 17,000-foot Mount Kenya, eighty miles north of Nairobi. Their last camp, at an altitude of 10,000 feet, was so cold that the water froze in the basins. At Neri, they were greeted by the District Commissioner, who organized a great

Kikuyu dance in their honor. Two thousand naked and half-naked warriors took part in the celebration. Some carried "gaudy blankets, others girdles of leopard-skin; their ox-hide shields were colored in bold patterns, their long-bladed spears quivered and gleamed." Many wore head-dresses made of a lion's mane or the black and white pelt of a Colobus monkey. Their faces were painted red and yellow. Those of the young men about to undergo the rite of circumcision were "stained a ghastly white, and their bodies fantastically painted." The women, "shrilled applause, and danced in groups by themselves."[13]

The next day the clouds lifted and they were able to see the high rock peaks of Kenya, one of the rare glacier-bearing mountains of the equator. Mearns and Loring stayed in the area to make a thorough survey, while Roosevelt, Heller and Cunningham spent a week tracking down elephant. This hunt was carried out in a great forest, from which a thick screen of wet foliage largely shut out the sun. It was only passable, single file, on the elephant paths that wound up hill and down and on which the men had to duck under flower covered vines and scramble over fallen timber. The rain-soaked ground forced Roosevelt to wear his hob-nailed boots. On the second day they came upon the fresh trail of a herd of a dozen or so elephants, including two big bulls, which it took another day's tramping to overtake. First came their "savage" 'Ndorobo guides, then Cuninghame followed by his gun bearer, Roosevelt and his own, with Heller and a dozen porters and skinners bringing up the rear. They left their first night's camp intact and traveled with food for three days and carried two small tents.

Before they could see them, they could hear the elephants as they moved through the forest, the boughs cracking under their weight. TR was also struck by the clearly audible and "curious internal rumblings of the great beasts." He tried when possible to step in the footprints of the huge animals where there were no unbroken sticks to crack under his feet. It "made our veins thrill," he wrote, "thus for half an hour to creep stealthily along, but a few rods from the herd, never able to see it because of the extreme denseness of the cover." Finally, thirty yards in front of them, the head of a big bull with good ivory, resting its tusks on the branches of a young tree, came into view. Using the Holland & Holland, TR aimed a little to one side of the left eye, hoping for a brain shot and a clean kill. The first bullet, however, only stunned the bull, and it took the second barrel to dispatch it. Before he could reload, the thick bushes parted before him and "through them surged the vast bulk of a charging bull elephant" so close he could have "touched me with his trunk." TR dodged aside as Cuninghame opened fire, driving the wounded bull into the forest. He "trumpeted shrilly, and then all sound ceased."[14]

Pursuing the wounded animal would have to wait as they had first to preserve the skin of Roosevelt's bull, which would take some time and had to be done immediately. The tusks of his first elephant weighed a respectable one hundred and thirty pounds and the gun bearers and porters wildly celebrated the kill. The workers were soon "splashed with blood from head to foot" by the skinning which continued until stopped by darkness. One of the 'Ndorobo trackers took off his blanket and "squatted stark naked inside the carcass the better to use his knife." All the men cut off strips of meat for themselves, hanging them in "red festoons from the branches round about." Until late that night, around the camp fires, the men feasted and sang "in a strange minor tone." The flickering light left them "at one moment in black obscurity, and the next brought them into bold relief their sinewy crouching figures, their dark faces, gleaming eyes and flashing teeth." In a primitive rite his own Pleistocene ancestors would have appreciated, the Colonel feasted on slices of elephant heart roasted on a pronged stick. He found it "delicious; for I was hungry, and the night was cold."[15]

Leaving Cuninghame and Heller behind to finish the preservation, and to track down Cuninghame's wounded bull, Roosevelt returned to Neri to organize a hunt of his own for the first time. It took several days to find enough Kikuyu porters, and in this he enlisted the help of two young Scots who spoke the language. While he waited, Acting Governor Jackson arrived at Neri and Roosevelt was able to tell him of his bull elephant as well as the birds and mammals they had trapped. A great "ingowa" or war dance was organized in Jackson's honor, the sight of which TR found "one of interest and a certain fascination."[16] Since the fifty Kikuyu finally assembled could not handle the loads of the regular porters, the Colonel hired donkeys to carry the food required to the elephant camp. Continuing the quest for elephant and other game, in the end he pushed almost a hundred miles further north to the headwaters of the Guaso Nyero River. Though it was supposed to be the dry season, the weather continued very wet and during one evening's violent storm a funnel cloud snaked its way across the skies in sight of their camp, luckily moving away from them.

On this solo hunt they encountered no elephant but many antelope, in particular eland, the "king of the antelope," and the "strongly built and boldly colored" oryx, with long, black, rapier-like horns. A good bull eland head was among the few trophies Roosevelt desired for himself and he was pleased to be able to shoot, at three hundred yards, a "magnificent bull" with a fine head of the variety called Patterson's eland. Trying to find a similar specimen for the museum, Roosevelt came upon a herd of the large antelope, no faster than the range cattle he was used to, in open country. He galloped towards the herd on his brown zebra-shaped horse and, for the next fifteen or twenty minutes, felt as though he was a youth again in the "cow camps of the West, a quarter century ago." Twice he rounded up the herd, just as once in Yellowstone he had rounded up a herd of elk for John Burroughs to look at. Among the eland, however, there were no big bulls, only cows and young stock. He nevertheless "enjoyed the gallop."[17]

Next TR turned to oryx, which proved maddeningly elusive. Finally, after missing at four hundred yards, and feeling "rather desperate," he unleashed a fusillade, emptying his magazine "on the Ciceronian theory, that he who throws a javelin all day must hit the mark some time." This stratagem yielded an oryx cow with a handsome dun gray coat, long tail and horns, and bold black and white markings on its face. Roosevelt assigned four Kikuyu to skin the animal and carry in the meat. He was amused at the condescension with which his four regular attendants, his gun-bearers and sais, treated "their wild and totally uncivilized brethren" whom they called "shenzis," savages or bush people, and would not associate with in any way.[18]

Though the Colonel claimed to thoroughly enjoy "being entirely by myself, as far as white men were concerned" for this period of more than two weeks, he was pleased when, on the afternoon of September 3, Cuninghame, Heller and the main safari caught up with his party.[19] The combined expedition then set out for Meru boma, a small settlement in the snowy northeast slopes of Mount Kenya, directly under the equator, where three days later they were reunited with Kermit and Tarlton, who had been exploring the lower reaches of the Guaso Nyero. They also had found no elephant, but did kill lion, cheetah, oryx, and buffalo, and collected examples of several new animals including the aard-wolf, a miniature hyena; the gerenuk, a small giraffe-like antelope; and Grévy's zebra, as big as a small horse.

Roosevelt wanted another cow and bull elephant for the National Museum and they were fortunate at Meru boma to receive a report of three cows raiding the fields of the local people that had charged when an attempt was made to drive them away. The party found the animals in a practically impenetrable jungle of ten-foot tall "rank growing bushes" which was not good ground for hunters. They could only travel on the elephant trails while their prey could move in any direction, "with no more difficulty than a man would have in a hay-field." Luckily the party came upon the trunk of a great fallen tree and scrambled up it to a platform six feet above the ground. Balanced on this perch, TR was able to get a glimpse of the elephants. At sixty yards he opened fire at the largest with the Holland & Holland, the blast of which, he recorded, was "none too pleasant for the other men on the log and made Cuninghame's nose bleed." It was even less pleasant for the stunned animal, which he finished with his Springfield. The elephant turned out to be, not a cow, but a herd bull with forty-pound tusks. This specimen TR gave to the University of California.[20]

Back at Meru boma, Roosevelt reported to Lodge the "great comfort" the pigskin library gave him. The same was true, he said, about writing his own book, which he must finish before he reached Khartoum, for "I am now too old to be able contently to spend a year living only as a hunter and with my brain lying fallow." He told his friend that he and his wife Nannie would be amused to hear that in Africa he had "come into my inheritance of Shakespeare." He had never before cared for more than one or two of the plays, but for some reason the "sealed book was suddenly opened to me on this trip." Roosevelt supposed that when a man who was fond of reading was for long periods in a wilderness with but a few volumes he "inevitably grows into a true appreciation of the books that are good." He still balked at three or four of the plays, but most of them he had read over and over again.[21]

While the Colonel rested at Meru boma, a native runner brought the news that Captain Robert Peary had succeeded in reaching the North Pole. At Oyster Bay a year before, TR had gone on Peary's ship, *The Roosevelt*, to wish him "God-speed" for the effort. Several months later the Captain had sent to the White House what young Quentin called "treasures" from the arctic. These included a narwhal horn for the President, "wonderful and beautiful" fox skins for Edith and whale's ears for Quentin, who was, Roosevelt explained to Peary, the "first individual who recognized what those last treasures were."[22]

On September 12, 1909 TR instructed Foran that if the news about Peary's reaching the North Pole was "unquestionably authentic," to have the following published for him: "I rejoice over Captain Peary's great achievement. Too much credit cannot be given to him; he has performed one of the great feats of the age, and all his countrymen should join in doing him honor." About the safari, Roosevelt added that since he had written last he had killed two more elephants and Kermit one. Soon Kermit was going off west towards Lake Harrington and across to the Guaso Nyero. He asked Foran to share this with the Reuters news service people.[23]

As Kermit and Tarlton traveled west, TR and Cuninghame trekked directly north towards the Guaso Nyero District where they arrived on September 25. To insure there would be enough food for the porters they again took a small donkey safari with extra supplies. Along the way, the periodic rattle of the tall dry grass in the wind reminded the Colonel so much of the rattlesnakes of the West that, even though he knew no African viper made such a noise, each time the sound brought him instantly to attention in his saddle. Among the new animals TR shot were reticulated giraffe and ostrich, whose heart, liver and eggs he found excellent eating. The porters brought in ostrich chicks and two genet kittens, "much like ordinary kittens, with larger ears, sharper noses and longer tails." He became fond of the "dear" little cats, which perched on his shoulder or sat in his lap while he stroked them. He tried to raise them but failed and was very sorry when they died.[24]

Their picturesque camp on the banks of the Guaso Nyero was on the edge of an open glade in a shady grove of giant mimosas. The river ran across the equator, through a desert country eastward into the Lorian swamp where it disappeared. At their location it was a broad, rapid, muddy stream infested with crocodiles, which TR loathed as man killers and shot when he could. From this camp he collected a pair of gerenuk, the "queer long-legged, long-necked antelope" with the curious habit of rising on their hind legs to browse among the bushes, unlike any other antelope he saw. Roosevelt also had a remarkable encounter with a napping cow giraffe, which awoke and stared at him as he stalked within forty yards. When he stopped, she dozed off again and allowed him to come within ten feet. The giraffe then re-awoke from its slumber and reared slightly, striking at him with her left foreleg, but the blow fell well short. The others came up shouting but the cow would not run away. "She stood within twenty feet of us," TR recorded, "looking at us peevishly, and occasionally pouting her lips at us, as if she were making a face." They all found the whole situation so strange and humorous that shooting the giraffe was out of the question. In the end, after three or four minutes, it took a pelting of sticks and dirt clods for the animal to canter off fifty yards and then to take up a leisurely walk. No other giraffe had allowed them to get within two hundred yards and all four men found her "utter indifference" to them inexplicable.[25]

Back at Nairobi on October 20, Theodore was reunited with Kermit, who had his twentieth birthday while off hunting with Tarlton. Their bag included Neuman's Hartebeest and the stately, handsome, and hard to get, great koodoo. En route TR had received a parcel of letters, including two from his sister Anna, who had written of the tragic death of Henry Cabot Lodge's son, by which news he was "inexpressively shocked and grieved" and wished he could be on the "same side of the water" to console his friends. About their trip Theodore reported that Kermit was now a better hunter than was he, "for Twenty is hardier and more active and endowed with better eyes than Fifty One." He hoped that in his articles he had been able "measurably to reproduce what we have seen, and the wonder and the charm of the life." In two months they would be leaving for Uganda and the Nile, "and then our time of discomfort and trouble begins."[26]

After enjoying five days of rest at Nairobi, Roosevelt departed for the Uasin Gishu plateau and the 'Nzoi River which flowed not far from the foot of Mount Elgon. While on this hard march TR passed his fifty-first birthday, but they were unable to pause for the celebratory hunt as he would have liked. The landscape reminded him of northern California or southern Oregon rather than any tropical country. The nights were so cold that he had to wear a lumberman's mackinaw he had not expected to use in Africa. The party arrived at the plateau on November 1, and from their first camp, shot giraffe, hartebeest, and oribi antelope for the Smithsonian. The giraffe camp was two days from the 'Nzoi River which emptied into Lake Victoria Nyanza. They had crossed the divide to the Nile side of the watershed and the rivers no longer flowed into the Indian Ocean.

On the trek to the 'Nzoi, TR was more interested in the honeyguides than the game. John Burroughs had especially charged him to look personally into the habits of these extraordinary little birds, the existence of which Burroughs was "inclined to disbelieve." But their experiences in Africa confirmed the stories. In fact the birds at times became a real nuisance with their constant harsh chatter. Besides bee hives, they were also reputed to lead men to a serpent or wild beast, which Mearns experienced first hand when one of the honey-guides led him face to face with a rhinoceros.[27]

Mearns and Loring had stayed behind in Nairobi, preparing yet another shipment for the National Museum. Though they were treated extremely well by the British, the claims of the discovery of several new species by the American expedition in their domain irked some Englishmen who believed such finds should be reserved for the British Museum (Natural History). Consequently, an international race of sorts developed. Mearns confided to Walcott's assistant at the Smithsonian that Roosevelt was "awfully pleased to have us get new species and describe them first" and wanted "quick action" on the fox of Naivasha. He asked the museum to "work up" the fox and "describe it, if new, without delay." The English had scrambled to get ahead of them at every turn and the local game ranger, who had seen the fox, claimed it was the first ever taken. The British expected to bag their own specimen and were prepared to put it on the same steamer which would carry Mearns' letter. Further, the English had rushed to send a collection of the fish of Lake Victoria to the British Museum (Natural History) when they learned he planned to collect there.[28]

Meanwhile, from his camp on the 'Nzoi, TR's expedition ran across the only other safari they would meet in almost a year in the wilds, that of Carl Akeley, who was hunting elephant for the American Museum of Natural History in New York. He and Roosevelt had planned to meet in Africa, but his departure had been delayed and he had thought TR had gone on to Uganda. The Colonel had already shot a bull elephant for the New York museum, but Akeley wanted Roosevelt to add a cow. As it happened, TR's party had passed an elephant herd the day before which, since they already had their quota of the great beasts, Kermit only photographed. They all joined forces in pursuit of this herd, which was soon located. Using a huge anthill for cover, TR stalked to within sixty yards. Akeley expected Roosevelt to shoot at the cow he pointed out to him from behind the anthill, but instead the Colonel walked around it and began advancing towards the herd. He had an impulse to "climb on Roosevelt's shoulder and whisper that I wanted him to shoot her, not take her alive."[29] TR got within thirty yards before the elephant saw him and when he opened fire, the herd charged. To stop this they were forced to kill one more cow than the two Akeley wanted for his museum. After the herd was turned Kermit shot a bull calf to complete the collection.

While Tarlton and Kermit returned to the camp to fetch the equipment and men needed to preserve the elephants, Akeley and Roosevelt rested in the shade of an acacia tree. TR talked of Edith and his children at home. He had not seen anyone from the United States for many months, while Akeley was fresh from America and had visited Oyster Bay before he left. In those three hours, Akeley later wrote, he got a "new view of Theodore Roosevelt." It was then that he "learned to love him." It was then that he realized he could "follow him anywhere; even if I doubted, I would follow him because I knew his sincerity, his integrity, and the bigness of the man."[30] Akeley also passed along an invitation to come to Constantinople for TR from his old friend Oscar Straus, who had accepted the Ambassadorship to Turkey. This his schedule would not allow. Instead the Colonel asked Straus and his wife to meet him at Cairo in March.[31] His friend had also sent a bottle of cognac, which TR passed along to Cuninghame, who had a greater appreciation of such things.

Once the men and supplies returned, they pitched camp a hundred yards from the elephants and, TR recorded, Akeley and Tarlton, working like demons, "had the skins off the two biggest cows and the calf before nightfall." That night they listened to the raucous chorus of the hyenas fighting among themselves as they gorged on the carcasses. Near morning a lion came along and "uttered a kind of booming long drawn moan, an ominous and menacing sound." The hyenas replied with an "extraordinary chorus of yelling, howling, laughing, and chuckling, as weird a volume of noise" as any the Colonel had ever heard.[32] At dawn he and Akeley crept out in their pajamas hoping to get a shot at the lion, but it was gone. As they came towards one carcass a hyena raised its head from inside and Roosevelt promptly shot it with his Springfield. But he need not have bothered as the animal had managed to push his wedge shaped head between a wall of muscle in the elephant's stomach and then was unable to extract it. The hair was worn thin on his neck from his efforts but, Akeley wrote, he was "literally tied up in the thing that he loved best."[33]

After saying his farewells to Akeley and his party, Roosevelt had the opportunity to witness a lion hunt of a different kind, carried out with spears by Nandi warriors. This was arranged by the district commissioner at Sergoi Lake, Mr. Corbett. Like the Masai, to whom they were kin, the Nandi were warlike pastoralists who, with intertribal warfare ended by British rule, were limited to lion killing as a rite of passage for their young men. Eight hundred warriors had volunteered and seventy were chosen for the privilege. On this hunt, across a rolling grass plain, Roosevelt's duty was only to "round up the lion and hold him" for the advancing Nandi whom he described as

> splendid savages, stark naked, lithe as panthers, the muscles rippling under their smooth dark skins; all their lives they had lived on nothing but animal food, milk, blood and flesh, and they were fit for any fatigue or danger. Their faces were proud, cruel, fearless; as they ran they moved with long, springy strides. Their headdresses were fantastic; they carried ox-hide shields painted with strange devices; and each bore in his right hand the formidable war spear ... the narrow spear heads of soft iron were burnished till they shone like silver; they were four feet long and the point and edges were razor-sharp ... each sinewy warrior carried his heavy weapon as if it were a toy, twirling it till it glinted in the sun-rays.[34]

At last they found their lion, a large, black-maned male in his prime lying near a hartebeest on which he had been feeding. TR was sorely tempted to shoot the magnificent beast himself but could not break faith with the Nandi who had come only on the condition that they could make the kill. One by one the spearman approached, forming a ring around the lion, each man crouching behind his shield, his spear in his right hand. The lion's "mane bristled and his tail lashed" as he held his head low, facing first one way and now another, never ceasing to "utter his murderous grunting roars." Once the ring was complete the Nandi closed in, the leader bounded ahead of his fellows to throwing distance, driving his weapon three feet deep, through the lion's shoulder and out the opposite flank near the thigh. The mortally wounded lion nevertheless sprang on the man who covered himself as best he could with his shield as his fellows closed in with their own spears flashing to join the fight. Several other weapons were driven home but before the lion succumbed he managed to wound another Nandi and gripped a spearhead in his jaws with such force that it bent double.[35] It was a wild sight Roosevelt would never forget and became perhaps his most recounted African story.

By this time back at home, a serious crisis over conservation policy, dubbed the Ballinger-Pinchot affair, had been added to Taft's political troubles over the tariff and other matters.[36] TR's man Gifford Pinchot, still the chief of the Division of Forestry in the Agriculture Department, had come into conflict with Taft's Secretary of the Interior, Richard Achilles Ballinger, over allegations of wrongdoing when Ballinger's department allowed the allocation of coal lands in Alaska to a Morgan-Guggenheim syndicate. With Roosevelt in Africa and his ally Garfield gone from the Interior Department, Pinchot saw himself as the sole protector of his and TR's policies. Further, he feared Taft and Ballinger's deliberate and legalistic view of things gravely jeopardized the advances made under Roosevelt, which had often been carried out through presidential commandments that stretched the boundaries of legality—to say the very least.

The firing of the investigator who had brought the charge against Ballinger set in motion a chain of events that in the end prompted Pinchot to send a scathing letter about the whole affair to a conservation ally, Iowa Senator Jonathan P. Dolliver, who famously described Taft as an "amiable man surrounded by men who know exactly what they want."[37] Almost completely forgotten today, Dolliver was one of the most celebrated orators of his time and a leader of the congressional insurgents in the losing effort against what became the Payne-Aldrich Tariff. The chief forester was well aware that his letter, which Dolliver would read out in the Senate, had been sent in direct violation of a presidential edict that any such communications must be made through the department heads. It was only a matter of time before Pinchot's own head would roll. Robert Bacon, an old Harvard friend of Roosevelt's who had reluctantly replaced Henry White as U.S. ambassador in Paris, wrote TR, "Is it possible that Gifford, good old Gifford, has got to go too?" He hoped that the rumor was untrue, telling Roosevelt, "It would be a real calamity to have him go wouldn't it!"[38] The Colonel undoubtedly agreed. Three days before he left office he had written Pinchot, "I cannot think of a man in the country whose loss would be a more real misfortune to the nation than yours would."[39]

Taft was also very well aware of the close bond between the ex-president and the chief forester. On a tour through the Midwest out to the West Coast meant to rally support for his actions, Taft only added fuel to the fires at a speech at Winona, Minnesota, made in support of standpatter congressman James Tawney. The president threatened the insurgents with expulsion from the party, praised Aldrich, and declared that on the whole he thought the tariff "the best bill that the Republican [P]arty ever passed."[40] This insulting gaffe only increased the already open talk of bringing back Roosevelt in 1912.

In a letter written from the West, Taft complained to his wife Nellie that he had received a "screed" from Silas McBee, the influential editor of *The Churchman*, which supported Pinchot and did "gross injustice" to Ballinger. McBee, Taft told his wife, was "one of those impressionist artists that are so often carried off their feet by Roosevelt's sermons and preachments and that have very little regard for the substantial methods of making progress through statutes and by lawful steps." Pinchot had "spread a virus" against Ballinger widely and had used the publicity department of his bureau for the purpose. The chief forester would deny it, but Taft saw traces of this in talks he had with newspapermen, "who assume Ballinger's guilt, and having convicted him treat any evidence showing that he is a man of strength and honesty as utterly to be disregarded."[41] Dolliver commented to his fellow senatorial insurgent Albert Beveridge that he found it an "incredible thing that as sensible a man as Taft should start out by tying the Aldrich millstone about his neck and traveling like a peddler of damaged goods." With Pinchot "knocked out and Aldrich in command I think you can hear a lion roar in East Africa."[42]

This may have been only wishful thinking on Dolliver's part, but by this time Roosevelt was growing restive on account of the messages he was receiving, some criticizing Taft and others advising him to stay abroad until after the fall 1910 elections.[43] This impatience was reflected in a letter to Lawrence Abbot at the *Outlook* in which TR declared, "As much as I should hate for the White House to see Cannon, Tawney, et al., defeated, I fear I will be unable to delay my return on that account." To Abbott this clearly signaled that Roosevelt meant to return and speak against them.[44] On a more personal level, the Colonel told his sister Anna that he hadn't the "slightest intention of allowing myself, & poor Edie, to be kept longer away from our home and children."[45] Safely back at Sagamore Hill from her European tour, Edith notified Kermit that the country was "crazy mad about Father" and poor Taft was having a horrid time. Newspapermen in New York, she went on, hungering for TR's return, had formed a "Back From Elba" club and formally drank the toast at every Saturday meeting.[46] On the other hand people close to Taft were telling her to keep her husband out of the country for a year and half longer. When he heard of this, Henry Adams commented, "Why not for life? The ostrich business won't work forever even among the Hottentots."[47]

On November 27, TR's party began a four-day journey to Lord Delamere's Equator Ranch at Njoro, where they would complete their hunting in the protectorate. On this march, at the Londiani rail station, Roosevelt dismissed most of the safari's men as they could take along to their next destination, Uganda and the Nile Valley, only their tent attendants, saises, and the skinners Heller had trained. TR recorded with genuine regret that he was "really sorry to see the last of the big, strong, good-natured porters," who had been with them for seven months and had behaved well. Much of this he credited to the management of Cuninghame and Tarlton. The Colonel was proud that they had not lost a single man. One had been tossed by a rhino, one clawed by a leopard, and others had been in hospital for various sicknesses, but none had died.[48] They would not be so fortunate in Uganda.

Roosevelt's final host in British East Africa was also the protectorate's most colorful character and largest landholder—Hugh Cholmondeley, the Third Baron Delamere. Since 1897 Delamere had poured a fortune in borrowed money into his one hundred thousand acre ranch in the Njoro District, trying and failing at various agricultural experiments, from sheep to cattle. Only recently, after many missteps, had he succeeded in producing a hybrid strain of wheat that would become the staple crop. Since 1904 the baron had been President of the Colonial Association and the spokesman for the settler community in Nairobi and London. He was a tireless champion of the idea of British East Africa as a "white man's country" and a prospective miniature dominion on the lines of New Zealand.[49] An unusual aristocrat, Delamere allowed his red hair to grow down to his shoulders and crowned his locks with an enormous sun helmet, the largest in East Africa, that both obscured his face and accentuated his slight figure. Roosevelt became very fond of the eccentric baron, who, eschewing British upper-class decorum, did not dress for dinner and whose usual costume was a worn pair of khaki pants and a wool sweater. His ranch house was not as grand as that of the McMillans, but TR enjoyed its well-stocked library containing the books of Delamere's wife Florence, a daughter of the Earl of Enniskillen.

In the deep forests of the Delamere ranch, Roosevelt and his host went after the rare and elusive bongo antelope, which no white man had ever shot. Along the way TR was amused to find that the tree hyraxes, "squat, wooly, funny things" that lived in hollows high in the big trees and produced an eerie moaning wail at night, were dubbed "teddy bears" by the locals. Delamere hoped to produce a bongo for his guest, but failed. Kermit, however, hunting on his own with Barclay Cole, Delamere's brother-in-law, had more luck. Not only did he bag several bongo, but also jet-black sable with scimitar-shaped horns, considered after the koodoo the most beautiful of the antelope. Though TR was disappointed in the hunting on Delamere's land he described the baron as the "most useful settler, from the standpoint of the all-around interests of the country, in British East Africa." Though an accomplished big game hunter, the baron went beyond being a "mere sportsman" to become a "leader in the work of taming the wilderness, of conquering for civilization the world's waste spaces." In Roosevelt's view, no career could be "better worth following."[50]

Returning to Nairobi for the final time, TR dispatched a report on the success of the expedition's British East African leg to Walcott at the Smithsonian. The naturalists were shipping home a treasure trove of 550 large mammals, 3,379 small mammals, 2,784 birds, about 1,500 reptiles and amphibians, and about 250 fresh water and marine fish. The shipment also contained a large number of mollusks and other invertebrates, several thousand plants, 2,000 photos, and anthropological material gathered by Mearns.[51] The specimens collected after they left British East Africa would be dispatched from Khartoum.

At Nairobi TR was also able to compare views on imperialism with the newly arrived Governor, Sir Percy Girouard, who had spent many years in Africa, the last as Governor of Northern Nigeria. After a dinner with the Governor and his wife, Lady Girouard reported to her father in London, Sir Richard Solomon, that she had a "perfectly delightful evening" and that TR, though "extraordinarily ugly," was "one of the most stimulating, clever and vital" men she had ever met, as keen and full of enthusiasm as a boy. She went on that Roosevelt claimed his politics were "Radical internally, tremendously imperial externally." They had a long serious talk after dinner and the rest of the time TR regaled them with "thrilling stories of Texas and the war and his regiment." Roosevelt, Lady Girouard told her father, really was "a man to meet" and she was "so thankful" to be there when he came.[52]

Sir Percy was at first inclined to view Roosevelt as a busybody and a threat to his authority, but after several encounters the Colonel's energy, astounding breadth of knowledge, and sympathetic view of the British Empire, won over the Governor, who read aloud to him parts of his own manuscript, "The Imperial Idea." The Colonel later told Girouard that this was the "best presentation of the case" he had seen and gave a coherent policy for what the Governor called "Democratic Imperialism" and TR called "Democratic Nationalism."[53] Along these lines, Roosevelt reported to Arthur Lee that he was, as he had expected he would be, "a pretty good imperialist!" And when he saw Lee in England he would have lots to tell him about the possessions through which he was passing. In most points the British administration was admirable, and he had a genuine respect for the officials, but he wished to make one or two suggestions from the point of view of the actual settlers, who reminded him so much of his beloved westerners that he felt "absolutely at home among them." And unless he was mistaken they in turn cordially received him "as a natural friend."[54]

Before TR got to England one such "friend," Florence Delamere, confided to him that he could "help us back here by telling the people at home" to support Governor Girouard, whom she and her husband thought was doing well, "and let him have a free hand." Everyone believed in Girouard and thought he had "done a lot towards putting things straight already" and would do "wonders if encouraged." She was sure that Roosevelt would "try to make the people at home understand that this has got to be a White Man's country and not an Indian preserve." Churchill would "talk nonsense to you about the Indians being here first regardless of the facts" but in her view adding an increased Indian population to the existing black/white balance would be "folly." However, she was sure he could "see it all twice as clearly as I can," so there was "no sense in writing pages about it."[55] TR replied that he would do his part and knew "that you and D. have the large outlook, that your own success comes second to the feeling that you have taken the lead in adding to the Empire the last province that can be added to the white man's part of it." In his opinion, her husband Delamere had "rendered to East Africa and therefore to Greater Britain a literally incalculable service." He only wished "that in England there was a fuller appreciation of the service."[56]

On December 18, 1909 Roosevelt's party boarded a train at Nairobi for Lake Victoria and the last leg of the safari, into the British Uganda Protectorate and briefly the Belgian Congo, to be followed by a journey down the Nile through the Sudan and Egypt to Cairo.

Chapter 4

White Rhino and Giant Eland

On December 19, 1909, Roosevelt's party arrived at Port Florence on Lake Victoria Nyanza. In this last leg of the African adventure, the aim was to hunt first the legendary white rhinoceros, and then the little-known giant eland. These were sought over the following two months in forays from Uganda into the Lado region of the Belgian Congo, the safari's only detour outside the British Empire. Twenty-four hours in a "smart little steamer" took the party across the smooth surface of the immense lake to Entebbe on its northern shore. Along the way, TR pointed out the grebe and cormorants to Mearns and they passed many green and forested islands, "empty with the emptiness of death" from the scourge of the sleeping sickness which had killed at least two hundred thousand people before what remained of the population was relocated. The Colonel found Entebbe a "pretty little town of English residents, chiefly officials; with well-kept roads, a golf course, tennis-courts, and an attractive club-house." The whole place was "bowered in flowers, on tree, bush and vine, of every hue—masses of lilac, purple, yellow, blue and fiery crimson."[1] At Entebbe, the head-quarters of the British administration in Uganda, they were the guests of Acting Governor Boyle.

Two days later TR and Kermit left for Kampala, seat of the native king and council, where Cuninghame was organizing the new safari. The houses of Kampala had mud walls and thatched roofs, and the gardens were surrounded by braided cane fences. All the people were very polite and ceremonious, both to one another and strangers. Now and then they met parties of Sikh soldiers, "tall, bearded, fine-looking men with turbans"; and there were also Indian and Swahili and even Arab and Persian traders. The first night, in a torch-lit ceremony accompanied by pounding drums, Roosevelt called on the boy king, who was being trained by an English tutor and whose comfortable house was furnished in British fashion. He also met the king's native advisors, "shrewd, powerful-looking men"; and was greeted by the council of "substantial looking men, well-dressed in the native fashion, and representing all the districts of the kingdom."[2] TR reported to his daughter Ethel that he found the little king's prime minister "exceedingly competent" and "gorgeously dressed." The man reminded Kermit of a "rather civilized Umslopagaar—if that is the way you spell Rider Haggard's Zulu hero." Roosevelt went on that in the native town they were driven around in rickshaws, "each with four men pushing and pulling," who uttered a "queer, clanging note of exclamation in chorus, every few seconds, hour after hour."[3]

Kampala was also headquarters of the Church of England and Roman Catholic missions both of which TR made a point of visiting. The people of Uganda had proved the most receptive to Christianity of any in tropical Africa and made it the dominant creed. At the Anglican mission, Bishop Tucker greeted them, and at the two Catholic establishments, bishops Hanlon and Streicher. At all of these the American and British flags were unfurled and TR was amused by native children's phonetic renditions of the "Star Spangled Banner." He was much impressed by the high school and the admirable medical mission he toured, as he was by the handsome cathedral built by the native Christians themselves without outside help or money. At Hanlon's mission he had lunch with a fellow New Yorker, Mother Paul, whom he had promised to see in Africa before he left the United States. She was involved in industrial training, "taking especial pains" to develop those industries natural to the Ugandans that would be useful when they returned to their own homes. Both the Catholic missions were teaching the native men to cultivate coffee, and various fruits and vegetables.[4]

In TR's view it was fortunate for the Ugandans that the British had established a protectorate over them and that both the government officials and missionaries were wisely "developing them along their own lines, in government, dress and ways of life, constantly striving to better them and bring them forward." In this the British were not "twisting them aside from their natural line of development, nor wrenching them loose from what was good in their past, by attempting the impossible task of turning an entire native population into black Englishmen at one stroke." It was plain to Roosevelt that Uganda could never be a "white man's country" as was hoped for the highlands of British East Africa, where the primary need was to build up a "large healthy population of true white settlers" who would "take the land as an inheritance for their children's children."[5]

Uganda's geography, climate and population made it a "black man's country" and the task of the "intrusive and masterful" British "must be to bring forward the natives, to train them, and above all to help them train themselves, so that they may advance in industry, in learning, in morality, in capacity for self-government." It was "mere folly" in TR's opinion to talk of " 'giving' a people self-government; the gift of the forms," when the inward spirit was lacking. All that could be done was "patiently to help a people acquire the necessary qualities—social, moral, intellectual, industrial, and lastly political—and meanwhile to exercise for their benefit, with justice, sympathy and firmness, the governing ability which as yet they themselves lack."[6]

Before they left Kampala the district commissioner, Frederick Knowles, arranged a successful situtunga hunt in the nearby marshes. This antelope was a larger relative of the bushbuck with very long hooves and shaggy hair like a water-buck. The following day, Christmas Eve, the newly formed expedition marched out of Kampala to begin its trek northwest more than a hundred miles to Lake Albert Nyanza. To the handful of men they brought from British East Africa, Cuninghame had added Ugandan porters and askaris from the local constabulary. One of the new porters carried nothing but a big Ugandan drum that he beat at the head of the column in company with the flag bearer.

On New Year's Day 1910, TR reported to his friend Lodge that they were on the "final stretch of our journey" and he might get no more mail before reaching Khartoum, while the chance for writing would be small. They were between the two great Nyanza Lakes just north of the equator in a strange and interesting land. After so long in the cool highlands, TR was now in "a bit of the true tropics" filled with palms, monkeys, parrots, deadly snakes, and man-eating croco-diles. It was a beautiful country, but also the country of the spirrilum tick, whose bite brought paralysis, and of the sleeping sickness and black water fever. They were taking great care and he did not antici-pate any serious sickness, in fact he and Kermit were in perfect health, the only members of the party who had not had a touch of trouble in Uganda. The natives were "semi-civilized and Christian of a sort," quite unlike the naked, warlike savages they encountered in British East Africa. It was all "most picturesque and interesting" and Kermit had "certainly had a wonderful experience."[7]

Ten days out from Kampala the safari crossed the Kafu River and entered the native kingdom of Unyoro, still part of the British Protectorate, but a separate kingdom. They stopped for a day at the capital, Hoima, where the Christian king lived and the British officials and the missionaries all had outposts. TR gave tea to the king and the British commissioner. On January 5, 1910, the party reached the village of Butiaba on Lake Albert Nyanza where they boarded a "crazy little steam-launch," two sailboats, and two large rowboats for their trip across the lake and down the White Nile. Two days later the flotilla landed on the west bank of the parched Lado Region of the Belgian Congo and made camp in a thin grove of scattered thorn trees. The next morning, led by Quentin Grogan, a young British guide, they set off in pursuit of the great square-mouthed, called white, rhinoceros. Their goal was to collect one family group for the Smithsonian, another for the American Museum in New York, and a head for the National Collection of Heads and Horns started by William Hornaday at the New York Zoological Gardens.

The square-mouthed rhinoceros differed from the ordinary African prehensile-lipped variety (the upper lip of which looked like the hook of a turtle's beak), in several other ways. It was less solitary and on the average larger, with a very prominent hump over the withers, and a still larger fleshy hump on the neck. Its "huge, mis-shapen head," in TR's opinion, differed as much from the ordinary rhino as the head of a moose differed from an elk. It fed exclusively on grass, unlike the more common variety. The square-mouth, once plentiful in South Africa, had been almost exterminated there and also had become rare in British East Africa. Consequently, Roosevelt ventured into the Belgian Congo where the animal was still found in some numbers. Nevertheless, he admitted that it would "be well" if all killing were prohibited "until careful inquiry" had been made as to its remaining numbers and exact distribution.[8] After, of course, he took his specimens.

Late on the first day out tramping through the dry grassland they came upon a group of rhino and were able to take several. From an ant-hill, TR spied the first lying asleep on its side, "looking like an enormous pig." When the full-grown cow heard something and rose up on its forelegs in sitting position, he opened fire with the Holland & Holland, killing it with one shot. At this four other rhinos rose and bolted right and left. As he watched them Roosevelt was struck by how much they resembled the paintings he knew from Sir William Cornwallis Harris's famous 1840 portfolio of South African game. On this occasion Kermit killed a bull, while his father added a calf for the Smithsonian family group. TR noted that the common rhino was a dark slate gray, while these animals were rather lighter in color, but he put this down to "a mere individual peculiarity" for the experts claimed they were the same.[9]

Leaving Heller and the skinners to do their jobs, TR returned to the main camp which he had to defend from two fires that swept towards them across the tinder-like, tall thin grass. He, Kermit, Mearns, Loring, and the porters cut a lane around their tents and started a back-fire which burnt out fifty yards from their camp and ended the danger. Shortly afterward, TR recorded, it was a "fine sight to see" when one of the fires against which they were guarding came over a low hill crest into view beyond the line of their back-fire, as "the long line of leaping, wavering flames advance toward one another." The fires burned in their neighborhood for several days and at night it was "splendid to see the line of flames, leaping fifty feet into the air as they worked across the serried masses of tall papyrus" across the bay.[10]

While TR bagged his first white rhino in the Belgian Congo, at home Senator Dolliver read aloud in the Senate a flagrantly insubordinate letter by Gifford Pinchot on the conservation controversy that forced Taft's hand. The president dismissed him on January 7, 1910, asserting that Pinchot's conduct had "destroyed your usefulness as a helpful subordinate."[11] Later that month a Joint Committee of both Houses began to look into the Ballinger-Pinchot controversy, and affairs generally in the Interior Department. From Sagamore Hill, Edith reported to Kermit that the investigation had begun and she was not happy with it for it put Taft, for whom she felt sorry, in "such a difficult position." In her opinion, his good qualities had become disadvantages. If he would have "roared" at them a bit, as would have Kermit's father, things might not have come to such a pass. Now, as it threatened to engulf her husband once again, she hated the political outlook more and more.[12] The news of Pinchot's firing reached TR by special runner ten days after the event. From the Lado he wrote to his friend that it seemed to him "absolutely impossible that there could be any truth in this statement" and that he did not know any man who had "rendered quite the service you have rendered." He asked Pinchot to write him "just what the real situation is" as he had been able only "very imperfectly" to follow things in Africa.[13] Such a letter had already been sent, a week before Pinchot's dismissal. TR did not receive this, however, until he reached Gondokoro in the Sudan the next month.

The day TR got the news of Pinchot's dismissal, January 17, he reported to Lodge from the Lado Enclave, "Here we are, camped on the banks of the White Nile, about two degrees north of the equator" in the "heart of the African wilderness." The previous night a hippo almost came into camp, lions were roaring and elephants were trumpeting within a mile. The day before he had shot two white rhinos which, he reported, were "not as white as they are painted." Ever since they had reached Lake Albert Nyanza the heat had been intense. In the evenings they had to use mosquito headnets and gauntlets and they slept under netting, "usually with nothing on, on account of the heat." Kermit remained "hard as nails" and both of them were in excellent health. They were now past the spirillum tick and sleeping sickness districts. He told Lodge that he earnestly hoped the news of Pinchot was not true. TR concluded that he was not sure when his friend would get the letter, as the postman was "a wild savage who runs stark naked with the mail."[14]

The layer of snow-like ash left by the widespread grass fires made tracking the game much easier. On a second foray after the square-mouthed rhino, they took along the small mammal expert Loring who had before this not seen elephant or rhino alive. This would soon be remedied as within a few hours of leaving camp they came upon a herd of elephant, which they skirted around, not wishing them to charge. A few hours later they came upon the spoor of two rhino they soon caught up with and Kermit captured with his camera before Roosevelt shot one, while the other dashed away to safety. Unlike the ordinary rhino, they found the square-mouth did not charge as often when attacked. They also had the habit of sitting on their haunches like a dog, the only kind of heavy game they saw do so.

Loring stayed behind to oversee the skinning, while TR and Kermit went on to follow a native who had come in with a report of another rhino nearby. This turned out to be, Roosevelt recorded, "a huge bull, with a fair horn; much the biggest bull we had seen; and with head up and action high, the sun glinting on his slate hide and bringing out his enormous bulk, he was indeed a fine sight." The color of the animal was exactly that of the ordinary rhino, but he was taller and heavier, being six feet high. The "stout" horn was over two feet long. Later, after first taking a series of photographs of her, Kermit shot a cow with a thirty-one inch horn, the longest they had collected, to complete the two pair needed for the museums.[15]

After this hunt, while Loring and Mearns stayed behind capturing in photographs, and in the flesh, the abundant bird and other life, TR, Kermit, Heller, Cuninghame and Grogan set off inland for a week's safari traveling as lightly as possible with only two tents. The grass was mostly burned, but they camped by a beautiful pond covered with white and lilac water lilies, with large acacias nearby to provide shade. They saw nine rhino, none of which carried notable horns, before Roosevelt shot one with a horn a little shorter than Kermit's cow for the National Collection of Heads and Horns. At the "zenith" of his trip, the Colonel reported the six white rhinos to his sister Anna, telling her that it was the animal he most wanted and their "tale of big game is now full." They were in the heart of wild Africa where there were not even any natives nearby. TR supposed that they were bound to come down with "some fever or other soon," but so far Kermit had been in robust health and he had not for years passed nine months in such good physical condition as he had the last nine in Africa.[16]

Breaking camp at the Lado, the party sailed down the Nile to Nimule where the boats were left behind for a ten-day march cross country through a "barren and thirsty land" to Gondokoro. After this tramp, TR reported to Lodge on February 5 that he and Kermit remained well, but "this was not a mere health resort" as all the other members of the party had been down with fever or dysentery. One gun bearer, one skinner, and four porters had died, two had been mauled by lions and, in a village along the way, eight had died of sleeping sickness during their stay.[17] Loring, adopting the style of epitaph they had seen on numerous headstones in Africa, left a rhyme in one of the native graves:

> Here lies the remains of skinner Dick
> Who died from the bite of the spirillum tick
> He trapped from Mt Kenia to the Athi plains
> And here in Uganda we leave his remains.[18]

Among the many letters awaiting TR at Gondokoro was Gifford Pinchot's explanation of the Ballinger affair and his firing. Though couched in careful language on account of Roosevelt's close friendship with the president, it amounted to a bill of indictment against Taft. Pinchot explained that he had not written before as he wanted TR to be "free for a time from the echoes of trouble." But now, in Pinchot's view, it was clear that, "We have fallen back down the hill you led us up" and there was a general belief that the special interests were "once more substantially in control of both Congress and the Administration." He did not go so far as to attribute the present situation to "deliberate bad faith on the part of Mr. Taft," but to a "most surprising" weakness and indecision, and to his desire to "act as a judge, dealing with issues only when they are brought to him," not as, what the president really was, at least in the view of TR and Pinchot, "the advocate and active guardian of the general welfare." Further, the reactionaries believed that Taft followed the advice of the last man who talked to him and had consequently "built a fence round him with their own men."

Pinchot then proceeded to list sixteen reasons he had come to these conclusions. To begin with, after his election, Taft had surrounded himself by Trust attorneys and other reactionary advisors in the Cabinet and Congress "who were necessarily in opposition to the Roosevelt policies" and from which he had never broken away. Consequently, in the tariff debate Taft had failed to support the insurgent Republicans in Congress, including many progressives who were "honestly trying to fulfill the party pledges and reduce the tariff" and now the president defended "a tariff bill made by the special interests, following the passage of which the cost of living rose beyond all precedent." On the conservation front, Taft had allowed the work of the National Conservation Commission to be stopped, which "seriously retarded the practical progress" of the movement. Through decisions by the attorney general, Taft had abandoned the principles TR had established of federal regulation and control, in the public interest, of waterpower on navigable streams. By the appointment of Ballinger, the president had "brought about the most dangerous attack yet made upon the Conservation policies—an attack now happily checked."

On a more personal level, Pinchot reported that Taft had allowed attacks on TR in Congress to continue "unchecked when a word from the incoming President would have ended them." Then, in a series of speeches, Taft had endorsed Roosevelt's bitterest enemies in the Congress, including Senator Aldrich and Speaker Cannon, while he "tried to read out of the Republican [P]arty," senators Nelson,

Beveridge, Cummins, and others "whose fight was made for equality of opportunity and a square deal." And finally, Taft had repeatedly put party solidarity above the public welfare while allying himself with the special interests and allowing "the great mass of the people to lose confidence in the President." Pinchot claimed not to have lost all hope that Taft might yet change course and vowed to support him "up to the point where my loyalty to the people of this country requires me to break with the administration." He assured Roosevelt that "the hold of your policies on the plain people" was as strong as ever and that because of Taft's actions many of TR's former enemies were now his friends. The issue at stake had become "immeasurably larger than politics or any man's political fortunes." It was a "straight fight for human rights." At least that was how it looked to him "on the last day of 1909."[19] And this is how it would look to Roosevelt two years later when he challenged his friend Taft for the Republican nomination.

At the time, however, TR replied to Pinchot that he had received his letter at Gondokoro and along with it the definite news that the chief forester had been removed. He assured Pinchot that his replacement by an able man, the forestry expert Henry Graves, in no way or to the least degree lightened the blow, for besides being the chief of the forestry department, Pinchot had also been the leader of "all the forces which were struggling for conservation, which were fighting for the general interest as against special privilege." He did not wish to be ungracious towards his successor, but he could not as an honest man cease to battle for the principles for which Pinchot, Garfield and other of their close associates stood. Roosevelt went on that he would of course say nothing at present but asked if there was any chance to see Pinchot in Europe. If not he asked to see him on the steamer to America as he wanted to talk to him before he "even in the smallest degree commit myself."[20] Three days after TR wrote this letter, on the first anniversary of Taft's inauguration, the Indiana newspaperman and reformer Lucius B. Swift sent "My Dear Roosevelt" a one sentence message which summarized the view of many: "Taft is a damn, pig-headed blunderer."[21]

All of Roosevelt's correspondents, however, did not condemn Taft. Two of his closest friends in fact, Lodge and Root, defended the president in their letters. Lodge, who also had been a supporter of the Payne-Aldrich Tariff, noted that no president could possibly have tolerated such a letter as their mutual friend sent to Dolliver. He thought Pinchot had been unwise as his first duty should have been to "the great service he has built up" and he ought not to have allowed himself or his subordinates to become involved with the muck-raking magazines that attacked Ballinger.[22] Root, whom Taft had consulted before he dismissed Pinchot, had become one of the president's closest advisors. Root revealed to TR that, for his sins, he had been placed on the committee investigating the Ballinger-Pinchot affair, which he considered a "very disagreeable row" between the two men. Taking Taft's line, Root asserted that there had been lots of gross distortions aimed at Ballinger and that "indiscreet friends" were making matters worse. In his view the scandal was hurting the administration and, he feared, Pinchot and the cause of conservation as well. Although he admitted Taft had not "yet altogether arrived," Root asserted that he was nevertheless "making a good President" and would eventually win his way 'into the public confidence." He compared the change in presidential styles from TR to Taft as between an automobile and a cab. Like the latter, Taft was "big and good natured and easy going and let things drift considerably."[23]

Back in Africa, there was still hunting to be done. While the sick members of the party recovered at Gondokoro, TR and Kermit struck off across the Nile again into Belgian territory for eight days spent in pursuit of the giant eland, not only one of largest and handsomest, but also the least known of African antelopes. The Belgian commandant of the Lado supplied seven askari to accompany the party, which had sixty Ugandan porters in train. The weather was very hot and the terrain a "waste of barren desolation." They saw elephant, giraffe, and buffalo along the way before, after three days, Roosevelt at last got a chance for a giant eland, a big bull with horns twisted almost like a koodoo's and a finely modeled head and legs. After a long stalk, at the end of which he had to crawl on all fours across the baked ground, TR shot his bull at one hundred yards with his Springfield. In the following days Kermit shot a bull and a cow. Eight days hunting yielded only these three of the elusive prey.

Their last major big game animals bagged, the hunters returned to Gondokoro, where they found waiting the steamer *Dal*, which Sir Reginald Wingate, the Sudan's governor-general, had arranged to take them on the two week voyage down the Nile to Khartoum and civilization. Along the way, at Lake No and near the Nile, and on short side trips down its tributaries—the Bahr el Ghazal and Bahr el Zeraf, the final few specimens collected included white-eared kobs and saddle-marked lechwes, commonly called Mrs. Gray's water-buck. When the numbers were totted up at the end of the safari, more than 11,000 specimens, large and small, had been captured and preserved. Many of the almost 5,000 mammals, 4,000 birds, 500 fish, 2,000 reptiles, and many invertebrates, remain in the Smithsonian and other museums and are still used regularly today for research and study.[24] The naturalists discovered new genera, species, and sub-species. To many of these, including shrews, rodents, monkeys, deer, antelope, gazelle, birds, and even a conch shell, they gave the name roosevelti. Outside big game, the expedition had been the first systematic and comprehensive investigation undertaken of the flora and fauna of the areas visited. From this the Smithsonian garnered the most complete collection of East African species in the world.

Roosevelt and Kermit personally accounted for 512 big game trophies, of which they kept only a dozen for themselves.[25] TR's bag included nine lions, eight elephants, thirteen rhinos, six buffaloes and fifty-three other species, 296 animals in all collected over nearly as many days. Game was so numerous that, had they been willing, they could have killed ten, or a hundred, times as many. In all the hunting, only two wounded animals that Roosevelt knew of were left unaccounted for in the field. Of all the letters he received applauding the expedition, the one the Colonel perhaps most cherished came from Selous, who congratulated TR on the "marvelous, unbroken success of your African journey." More than "anything else he had got," Selous envied him the giant eland trophy.[26] TR's and Kermit's achievements in Africa had placed them amongst the greatest big game sportsmen in the world. However, Roosevelt had had enough. The safari was meant to be the adventure of a lifetime and he had done a lifetime of shooting in ten months. He told his sister Corinne, "I do not care if I do not fire off my rifle again." He was also overjoyed at the prospect of seeing Edith and confessed he would "never go away from her again if I can help it."[27]

On March 10 the *Dal* reached Kodok, where the British had faced down a French imperial incursion a decade before in the so-called Fashoda Incident. Just before this they met the steamer of Sir William Garstin, a British engineer who had built the Aswan dam and for two decades had overseen the massive irrigation projects that ensured Egypt's prosperity. Garstin and the Colonel were able to talk for some time of Sudanese and Egyptian affairs. Roosevelt greatly admired the constructive work of Garstin, as well as that of Sir Reginald Wingate, both of whom he saw as fellow imperialists toiling in the vineyard without much support, particularly from the elected leaders at home. While still president he had written to Wingate that his own colonial experiences made him appreciate the governor-general's complaint that he was not getting the money that he needed for development in the Sudan. There was much TR would have liked to do in the Philippines that was impossible because Congress denied him the necessary funds. Roosevelt had years before read Wingate's 1891 book *Mahdism and the Egyptian Sudan* and, in addition to the hunting, he had written Wingate that he looked forward "with eager interest" to see what his people were doing in his domain, as in all the British possessions.[28]

On his journey down the great river, at village after village that had been "touched by the blight of the Mahdist tyranny," Roosevelt was struck by the lack of men of middle age, and by the children, all of whom were under twelve and known as "Government children" because under the previous regime most of them had been killed or died of starvation.[29] In his opinion, during the twelve years of British rule since the Khalifa's defeat at Omdurman, no place else in the world had shown "such astonishing progress from the most hideous misery to well-being and prosperity." By putting an end to the "wolf-pack" rule of the Mahdi, and his successor the Khalifa, the British had ended a "tyranny which for cruelty, blood-thirstiness, unintelligence, and wanton destructiveness surpassed anything which a civilized people can even imagine." Under such rule millions had died in an atmosphere of religious intolerance, slavery and murder.[30]

What he saw along the Nile in the Sudan made a strong imprint on TR, who came to equate the bloody jihadist regime of the Mahdi with Muslim rule in general. When he reached Khartoum, the Colonel told the American missionaries there that he felt they owed "a peculiar duty" to the Government under which they lived "in the direction of doing your full worth to make the present conditions perpetual." It was "incumbent on every decent citizen of the Sudan to uphold the present order of things; to see that there is no relapse; to see that the reign of peace and justice continues."[31] This meant continued British rule.

Lodge had warned TR that at Khartoum at least eight or ten newspapermen, some very hostile to Taft, would attempt to "rouse your indignation against him by what they say." Lodge thought it of the "first importance" that Roosevelt should stay "entirely aloof" and say "absolutely nothing" about American politics before he got home, where they could talk and TR could judge the facts himself. Edith had written to Lodge about those who wanted Theodore to stay away another year. With this Lodge disagreed, and he told his friend to "carry out your plans just as you intended" and come home in the summer.[32] The Colonel would heed Lodge's advice as best he could, but the journalists would not wait until Khartoum for their interviews. They hired boats and came up the Nile to intercept him on the way down.

Figure 1 TR, seated, with his mountain lion statue and "Tennis Cabinet." Notables include Captain Archie Butt at far left; Gifford Pinchot, fifth from left; French Ambassador Jules Jusserand, thirteenth from left; Elihu Root, behind TR's left shoulder; James Garfield to Root's left; Seth Bullock next to Garfield; John Callan O'Laughlin, fourth from right. Jack Abernathy is in a light colored suit. Courtesy the Theodore Roosevelt Collection, Harvard College Library.

Figure 2 TR and his chosen successor William Howard Taft at the 1909 Inaugural. Courtesy the Theodore Roosevelt Collection, Harvard College Library.

Figure 3 The Roosevelt family, Christmas 1908. From left, Ethel, Kermit, Quentin, Edith, Ted, TR, Archie, Alice, and her husband Nicholas Longworth. Courtesy the Theodore Roosevelt Collection, Harvard College Library.

Figure 4 TR, Sir Frederick Jackson, Frederick Selous, and Dr. Edgar Mearns on an engine platform en route to Kapiti. Courtesy the Theodore Roosevelt Collection, Harvard College Library.

Figure 5 TR with his first elephant, in Kenya. Courtesy the Theodore Roosevelt Collection, Harvard College Library.

Figure 6 Kermit, TR, and an African Cape buffalo, Courtesy the Theodore Roosevelt Collection, Harvard College Library.

Figure 7 TR and the German Kaiser, May 1910. Courtesy the Theodore Roosevelt Collection, Harvard College Library.

Figure 8 TR, on the far right, as Special Ambassador at the funeral of Edward VII, May 1910. Courtesy the Theodore Roosevelt Collection, Harvard College Library.

Figure 9   TR with a teddy bear at Cambridge Union, May 1910. Courtesy the Theodore Roosevelt Collection, Harvard College Library.

Figure 10   TR, waving his hat, welcomed back to New York in June 1910. His niece Eleanor and her husband Franklin Roosevelt stand by the smokestack. Courtesy the Theodore Roosevelt Collection, Harvard College Library.

A SITTER; OR, BIG GAME TO THE LAST.

Mr. Roosevelt. "STEADY, KERMIT! WE MUST HAVE ONE OF THESE."

Figure 11 *Punch* cartoon, March 23, 1910: TR and the Sphinx.

A SUGGESTED PRECAUTION.

IN VIEW OF PRESIDENT ROOSEVELT'S VISIT TO LONDON.

MUST MEETINGS.

You hear a great deal just now about May Meetings; let us tell you something about Must Meetings. One of the most frequented centres for Must Meetings is Bow Street Police Court. There is generally a full and orderly attendance; some of the most eloquent and talented speakers are to be heard there, pleading worthy causes or denouncing desperate evils, and the remarks of the gentleman presiding are always sure of respectful attention. A collection is a feature of these meetings; it frequently occurs that someone present, obviously not well-to-do, will contribute as much as forty shillings. A notable Must Meeting took place at the Law Courts (King's Bench IV.) last week, Mr. Justice CHANNELL presiding. The principal speaker was Mr. HALL CAINE, who dealt with the interesting subject of "The Unwritten Law." The meeting ended quite amicably, Mr. HALL CAINE shaking hands with one of the speakers who,

earlier in the meeting, was evidently at variance with him. It was noticed by the audience that no collection was taken, but we understand that a number of solicitors and barristers who happened to be present will attend to this matter in due course.

It is not unusual, excepting in the month of May, which is unlucky for the purpose, for Must Meetings to take place in churches. We ourselves took part in a meeting of this kind in a country church not long ago. The vicar presided. The meeting had been brought about by a young man of our acquaintance, who, however, strangely enough, at the last minute was reluctant to attend, urging as his excuse that he couldn't face all the trimmings. "You must," said his counsellors, and, pushing him into a cab, they got him at last to the church. In proof of the wisdom of their efforts they found that the meeting had waited ten minutes, refusing to proceed without its instigator. The young man was persuaded to say a few words during the pro-

ceedings. There was also an attractive young lady speaker; the organist played some well-written compositions, and the vicar's address will not readily be forgotten by those who paid attention to it.

The last of the series of Must Meetings for which we have space took place in the quiet of the study of the headmaster of a well-known boarding school for young gentlemen. Only two persons attended, the headmaster and one of the young gentlemen, who had proved himself to be more young than anything else. The subject of the meeting was the effect of arboriculture on the human anatomy, with experiments. The younger of the two took the chair, and was much affected by the proceedings.

According to a local paper the Beckenham Urban District Council has "decided to meet for three months every three weeks." This spirit is all very well at the start, but it doesn't last long.

Figure 12 *Punch* cartoon, May 11, 1910: Lion in Trafalgar Square with a sign reading "Not to be shot."

THE WISDOM OF THE WEST.

Figure 13 *Punch* cartoon, May 4, 1910: "Roosevelt's Straight Talk to Effete Civilisations."

Chapter 5

Down the Nile: Khartoum to Cairo

A few days before the *Dal* reached Khartoum, a flotilla of boats carrying the journalists barred from the safari intercepted Roosevelt on the Nile. Among the newspapermen was at least one friendly face, John "Cal" O'Laughlin of the *Chicago Tribune*, who, as an acting assistant secretary of state at the end of TR's administration, had been present at the final "tennis cabinet" gathering a year before. O'Laughlin recalled his first glimpse of a beaming TR on the deck of the *Dal*, dressed in khaki and under an American flag swinging his olive green helmet in reply to the frantic hat waving of the press who crowded the railing of his vessel, the *Abbas Pasha*. Roosevelt had lost the care worn look O'Laughlin remembered from the last White House days, his face was brown, his moustache lightened by the sun showing "more than a few gray hairs." He heartily welcomed the journalists as the "vanguard" of the civilization he had left behind a year before.[1]

The pressmen were eager to quiz the former president about his journey and to ask his opinion of President Taft, who had been left in charge explicitly to carry on Roosevelt's policies, but had instead, as we have seen, among other things supported the controversial Payne-Aldrich Tariff and dismissed TR's man Gifford Pinchot from the Department of Forestry. The Colonel, however, was willing to discuss such matters only "off the record" and told each as he spoke to them separately that anything they published would be denied. He would only authorize the statement that he had nothing to say about politics. Of course Roosevelt's silence only led to ominous headlines to that effect in the U.S. papers. Jusserand sent one such clipping to him along with a letter in which he declared that "It is pleasant to think that Africa has not changed you in any way... Mute you went into the desert, dumb you return." In addition to sharing the itinerary which he had drawn up for TR's visit to Paris, the Frenchman told Roosevelt that he had gone to the Smithsonian for a glimpse of the fruit of his labors. "But we found there under glass, only 2 or 3 skulls, 2 rats and one hedgehog." They were assured, however, that before long "your expedition would make a better show in the museum."[2]

At Khartoum on March 14 the local British officials once again greeted Roosevelt with "more than friendly enthusiasm." He stayed at the yellow stucco Governor's Palace, where twenty-five years before, General "Chinese" Gordon had been slain by the jihadist dervishes of the Mahdi. To TR's great regret the Governor-General, Sir Reginald Wingate, had been forced to Cairo by an illness and in his absence the Colonel's host was Sir Rudolph Slatin Pasha, the inspector-general. An Austrian soldier who had joined the Turco-Egyptian administration in the Sudan, Slatin had been imprisoned by the Mahdi and had endured more than a decade of captivity of one sort or another. He made his name (and that of Wingate who had played a part in his escape) by recounting his harrowing tale in *Fire and Sword in the Sudan*.[3] This Roosevelt had devoured and he peppered a surprised Slatin with questions and observations.

The *Dal* docked just in time for TR and Kermit to meet the train which carried Edith and Ethel south from Wadi Halfa. After their separation of just ten days less than a year, Theodore's homesickness and Edith's worries both vanished at the rail station. She found her husband in "splendid condition" and noted that he had "lost that look of worry and care" which had been "almost habitual" in the White House years. Edith was also heartened to see that the adventure in Africa had transformed her beloved Kermit from pale youth to tan and sturdy manhood.[4] She even approved of the wisp of a moustache he had grown. Edith brought along clothes for both men and at Khartoum Roosevelt shed his khaki safari accoutrements, donning a gray sack suit. As a reward for her forbearance of his yearlong safari, Theodore meant to give his wife a prolonged second honeymoon in Europe, which she had also scouted in her own peregrinations over the past year, but almost all their plans were scuppered by events.

At Khartoum, Roosevelt finished a "preliminary statement" summing up the accomplishments of the expedition, which he dispatched to Walcott. In this he noted that Heller had prepared 1,020 mammal specimens, mostly large, while Loring had prepared 3,163 and Mearns 714, for a total of 4,897 mammals. Almost 4,000 birds had also been prepared, almost all by Mearns and Loring. To these mammals and birds were added about 2,500 reptiles, amphibians, and fish, for a grand total of 11,397, not including thousand of invertebrates and plants.[5] TR also regretfully said goodbye at Khartoum to his companions of the last year, the expedition's hunters and naturalists, all of whom he came greatly to like and respect. He wrote to Leslie Tarlton a few months later, "you do not need to be told my feelings for you, and for that old trump R. J. [Cuninghame]. I shall always count you both as among my real friends."[6] In his report to Walcott, the Colonel declared that the hunters had "both worked as zealously and effectively for the success of the expedition as any other member."[7] Loring and Mearns had proved indefatigable collectors of small animals and birds, while Heller and Roosevelt collaborated on a two-volume study, published four years later as *Life-Histories of African Game Animals*, a significant contribution to the scientific literature. No three better men, TR wrote, "could be found anywhere" for such an expedition as theirs. He and Kermit also had a sad parting from "our faithful black followers, whom we knew we should never see again." It had been an interesting and a happy year but he was "very glad to be once more with those who are dear to me, and to turn my face toward my own home and my own people."[8]

From Khartoum, TR had hoped to travel as a private citizen and even to handle all the family's travel arrangements himself. However, as with the safari, he soon had to admit the impossibility of this notion and accepted the volunteer services of two members of the press contingent, who were also friends, Cal O'Laughlin, and Lawrence Abbott of the *Outlook*, which TR had agreed to join as a contributing editor once he returned to America. Roosevelt had invited Abbott to meet him at Khartoum and he had escorted Edith and Ethel down from Cairo. The pair acted as private secretaries to Roosevelt until he reached England.[9] Both men, with the Colonel's blessing, took advantage of their position to send home articles detailing the trip and TR's view of things, international and domestic.[10]

Roosevelt himself sent off the last installment of his own book. He wrote the "Foreword" at Khartoum, beginning the work (and continuing his rehabilitation in Shakespeare) with a quotation from

Henry IV, Part II: "I speak of Africa and golden joys." He went on with no mean nature prose of his own

> The hunter who wanders through these lands sees sights which ever afterward remain fixed in his mind. He sees the monstrous river-horse snorting and plunging beside the boat, the giraffe looking over the tree-tops at the nearing horsemen, the ostrich fleeing at a speed that none may rival, the snarling leopard and coiled python with their lethal beauty, the zebras barking in the moonlight, as the laden caravan passes on its night march through a thirsty land. In after-years there shall come to him memories of the lion's charge, of the gray bulk of the elephant, close at hand in the somber woodland; of the buffalo, his sullen eyes lowering from under his helmet of horn; of the rhinoceros, truculent and stupid, standing in the bright sunlight on the empty plain.
>
> These things can be told. But there are no words that can tell the hidden spirit of the wilderness, that can reveal its mystery, its melancholy, and its charm. There is delight in the hardy life of the open, in long rides rifle in hand, in the thrill of the fight with dangerous game. Apart from this, yet mingled with it, is the strong attraction of the silent places, of the large tropic moons, and the splendor of the new stars; where the wanderer sees the awful glory of sunrise and sunset in the wide waste spaces of the earth, unworn of man, and changed only by the slow changes of the ages through time everlasting.[11]

With his writing duties completed, Roosevelt was free to join his family in a busy schedule of sightseeing. In their three days at Khartoum they took a camel trip into the forbidding desert, visited the battlefield of Omdurman just across the Nile, where Lord Kitchener famously had defeated the Khalifa (the Mahdi's successor) in 1898, watched native dancers and reviewed an impressive parade of Sudanese troops. They were also extended a rare invitation to the Egyptian and Sudanese Officer's Club. Slatin saw this as an opportunity to enlist Roosevelt's aid with the officers whose continuing loyalty he and all the other officials questioned in light of a new menace, the growing power of the anti-British Nationalist party in Egypt, which had reclaimed the Sudan after Kitchener's victory. Three weeks before at Cairo, Boutros Ghali Pasha, the Coptic Christian Egyptian prime minister (whose namesake grandson would one day be secretary-general of the United Nations), had been assassinated by a Muslim Egyptian nationalist who saw Ghali as a tool of the British. This act not only stirred fears of unrest in Egypt, but also in the Sudan, where Wingate had been forced to stamp out a minor rebellion the previous year.

The youthful assassin of Boutros, though immediately captured, had not yet been tried and Roosevelt was asked at a dinner at the Governor's Palace what action he would have taken had he been the British Agent. To TR the matter was a simple one. He would immediately have brought the murderer before a drum-head-court-martial. As there was no question about the facts, which the Nationalists did not deny, he would have been sentenced to death and taken out and shot. Then, if the Home Government cabled, "in one of their moments of vacillation to wait a little while, I would cable in reply: 'Can't wait, the assassin has been tried and shot.'" The government could recall or impeach him if it wished, "but *that* assassin would have received his just deserts." After this remark, Lawrence Abbott recalled that one of the British officers, Colonel Asser, told him, "By Heaven! I wish that man were my boss!"[12]

Some Egyptian officers of the Sudanese army had greeted the news of the murder of Boutros Ghali with cheers and there was no little fear of disloyalty, understandable since the original British occupation of Egypt in 1882 had come in reaction to an officers' revolt at Alexandria which posed an unacceptable threat to the Suez Canal, Britain's lifeline to India and the Far East. Slatin asked Roosevelt to address the officers at Khartoum which, he believed, would do "a very real good." The Colonel readily agreed and told Slatin that the fact that he, an Austrian, was the British representative only underscored the fundamental truth that English rule in the Sudan was "really the rule of civilization, and that every believer in justice and progress all over the world should uphold it." Consequently, at the Egyptian Officers Club on March 17, Roosevelt urged the men to stay out of politics and tried his best to "use such language and arguments as would add to the self-respect of my hearers" while at the same time speaking with "unmistakable plainness as to their duty of absolute loyalty," and the "ruin which would come to both Egypt and the Sudan unless the power and prestige of English rule were kept undiminished."[13]

The day of his speech, Roosevelt's party boarded a special train for Wadi Halfa, where the government steamer *Ibis* waited to begin the next segment of the voyage down the Nile. By coincidence the steamer carried the same name as the luxurious lateen-sailed houseboat, complete with servants and crew, on which a thirteen-year-old

Theodore and his parents had sailed the Nile for two months thirty-eight years before. When he first saw Alexandria on November 28, 1872, he recorded: "How I gazed on it! It was Egypt, the land of my dreams; Egypt the most ancient of all countries; a land that was old when Rome was bright, was old when Babylon was in its glory, was old when Troy was taken! It was a sight to awaken a thousand thoughts and it did." On that trip, young Theodore was able to add Egyptian bird specimens to the "Museum" he had started in the family's Manhattan brownstone. He later wrote that his "first real collecting as a student of natural history" started in Egypt and at least three of the birds remain in the collection of the American Museum of Natural History in New York.[14]

In 1910, on the week-long journey to Cairo, the party paused at major and minor sites, the first being Abu Simbel, with its four colossal figures of Ramses the Great. Ethel read descriptions from their Baedeker's guide and her father was indignant to find initials carved in the rock of the ancient chambers. If he had his way the vandals would be treated as similar miscreants in Yellowstone Park, who when apprehended were forced to "return and remove every trace of their despicable work."[15] TR had apparently forgotten his own youthful sacrilege in 1872, when he shot birds from a column of the Ramesseum at Thebes. The *Ibis* stopped at the island ruins of Philae, formerly the garden-like "Pearl of the Nile," but sadly under water half the year since the 1902 completion the Aswan dam, a modern wonder they visited as well. At Aswan for the first time, crowds of American and English tourists gathered to see the former president.

From Luxor, the chief tourist center of Upper Egypt, they took an excursion to the nearby massive ruin at Karnak in a moonlight tour led by a British Egyptologist. Roosevelt also visited the American Presbyterian mission school for girls. There he praised the education of native women, who along with men, he asserted, must be elevated to a new status based on respect for the individual.[16] In the long run, the Colonel told the students, "a fig tree is judged by the fact that it produces figs and not thistles." Rehearsing a theme he would raise many times in the following months, he asserted that book knowledge was not all. Education must be practical as well. "You women must learn to cook and keep house, but at the same time you must have the literary knowledge and trained mind to enable you to take your proper place as counselor of the families." To O'Laughlin, however,

Luxor was most notable as the place Roosevelt received a warning that if he mentioned the assassination of Boutros in a planned speech at the new Cairo University he might suffer the same fate. This threat only ensured that the address, which the Colonel dictated at Luxor, included a pointed condemnation of the murder.[17]

Arriving at Cairo on March 24, the party was greeted by the American Consul-General Lewis Iddings and TR's old friend and "tennis cabinet" member Oscar Straus. Now the U.S. ambassador at Constantinople, Straus briefed his former chief both on conditions in Turkey and politics at home, where "much ground had been lost." The Colonel paid a call at the Abdin Palace on the Khedive Abbas, the titular ruler of Egypt, and in return he received Abbas at the American Agency, the first of many such reciprocal visits he continued across Europe. At the same time Mrs. Roosevelt and Mrs. Iddings called on the Khediva, described as a "beautiful woman of about thirty years, with sad eyes and a pathetic manner," who, if local gossip was true, "was about to be replaced by an Austrian woman who has first place in the affections of the Khedive."[18]

The Roosevelts stayed at Shepeard's Hotel, the home away from home of visiting Englishmen, and a powerful symbol of British rule which would be burned down forty-two years later during another nationalist uprising—one which would finally force out the British. The first night the family saw the Sphinx and pyramids in the moonlight. The next day they visited Saqqara, burial site of the rulers of ancient Memphis, the capital of Egypt's old Kingdom, twelve miles south of Cairo. Abbot recounted Roosevelt's reaction to a temple carving which showed a witness in a law court being horribly tortured before a judge to gain a confession. TR commented that he wished "that those pessimists who believe that civilization is not making steady progress" could see it. Here was a king "portraying as one of the virtues of his reign a state of vicious cruelty which would not have been tolerated by Tammany Hall in its worst days of corruption." The "water cure," he was sorry to say, had sometimes been practiced by Americans in the Philippines, "but it was practiced secretly, and no man who employed it would have been willing to have the fact inscribed upon his tombstone."[19]

That evening Roosevelt dined with the modern rulers of Egypt, Sir Eldon Gorst, the British agent and consul-general, and Sir Reginald Wingate, who in addition to being governor-general of the Sudan, was also Sirdar (commander) of the Anglo-Egyptian army which enforced

British policy on the ground. Wingate and Roosevelt agreed in the "methods of action" needed to maintain British rule and the Sirdar thanked him for "all you have done to help forward our task in the Sudan."[20] The more conciliatory Gorst, who spoke Arabic and had decades of experience in Egypt, had the bad fortune in 1907 to follow a legend in Lord Cromer, who for the previous quarter century had run Egypt, called the "Veiled Protectorate" because it had not been officially annexed by Britain, with an iron hand.[21] Theoretically, the British hierarchy only advised Egypt's ruler, the Khedive, and his government, staffed in the main by a non-Egyptian Turco-Circassian elite, headed by a prime minister. The Khedive in turn made a substantial yearly payment to the Sublime Porte for the privilege of ruling Egypt according to a firman (license) granted by the Ottoman Sultan at the beginning of his reign.

It was a curious system, in which, Cromer had commented in his 1908 book *Modern Egypt*, "one alien race, the English, have had to control and guide a second alien race, the Turks, by whom they are disliked, in the government of a third race, the Egyptians."[22] Roosevelt told Wingate that reading Cromer's "really great book" gave him a "fresh realization of Lincoln's saying, 'There is a great deal of human nature in mankind.'" Cromer's descriptions of the trouble caused in Egypt by "well-meaning but fatuous philanthropists at home" reminded TR of his own experiences with the same type concerning the Philippines. They filled Faneuil Hall in Boston with audiences "equally prepared to demand that the Filipinos be given the fullest democratic self-government, and to denounce us if any disorder follows even the most cautious and tentative move in the very direction they advocate."[23]

Gorst and Wingate frankly discussed the current state of affairs with Roosevelt, including the nationalist agitation for self-government, which had only been emboldened by Gorst's conciliation. The nationalists were also incensed by recent increases in the numbers of British officials in government service and demanded more jobs for Egyptians. Roosevelt reported to his friend Henry White that Wingate was "a fine fellow" and he had no doubt Gorst was also a good man, but he was "evidently afraid of acting," unless he was sure that he would be "backed up at home."[24] Other British officials in the post-Cromer regime also seemed to be "drifting, and uneasy and uncertain of their ground." They too complained to Roosevelt of the "mischief wrought by certain ignorant Members of Parliament" who had come to Egypt "under the belief they were championing the cause of human righteousness." This had ironically only inspired in the Egyptians "a touch of that most dangerous of all feelings, contempt" towards the English. Cairo was also the only place in Africa where TR was disappointed with some of the British army officers he met, who seemed to be absorbed, not in the task at hand, but in polo and tennis matches, and had "no serious appreciation of the situation or of their own duties."[25]

Outside the British hierarchy, TR also spoke with several deputations of local dignitaries and journalists. He noted the "curious" state of things in which the country had prospered greatly, both materially and morally, since his visit thirty-eight years before. However, in his view the "very prosperity had made the Jeshuren wax fat and kick." The noisy nationalist leaders were "merely Levantine Moslems in red fezes" and "quite hopeless as material on which to build." He did not consider them dangerous foes, but noted that, profoundly affected by the reforms gained by the Young Turks in Constantinople, they were given to "loud talk in the cafés and to emotional street parades."[26] Before he left the United States, TR had commented to Spring Rice on the Young Turk movement, which had forced a parliament and a constitution on the Ottoman Sultan, that he was "intensely interested in the Liberal movement in the Moslem world." He admitted that it was of course very complicated but he hoped that in Turkey the "parliamentary talkers and the army fighters" would be able to stay together and act "not only in harmony but with moderation." One of the things he feared was that they would be "misled by false analogies." In his estimation, the fact that reform was necessary in Turkey, did not mean that it was "now to the advantage of Egypt to have a parliament" or for that matter a constitution as the nationalists demanded.[27]

Roosevelt did not fear "Levantines in cafés" as much as what he considered the real strength of the nationalists—the "mass of practically unchanged bigoted Moslems to whom the movement meant driving out the foreigner, plundering and slaying the local Christian, and a return to all the violence and corruption" of pre-English rule. All those he spoke to, whether American missionaries, Greeks, Syrians, or Copts, agreed that the "overthrow of English rule would be an inconceivable disaster" and dreaded "keenly the murderous outbreak of Moslem brutality which was certain to follow." However, they were "cowed by the seeming lack of decision of the English authorities."[28]

The speech in the Sudan already had raised the ire of the "Egypt for the Egyptians" nationalists and now, despite the warnings of Iddings and others, Roosevelt further provoked them with another address at the new Cairo University. Entitled "Law and Order in Egypt," the speech, which had been approved by Gorst and Wingate, pointedly condemned the ongoing agitation and the assassination of Boutros Ghali. Before doing this, however, Roosevelt drew applause from his audience when he spoke of the great University of Cordova, which had flourished a thousand years before in Muslim Spain, as a "source of light and learning when the rest of Europe was either in twilight or darkness." The previous day he had visited the Al-Azhar, the historic Muslim university of Cairo, and seen the writings of Ibn Batutu in its library. He hoped the new and non-sectarian National University could be part of a "revival, and more than a revival, of the conditions that made possible such contributions to the growth of civilization."[29]

Preaching from a text he would repeat before other students at Cambridge two months later, Roosevelt argued that character was far more important than "mere intellect," which by itself was "worse than useless" unless it was "guided by an upright heart" with "strength and courage behind it." More important than "mental subtlety" in the make up of a people were "morality, decency, clean living, courage, manliness, self-respect." Striking at least a glancing blow at Egyptian aspirations for government jobs, Roosevelt also counseled the students to guard against the western tendency to train men at university "merely for literary, professional and official positions." In his view it was a "very unhealthy thing" for any country to "turn to such channels" more than a small proportion of its "strongest and best minds." At home he supported Booker T. Washington's Tuskegee Institute and vocational education in general. He was equally glad that industrial and agricultural schools had also been built in Egypt as it was essential to train people to cultivate the soil and to be engineers and merchants, men "able to take the lead in all the various functions indispensable in a great modern civilized state." The base and foundation of healthy life in any country or society, in his view, was "necessarily composed of the men who do the actual productive work."[30]

Comparing gaining an education to gaining self-government, TR asked his audience to remember that securing the first, "whether by the individual or by a people," was "attained only by a process, not by an act." You could no more make a man "really educated by giving him a certain curriculum of studies" than you could "make a people fit for self-government by giving it a paper constitution." The education of an individual was the work of years, just as the training of a nation to "fit it successfully to fulfill the duties of self-government" was a matter, "not of a decade or two, but of generations." Only "foolish empiricists" believed that granting a "paper constitution" conferred "the power of self-government upon a people." What was needed first was a "slow, steady, resolute development of those substantial qualities, such as the love of justice, the love of fair play, the spirit of self-reliance, of moderation, which alone enable a people to govern themselves." This was a long "and even tedious but absolutely essential process," in which he believed "your University will take an important part." Roosevelt then drew renewed applause from his audience by quoting in passable Arabic a proverb from Koran: "God is with the patient, if they know how to wait."[31]

Roosevelt himself waited until the end to address the assassination of the Coptic Christian premier Boutros Ghali, notably, given the occasion, by a Muslim pharmacology student recently returned from training in Britain. He told his audience that an important feature of the process of working towards self-government was the development of a spirit which condemned "every form of lawless evil, every form of envy and hatred and, above all, hatred based on religion or race." All good men of every nation, whose respect was worth having, had condemned the recent murder which Roosevelt believed "an even bigger calamity for Egypt than it was a wrong to the individual himself." Whether such deeds were committed under pretence of preserving order or of obtaining liberty, they were "equally abhorrent in the eyes of all decent men" and in the long run, "equally damaging to the very cause to which the assassin professes to be devoted." At a national university such as theirs, which knew no creed, there should be absolute equality between Muslim and Christian, as in the laws of the country. He hoped the university in future would "frown on every form of wrong-doing, whether in the shape of injustice or corruption or lawlessness and to stand with firmness, with good sense, and with courage for those immutable principles of justice and merciful dealing" between man and man, without which there could never be "the slightest growth towards a really fine and high civilization."[32]

Most of the audience could not understand Roosevelt's speech at the time and reacted only the next day after reading the published translation. His condemnation of the assassination, and support for those who preached delaying self-government, brought a nationalist student march in protest. Hundreds gathered outside Shepheard's Hotel to chant "Down with Roosevelt," "Down with the Occupation" and "Long Live the Constitution." Cal O'Laughlin sent an article home in which he declared that Roosevelt had "placed his finger on the quivering nerve of Egyptian Nationalism" by denouncing the killing of Boutros in "vigorous language." Both Sir Eldon and Lady Gorst had listened with "rapt interest" and all the English agreed regarding TR's "sincere earnestness and the delicate way in which he handled the difficult subject." One less friendly Egyptian paper, *Al-Moayad*, had in response quoted another Arab proverb: "They are able to make a donkey's tail look like an elephant's trunk when so inclined."[33]

Sheik Ali Youssuf, a journalist and president of the Constitutional Reform League of Egypt, replied in print to Roosevelt's words. On the Colonel's arrival at Cairo the Sheik had published an open letter in *Al-Moayad* criticizing the Khartoum speech and begging him to "respect the dignity of the Egyptian nation when in the country." At a meeting with Youssuf and other representatives of the local press the day before the Cairo speech, Roosevelt had condemned as "a lie" the rumor that he had wounded the feelings of the Muslim officers in the Sudan. He then told them that he did not want the "newspaper men to dictate to me. I am going to speak tomorrow in the Egyptian University. Wait till you hear what I shall say and then say what you wish to say." Afterwards, Youssuf was astonished that the former president of the "greatest nation in civilization at the present time" and "best friends of the liberty of nations" had chosen twice to insult the Egyptian people. First, by telling the officers in Khartoum to stay out of politics, and then by telling the students at Cairo that it would take generations to achieve self-government.[34]

As he had done in the press meeting, the Sheik took umbrage at Roosevelt's portrayal of Muslims, despite their history of toleration of minorities for thirteen centuries before the British arrived in Egypt, as fanatics who would massacre those of other religions if they gained power. He also noted that the Colonel refused to meet with several Muslim groups while finding the time to see Christian and other leaders. Despite Roosevelt's misstep, Youssuf declared that he believed Americans were still "in their country, the friends of freedom and are the friends of nations that are governed against their will."[35]

Undaunted by this criticism, the few expressions of thanks TR received from Muslim quarters led him to comment that the "really intelligent" men who "earnestly desired to have the Moslem world advance as far beyond what it had been and what it still was as the Christian world has advanced beyond the dark ages," agreed with his speech. As might have been expected the Coptic and Syrian Christians, as well as the American missionaries, joined the hosanna chorus.[36]

Gorst, who had been worried about the consequences of mentioning Boutros Ghali's murder, wrote to TR that he had "Immensely enjoyed" his address and was glad he had consented to speak. He went on that if anything could bring the nationalists "into a more reasonable frame of mind, your words should have that effect." In any case, Roosevelt had given him "renewed courage to go on with what I often feel to be a very hopeless task."[37] The Colonel was touched by Gorst's letter of thanks, and by another from Wingate, but reported to Henry White that what he had said would "do small good unless they have the nerve to back it up by deeds" and were "backed up at home." All in all, he had come away with "rather a contempt for the English attitude in Egypt."[38]

At the same time, Gorst informed his masters at the Foreign Office in London that Roosevelt's speech had caused "great dismay in the nationalist ranks." He admitted that TR had shown him the speech beforehand and that he "encouraged him to administer this unpalatable medicine." When the initial irritation had "worn away," Gorst believed "this plain speaking may do some good to those who are not entirely beyond redemption."[39] Wingate predicted that the speech would help to awaken the British government to the true state of affairs in Egypt. Roosevelt's words would "travel all over the world" and "do more than anything else to make our sleepy people realize that the situation in Egypt is not as it should be and that a strong hand is absolutely necessary."[40]

This is exactly the text that Roosevelt would preach in London. He confided to Whitelaw Reid, the U.S. ambassador to the Court of St. James who was furiously trying to arrange the Colonel's crowded English itinerary, that when he arrived in London he would have much to tell him about his time in the Sudan and Egypt. He announced that there were "plenty of jobs for which I am not competent," but he had to say that he would "greatly like to handle Egypt and India for a few months." At the end of that he doubtless would be "impeached by the

House of Commons but I should have things moving in a fine order first."[41]

Over the previous months, TR had also corresponded with Reid concerning the forthcoming European campaign in support of Andrew Carnegie's plan for world peace. Taking advantage of Roosevelt's gratitude for his additional support of the safari, Carnegie persuaded him to broach his initiatives, including a league of peace, arbitration and arms limitation, particularly with the Kaiser at Berlin. The plutocrat also assured TR that his efforts in promoting universal peace would have the blessing of Taft, who sent Carnegie a letter to this effect.[42] The Colonel in return assured Carnegie that he was willing sincerely to "fight for peace" and that "with the big statesmen of Europe, emperors, Kings, Ministers of State," he would do what lay in his powers "to help secure the adoption of the policies," in particular international arbitration, for which Carnegie and Elihu Root both stood. He would do all he could to "bring about such a league of, or understanding among, the great powers as will forbid one of them, or any small power, to engage in unrighteous, foolish or needless war." He would also seek to secure "an effective arbitral tribunal, with power to enforce at least certain of its decrees" and to secure "an agreement to check the waste of money on growing and excessive armaments." If, as Roosevelt believed probable, the proposals could not be secured at once, he nevertheless promised to do all he could "help the movement, rapid or slow, towards the desired end." He pledged that in France, Italy, Austria, and in Germany especially, he would "go into the matter at length with the men of power," and would "report to you in full in England."[43]

The greatest immediate threat to peace, in almost everyone's view, lay in the Anglo-German naval arms race and Carnegie used his influence to ensure that after his talk with the Kaiser, TR would not only report to him but to a conference of British statesmen of both parties. Roosevelt left all the arrangements to Carnegie, who coordinated with Whitelaw Reid in London, and Viscount Morley of Blackburn, a member of the British Cabinet sympathetic with their peace aims. Consequently, a late May 1910 weekend meeting was set for Wrest Park, the English country estate of Reid. The British representatives who agreed to attend a "quiet conference" to discuss Wilhelm's response included the prime minister, Henry Asquith, the foreign secretary, Sir Edward Grey, and the former Conservative prime minister and current leader of the opposition, Arthur Balfour.

Carnegie and Roosevelt both saw Wilhelm II as the key to any progress on the peace front and TR pledged to Carnegie from Africa that when he saw the Kaiser he would "go over the matter at length" and reveal that he meant to repeat the entire conversation in England. Roosevelt confided that he considered the proposed meeting as "most important."[44] For an approach to Wilhelm, TR asked Carnegie to solicit the advice of Root, whose "gift of phrasing things" was unequalled. He asked Carnegie to have his trusted advisor put his thoughts in writing and send them to him.[45] Carnegie did as TR wished, and in his letter Root first cautioned Roosevelt not to seem to be lecturing Europe on its duties and not to assume the functions of the State Department. He suggested a friendly, informal talk with the Kaiser. It seemed plain to Root that TR could do nothing in England unless he was able to first accomplish something in Germany. He believed the British were willing to quit the arms race if Germany would but to urge her public men to do so except on that basis would be "merely to irritate them."[46]

In Root's opinion the crux of the matter was in Berlin and the only course was to say to Wilhelm: "One of those great opportunities which have been presented to a very few men in history lies before you at this moment. If you ignore it your name will live on only as one of a great multitude of men who have raised and trained armies and governed states and have been forgotten because everything they have done has been what thousands of other men have done equally well." If Wilhelm seized the moment he would "render a service to mankind of such signal and striking character" as to place him "forever in the little group of the supremely great" who were seen "rising above the great mass of the ordinary great." Having the "greatest and effective army that ever existed," having the means and constructive capacity for an "unsurpassed" navy, the Kaiser could say to the world: "I will lead you to peace. Let us stop where we are, and let us end now the race of competition in enlargement and provision for war."[47]

In addition, Root suggested that Roosevelt might discreetly intimate to the Emperor that, if the idea was entertained, aid could be given in sounding the other powers without committing Germany. And if this course was entertained by Wilhelm, then TR truly would have something to talk about in England and he had no doubt the British would give informal assurances of support to prepare the way. Root was convinced by the failures of the 1907 Hague Conference that this "Gordian method of cutting the knot is the only one that affords any possibility of success." The only way to quit was to quit and only the Kaiser could do it. He could think of no one better suited to "make a lodgment in the Emperor's mind with this idea than Theodore Roosevelt."[48]

Root's letter, TR confessed to Carnegie, was exactly what he wanted and, he gushed, "How wise he is!" He asked Carnegie to tell Root that he would not fall into the errors against which he warned. He would not "seem to interfere with the regular American diplomats," nor look as though he was "trying to teach Europe how to behave." All he could do he would do and, as Carnegie suggested, TR's Nobel speech would be made "with special reference to my call at Berlin afterwards." He was momentarily at least optimistic and told Carnegie, "What an interesting meeting we shall have at Wrest Park."[49]

Roosevelt and family departed Cairo on March 30, 1910 for Alexandria where they took ship the next day on the "dirty and uncomfortable" steamer *Prinz Heinrich* for Naples. TR reported to his old friend Lodge, that the British government was "showing an uncomfortable flabbiness in Egyptian matters." In the Sudan and Egypt, much to his amusement, "everybody turned to me precisely as if I were in my own country," hoping and praying for leadership. And ever since "striking Khartoum," he had been in "almost as much of whirl as if I were on a Presidential tour at home."[50] This "whirl" would continue in the European leg of his odyssey.

Chapter 6

European Whirl

Roosevelt's reception on April 2, 1910 at Naples gave a foretaste of the hubbub he would create across Europe, at least until he reached the regimented confines of Germany. That first night, at the Naples Opera, the Colonel received a ten-minute standing ovation and so many people came to his box to be introduced he hardly saw any of the performance. A representative Italian paper gushed that in politics Roosevelt was a supporter of vigorous reform at home and aggressive imperialism abroad, and personally, "a man with a masculine appearance and a handsome, muscular and dynamic figure, formidable Teddy."[1]

After his embarrassingly popular Neapolitan reception, at Rome there was a dust up with Pope Pius X, who made it a condition of an intended audience that Roosevelt not meet with American Methodist missionaries, a few of whom had attacked the Vatican. A year before there had been an embarrassing incident when the Pope cancelled an audience with TR's vice president, Charles Fairbanks, simply because he was to meet with the offending Methodists. Roosevelt had had cordial relations with the previous Pontiff, Leo XIII, but deemed Pius, though worthy, a "narrow-minded parish priest"; completely under the control of his Secretary of State, Cardinal Rafael Merry del Val, whom he considered a "furiously bigoted reactionary, and in fact a good type of a sixteenth century Spanish ecclesiastic." Although the Holy See was incensed by the Methodist encroachment at its very doorstep, to Roosevelt it only added a healthy "spirit of rivalry" in service and good conduct which in the long run was "as advantageous to the church as to its people," but was "peculiarly abhorrent to the narrow and intolerant priestly reactionaries."[2]

Some of the Methodist missionaries in Rome, Roosevelt believed, were "really excellent men, who were doing first class work." At their Sunday School, he discovered that one of the teachers was a grand-daughter of the Italian patriot Garibaldi and one of the graduates a grandson. On the other hand, one of the Methodist leaders, with the Dickensian name Ezra Tipple, was a "crude, vulgar, tactless creature, cursed with the thirst of self-advertisement," who found that he could "attract attention best by frantic denunciations of the Pope." In addition to preaching sermons in which Pius became the "whore of Babylon," Tipple also attacked Rome's other Protestant denominations, Episcopal, Presbyterian and the Young Men's Christian Association.[3]

If he had associated himself with Tipple, Roosevelt would have understood Pius's refusal to see him but felt he had "no right what-soever to expect that I would be willing to see him if he made it a condition that I should not see the entirely reputable Methodists." This was the response Roosevelt gave to a letter from Merry del Val received in Cairo. At Naples, he sent Cal O'Laughlin, an Irish Catholic, on to Rome for an audience in an attempt to solve the dilemma. The Cardinal then only made matters worse with an offer not to make it public if Roosevelt would secretly agree not to see the Methodists. This "piece of discreditable double dealing and deception" TR condemned as so reprehensible that even a "Tammany Boodle alderman" would have been ashamed to make it.[4] When Merry del Val revealed his proposal, Roosevelt also published their correspondence and had Lawrence Abbott put an article in the *Outlook* which fully explained why he would not see the Pope.[5] In the end, when they also displeased him with public utterances on the affair, TR cancelled a planned public reception with the leading Methodists. All this led him to comment to Arthur Lee that since reaching Khartoum he had been "dragged into every kind of mess. I trust the balance of my trip in Europe will be more peaceful."[6]

To Roosevelt, Rome presented the "very sharpest contrasts between the extremes of radical modern progress, social, political and religious, and the extremes of opposition to all such progress." The Vatican represented the last. The first he found at a reception and dinner at the Campidoglio with the "Jew mayor, a good fellow, and his Socialist backers in the Town Council." Ernesto Nathan, whose official title was "Syndic" of Rome, spoke excellent English, was "apparently a good public servant" and in TR's view would have been "quite at home as Reform Mayor of any American city of the second class."[7] Nathan, whom the American Ambassador John Leishman had informed TR was an "embryo Disraeli," a friend of the United States and a personal admirer, lauded Roosevelt as akin to the warrior philosopher Marcus Aurelius.[8]

As president, TR had often railed against radical socialists, a minuscule party at home, but as he would see firsthand, much more powerful and prevalent across Europe. One of the socialist journalists present at the Roman reception wrote that beneath the Colonel's rather nondescript blonde "Teutonic profile," he found what he was searching for. "Behind his thick glasses" was a "strong, confident and investigative eye," that penetrated and probed. "An eye that sees and foresees: acute, imperious, immense despite its smallness, as bright as an emerald. An eye of polished steel like his soul." Behind TR's glasses, he "saw the man, the great man."[9] What Roosevelt saw of Italy made him feel that there was "infinite need for radical action towards the betterment of social and industrial conditions." He felt a "very strong sympathy with some of the Socialistic aims," but at the same time had "a very profound distrust of most of the Socialistic methods."[10]

Roosevelt placed Italy's king, Victor Emmanuel III, somewhere in between the two extremes of socialism and reaction. The "most companionable" monarch had invited TR a year before to hunt ibex and now showed him his impressive collection of trophies, including a very rare South Italian chamois, but the two also spoke of social reform. About the last Roosevelt found the King "deeply and intelligently interested" and not only "astonishingly liberal, but even radical, sympathizing with many of the purposes and doctrines of the Socialists." Victor Emmanuel's understanding of the social and civil needs of the country, combined with his knowledge of military affairs, prompted TR to comment that he did not see how Italy could have "a more intelligent, devoted and sympathetic ruler" and he told the King he wished he had a "few more men like him in the Senate!"[11]

Roosevelt repeated this sentiment in his reply to an appeal from Lodge, who solicited his friend's aid for the fall congressional elections. TR's continued silence on U.S. politics, combined with the unpopularity of Taft and the Republican party, had garnered much comment. The *Washington Post*, for example, noted the "stress" the party was under and the need for Roosevelt's help, while his attitude toward the Taft administration remained an "Unknown Quantity."[12] To this point, Lodge had strongly advised TR to stay out of politics altogether on his return. But now, in particular to counter the unpopularity of the Payne-Aldrich tariff, which was being blamed for the country's economic problems, he proposed to send the former president on the stump. Roosevelt responded that he would be happy to do what he could for Lodge in Massachusetts, but a general appeal was "impossible" and would only eliminate him as a factor afterwards. Based on what he had been told by Lodge and others, TR had been "at first inclined to think that as much had been done with the tariff as possible." But now, with additional knowledge, he believed the tariff issue was "not met as it was necessary to meet it; that certain things that ought to have been done were left undone, and that the whole was done in a way that caused trouble." Therefore, the Colonel did not intend to spend his political capital defending it. He also told Lodge that "under no circumstances" would he accept either of the New York jobs widely rumored to be available to him—the governorship or a senate seat.[13]

After Rome, while Ethel and Kermit went on to Pisa, Theodore and Edith attempted to reprise, in reverse, their honeymoon trip of twenty-three years before along the Italian Riviera. However, the local populations and authorities refused to cooperate. On the first, and only, "delightful" day of privacy they drove a three horse carriage in "sun and shadow" from Spezia to Rappallo and then on to Sestri Levante, where they stayed at an old hotel. The next morning, however, the local residents descended, and on the way to Chiavari, brass bands, locals, and tourists lined the route, festooning their carriage with flowers. There would be precious little more privacy until the final day before departing for America. After a few hours hurried sightseeing at Genoa, the couple were rejoined by the children and the two secretaries for the seventy mile journey to picturesque Porto Maurizio and Edith's sister Emily's seaside house, Villa Magna Quies (Villa of Great Quiet), which hardly lived up to its name during Roosevelt's visit. Six thousand spectators filled the small seaport to see Mayor Carreti greet the Colonel as "the first citizen of the American Republic, but above all a great humanitarian." He was given the freedom of the City and opened a new boulevard named in his honor.[14]

The most notable of the multitude of visitors who descended on scenic Porto Maurizio was Gifford Pinchot, who on April 11 reported to his old chief on President Taft's apostasy and gave his version of the Ballinger-Pinchot affair that had cost his job and of which he had already written. The papers at home were abuzz that Roosevelt had sent for the former Chief Forester, and the visit was widely viewed as the beginning of the "Back From Elba" movement.[15] Pinchot recorded in his diary that the Porto Maurizio meeting, which lasted nearly all day, was "one of the best and most satisfactory talks" he had ever had with TR.[16] He wrote to James Garfield that he found "everything exactly as you and I had foreseen. There was nothing changed. Nothing unexpected." Pinchot admitted that their discussions left the ex-president "in a very embarrassing position, but that could not be helped."[17]

For extra ammunition, Pinchot had brought along a "sheaf of letters," including appeals from Garfield and the insurgent senators Jonathan Dolliver and Albert Beveridge, all of whom reported on the gloomy state of political affairs and the present insurgent movement of progressives in the party against Taft.[18] In perhaps the most eloquent of these, after comprehensively condemning the Taft administration's record, Dolliver added a more personal, and damning, indictment of the president for turning over the "certificate of character which Mr. Roosevelt had given him" to Senator Aldrich. If Pinchot saw the former president, Dolliver went on, he wished he would tell him that "the next certificate of character he issues ought, for the sake of caution, to be marked 'Not Transferable'." Dolliver ended with an appeal that Roosevelt, who was about to receive on his return a "popular welcome unparalleled in our history," not give his "affirmative approbation of the things which went on here last summer and the things that are going on here now." Instead, Dolliver appealed for TR to support the "little group of us in both houses of Congress" who were "fighting for public rights, under the inspiration which we gained in other years serving in the ranks under his leadership."[19] To Roosevelt, the political cartoons showing Taft carrying his policies out "on a stretcher" must have begun to seem all too accurate.

Neither Pinchot nor Roosevelt would comment on the substance of their meeting for publication, but TR did announce that he planned to give a speech on conservation in Colorado on August 27. He also permitted O'Laughlin to state, in a *New York Times* article, that "No event in Col. Roosevelt's trip has been of greater importance or interest to the American people" than the conference between the two men. TR was "very much attached to Mr. Pinchot," was very glad to see him, and listened to everything he had to say, "as I shall listen to any friend of mine or any side of any public question." Before any conclusions were reached, O'Laughlin felt it safe to say that he believed Roosevelt would also consult with Elihu Root and Henry Cabot Lodge. He went on to note that TR's refusal to talk about politics did not prevent him from remaining as deeply interested in all questions relating to conservation as when he was in the White House. The ex-president also felt it vital that the policies that he "inaugurated in this connection shall be carried to fruition." He had thought when he retired from the presidency that "such a splendid impetus had been given to these policies that they could be regarded as fixed principles, and as such loyally observed and carried out." Further, he believed that the people realized the importance of the things he advocated and would "insist upon their accomplishment in every respect."[20]

The day of Pinchot's visit, TR wrote a long letter to Lodge, who had not wanted him to receive the ex-chief forester. Though he tried to give Taft the benefit of the doubt, the Colonel told Lodge did not see how he could help him or the congress to victory in 1910 unless it was "on the ground that they are approved by the nation for having on many important points completely twisted round the policies I advocated and acted upon." He refused to win any more elections for congressional leaders he afterwards found "cynically indifferent, or rather cynically and contemptuously hostile to doing themselves anything" and without the "slightest regard" for what Roosevelt had promised. Taft, TR reminded Lodge, had been nominated "solely on my assurance to the Western people especially, but almost as much to the people of the East, that he would carry out my work unbroken." Now there was a widespread feeling that TR had, "quite unintentionally," deceived them.

Roosevelt could not help feeling that "even though there has been a certain adherence" to the objects of the policies which he "deemed essential to the National welfare," those objects had been pursued by the administration in a "spirit and with methods" which had rendered the effort "almost nugatory." He did not think that under the "Taft-Cannon-Aldrich régime" there had been "a real appreciation of the needs of the country" and he was certain there was "no real appreciation of the way the country felt." The Colonel told Lodge that he "earnestly hoped that Taft would "retrieve himself yet" and be the next nominee.

TR had played his part and had "the very strongest objection to having to play any further part." If, from whatever causes, the present political position of the party was hopeless, he "most emphatically" desired that he should "not be put in the position of having to run for the Presidency, staggering under a load which I cannot carry, and which has been put on my shoulders through no fault of my own."[21]

Leaving the ladies behind for a few more days at Porto Maurizio, TR and Kermit went on to Venice, Vienna, and Budapest. At the first, they took lunch with the American consul on a gondola excursion under the Bridge of Sighs and on to the statue of Colleoni which Roosevelt regarded as the most imposing sculpture in the world. During a whirlwind day they also visited St. Marks, admired the old masters at the Palace of the Doges and toured the Academy of Bella Arti with its masterpieces by Titian, Veronese, Bellini, Carpaccio, and Tintoretto. As he left for Austria, Roosevelt commented "If there were only one country in the world outside our own I would send my sons to Egypt; if there was only one city, I would send them to Venice."[22]

At Vienna, the popular reception outdid Rome. Everywhere the streets were lined as if Roosevelt were visiting San Francisco or St Louis. From this point across Europe, at capital after capital, the people and their rulers viewed him as "still the great American leader, the man who was to continue to play in the future of American politics something like the part that he had played in the past." In the end he finally gave up trying to disabuse them of this notion. Roosevelt was greeted by the Austrian Ambassador to the United States, Baron Hengelmuller von Hengervar, and Richard Kerens, the American Ambassador to Austria-Hungary. He made a formal call on the Archduke Franz Ferdinand, the heir to the throne of the Dual Monarchy. The archduke, who would be assassinated at Sarajevo four years later, was the only royal TR met that obviously did not like him. He in turn dismissed Franz Ferdinand as an "ultramontane, and at bottom a furious reactionary in every way, political and ecclesiastical both."[23]

Roosevelt had a much higher opinion of the Austrian foreign minister, Count von Aehrenthal, whom he thought a man of strength and ability. Two years before, the Austrian government had been appreciative when the then president "cordially approved" of their annexation of Bosnia and Herzegovina, which he considered more a "changing of the title, although not really the substance, of the Austrian occupation." At some point he hoped the Balkan states might stand on their own but the example of Serbia was "not sufficient encouraging" to make him believe the two small states would make more progress alone than under Austria, whose rule was infinitely preferable to that of Turkey.[24] Neighboring Serbia, however, and her friend Russia, looked upon the annexations with hostility and a fuse had been lit in 1908 which would explode with cataclysmic fury six years later.

Carnegie had let it get into the newspapers that Roosevelt was to speak to Wilhelm II about his peace plans and this had alarmed the German Foreign Office and the Kaiser. Consequently, when he called in Vienna on the prime minister, Richard von Bienerth, the Austrian broached the subject for his German ally. TR informed von Biernerth that when he was president he had sounded all the powers to see if something might be done to limit the size of armaments, at least by limiting the size of ships, but he had found that England and Germany would not consent. He added that, though he had no proposal of his own, he did "wish that the German authorities would seriously consider whether it was worthwhile for them to keep on with a building programme which was the real cause why other nations were forced into the very great expense attendant upon modern naval preparation." Two days later the Berlin papers revealed that Roosevelt wished to talk to the German Foreign Office about the subject of universal peace and disarmament, but they declared they did not believe for a moment that he would be "so lacking in the requirements of the situation" to take advantage of his friendly personal visit to "broach a subject which would be very distasteful and which the government authorities would have to refuse to discuss."[25]

In Vienna Roosevelt also had an audience with the Austrian Emperor Franz Joseph, who had been on the throne since the revolutions of 1848. The two chatted in French about hunting and politics. The Emperor struck Roosevelt as an interesting, although not very able, gentleman of good instincts who in his long reign had "witnessed the most extraordinary changes and vicissitudes." He in return told TR that he had been particularly interested in seeing him "because he was the last representative of the old system, whereas I embodied the new" and that he had wished to "know for himself how the prominent exponent of that movement felt and thought."[26] Franz Joseph extended to Roosevelt the signal honor of hunting in the royal game preserves, should he wish. All were shocked when the Colonel, pleading that his overfull itinerary would not allow it, asked to be excused from the privilege, which had never before been offered to a commoner, much less turned down by one.

When Roosevelt arrived at Budapest on the Danube at nine in the evening on 17 April there was, despite a driving rain, a crowd of thousands on hand at the train station. After a reception hosted by the Archduke Joseph at the palace the next day, Count Apponyi and a delegation representing the International Peace Union gave TR a formal welcome at the historic Parliament House. There he was presented with an illuminated address which recorded his achievements on behalf of human rights, human liberty and international justice. In his remarks, the gifted orator Apponyi called Roosevelt "one of the leading efficient forces for the moral improvement of the world." The Colonel in return praised Hungary for the "tremendous influence it has exercised upon the world in beating back, by the dauntless courage of its warriors, the hordes of barbarians who sought to overwhelm Europe."[27]

At Budapest, Kermit and TR boarded the Orient Express for Paris, where the family was reunited on April 21. They stayed with their friends, the new U.S. ambassador, Robert Bacon, and his wife Martha. This luxury made the city "an oasis in a desert of hurry and confusion." Roosevelt and Edith were able to get away to revisit several museums and art galleries, including the Louvre, where, he told Bacon, "I shall keep clear of the Rubens gallery, which I loathe, but there are some of the pictures which I must see."[28] The couple met the sculptor Rodin at his house and were able to see *Manon* and *Samson and Delilah* at the Opera and *Oedipe Roi* at the *Comédie-Française*, where they experienced another embarrassingly long ovation. TR made a much watched visit to Napoleon's tomb, which set off a renewed avalanche of editorial cartoons showing him in Napoleonic garb returning from Elba, some with the dark cloud of Waterloo in the distance.

Roosevelt enjoyed the company of all the Frenchmen he met, including the premier Aristide Briand, the president Armand Fallières, and various other members of the government and the opposition. After Fallières gave him a dinner at the Élysée Palace, one French newspaper cartoon depicted a scene with the president in which the Colonel is giving his host an account of his life in Africa. Roosevelt says: "Of evenings I used to read the Pensées de Pascal aloud; and the first hippopotamus that dared yawn—Bang! In His Jaw!"[29] TR later put down to his "complacent Anglo-Saxon ignorance" the fact that he had previously considered French public men "people of marked levity." During this visit he found them "just as solid characters as English and American public men" with the added "attractiveness" which to his mind made the "cultivated Frenchman really unique." He came to realize that it was "not they who were guilty of levity," but "the French nation, or rather the combination of the French national character with the English parliamentary system" instituted after the fall of Napoleon III. In his opinion the English system had not worked well "in a government by groups, where the people do not mind changing their leaders continually," and were "so afraid of themselves that, unlike the English and Americans," they did not trust "any one man with a temporary exercise of large power for fear they will be weak enough to let him assume it permanently."[30]

In Africa the Colonel had been notified of his election to the French Académie des Sciences Morales et Politiques, one of the five Academies forming the French "Insitute," and he officially took his seat while in Paris. Jusserand reported to him that this was not simply an honorary achievement, his credentials had been seriously debated and that in the end "everybody agreed that if there was one man who should become a member as having devoted his life to politics and morals, never dividing the one from the other, it was you."[31] Roosevelt met a number of men of letters whom he greatly admired, including Victor Bérard, translator of *The Odyssey*, as well as a talented writer on contemporary politics. An enchanted TR gushed, "What a charming man a charming Frenchman is!" In return he was received warmly, in fact he captivated the normally blasé city for the entire eight day visit. Only the royalist press, being Catholic, was cold because of his trouble with the Vatican.[32]

Before leaving America, Roosevelt had agreed to give a speech at the Sorbonne, which he praised to his audience as the "most famous university of mediaeval Europe at a time when no one dreamed that there was a New World to discover." For his text TR chose individual citizenship. This was because, for republics such as France and the United States, "the question of the quality of the individual" was supreme. In the long run, success or failure depended upon the way the average man and woman did his or her duty as a citizen. To be a good citizen needed "a high standard of cultivation and scholarship," underpinned by a sound body and mind, but above all stood character. This Roosevelt defined as "the sum of those qualities which we mean when we speak of a man's force and courage, of his good faith and sense of honor." Education for all the people, beyond book learning, should also foster "the great solid qualities" such as self-restraint, self-mastery, common-sense, the power of accepting individual responsibility, and yet of acting in conjunction with others, courage and resolution. These were the qualities which "mark a masterful people."[33]

Roosevelt also praised the "commonplace, every-day qualities and virtues," including "the will and the power to work, to fight at need, and to have plenty of healthy children." The average man must earn his own livelihood and the good man should be strong and brave, to be able to serve his country as a soldier. To the "well-meaning philosophers" who declared all war unrighteous, TR replied that war was a dreadful thing and an unjust war was a crime against humanity, but because it was unjust, not because it was a war. The question must be, Is the right to prevail? Every honorable effort should be made to avoid war, but no self-respecting nation, "can or ought to submit to wrong." The greatest of all curses to Roosevelt was not war, but sterility. The "chief of blessings for any nation" was that it should "leave its seed to inherit the land."[34]

Another threat, which could not be overstated in the Colonel's opinion, was the "deadening effect on any race of the adoption of a logical and extreme socialistic system." This would "spell sheer destruction; it would induce grosser wrong and outrage, fouler immorality than any existing system." However, this did not mean that "we may not with great advantage adopt certain of the principles professed" by some who happened to call themselves socialists. To be afraid to do so would be a "mark of weakness on our part." He was a "strong individualist by personal habit, inheritance and conviction"; but it was only common sense to recognize that "the State, the community, the citizens acting together, can do a number of things better than if they were left to individual action." But, he warned his audience, let us "not be misled into following any proposal for achieving the millennium" until it had been subjected to "hard-headed examination." If any idea seemed good, try it. If it proved good, accept it; otherwise reject it. There were plenty of men in his experience who called themselves socialists with whom it was quite possible to work.[35]

The speech delighted French Republicans, in the Colonel's opinion, because it came from a fellow "radical republican" and because they were "getting very uneasy over the Socialist propaganda, or at least over the mob work and general sinister destruction" in which it was "beginning to take practical form." He felt the same kinship with many of the French Republicans that he did with many English Liberals and American progressives. Fundamentally, it was the "radical liberal" in all three countries with whom he sympathized. They were all at least "working towards the end" for which he thought "we should all of us strive."[36] Others credited the Sorbonne speech for the stiffened attitude of the Briand government which, with elections looming, banned a mass socialist demonstration planned for May 1, 1910 and authorized the police and troops for the first time in years to use their weapons in self-defense. At the very least the attack on doctrinaire socialism in the Sorbonne speech got Roosevelt back in the good books of the royalist press, while the pro-government *Le Temps* published 57,000 copies for distribution to the teachers of France. Thus, his friend Jusserand commented, TR's words were "sure to reach the whole of the coming generation and it will do it an immense good."[37]

The Colonel's friend, still the French Ambassador at Washington, came over to act as a companion and guide at Paris. Though he was very fond of him, TR commented that Jusserand seemed to think "he was not doing his duty if I had one hour to myself." The Colonel had declined an invitation to review French troops, but Jusserand convinced him that, since everyone knew he was to do so with the Kaiser in Germany, it would be an insult to French Arms if he did not change his mind. This he agreed to do, watching a sham battle at Vincennes from horseback after borrowing a mount and riding breeches at the scene. Roosevelt was touched to receive a letter sent on behalf of the enlisted men of the squadron from which the horse was fetched, informing him they planned thereafter to take special care of the animal and to commemorate the event. He sent the men a signed photo, in his Rough Rider regalia, which they hung in a place of honor in their barracks.[38]

From Paris, Roosevelt reported to Carnegie his doubts concerning the prospects of any peace initiative, "even along the cautious lines of conduct" which Root had suggested. He took for granted that Carnegie had seen the Berlin papers and that, consequently, his "anticipations of the difficulties came far short of the actual facts." He felt Carnegie had been very wise in his suggestion about the Nobel speech, which Roosevelt now feared would "represent very nearly all that is efficient and useful that I can accomplish." Nevertheless, as he wanted to see

Carnegie before the Wrest Park meeting, he invited him to dine "alone and entirely informally with us" at Dorchester House, Ambassador Reid's London home, on the first night he arrived in England.[39]

After a week and a day in Paris, the travelers departed for Brussels, where they would spend only twenty-four hours. Roosevelt gave an address at the Brussels Exposition, in part to make amends for the rather embarrassing fact that the United States had not sent an exhibit. This was on account, in TR's estimation at least, of the failure of the skinflint Congress to provide the paltry funds needed. The recently crowned Belgian King Albert was on hand and Roosevelt described him as "a huge fair young man, evidently a thoroughly good fellow, with excellent manners and not a touch of pretension." Albert drove the Colonel through the streets in his carriage "as if he had been one of his own subjects," and was "greeted by the people in cordial democratic fashion." When they met later at the Laeken Palace for dinner, Queen Elizabeth "proved really delightful, really cultivated and intellectual." Every evening, she told Roosevelt, she read aloud to Albert books "in which they were both interested" and in his opinion "altogether they led a thoroughly wholesome life." Much in contrast, it may be said, to the behavior of the previous King, Albert's uncle Leopold. In this brief visit to Belgium Roosevelt was very favorably impressed by all he met.[40]

The same could not be said, at least at the top, for Holland, Roosevelt's ancestral home and the next stop on their journey. Lodge had exhorted TR to visit Holland, telling him he was one of "the half dozen great men whom that little country, or rather race, has given to the world."[41] On their way to The Hague the family visited the Het Loo Palace for lunch with Queen Wilhelmina. She was the only royal for whom they had felt much sentiment in advance and she ended by being the only monarch they did not like at all. Roosevelt had supposed that the Queen, who had come to the throne as a child of ten in 1890, would be "a very nice attractive little woman in a difficult position" and had sympathized with "her apparent loneliness, and had been glad at the birth of her little daughter" only the previous year. However, instead of being "attractive, sweet-tempered and dignified," they found her "excessively unattractive and commonplace" while "conceited and bad-tempered" to boot.[42]

The "almost freezing hauteur" displayed by the bourgeois Wilhelmina led Roosevelt to tell Arthur Lee that he felt inclined to say to her, "If you ever come to my country, Madam, I should like to

introduce you to the wife of the Lieutenant-Governor of Oklahoma."
She reminded TR of nothing more than a "puffed up wife of some
leading grocer" such as he had met in many American towns. He would
not have minded her "lacking refinement and being both common and
commonplace if only she had not been pretentious." It was this trait in
his estimation that made her ridiculous.[43]

Aside from this clash of personalities with the royal family,
Roosevelt thoroughly enjoyed his stay in Holland, both at Amsterdam,
where he viewed the many Rembrandts at the Ryk's Museum, and The
Hague, where he found a surprising number of people spoke English.
As elsewhere he was treated as if he were still president and at home in
America. At Amsterdam the Colonel told an audience that it had been
nearly three centuries since his people left Holland and now he was
back with his son who represented the ninth generation in America.
His family had taken part in the foundation of what was then the tiny
trading post of New Amsterdam. He was "very sorry they ever changed
the name" and his "forefathers had done what they could to stop it."
Roosevelt unfortunately did not speak Dutch but could recall a nursery
rhyme he learned from his grandfather that he recited to the applause
of the audience.[44]

Before taking ship for Norway, where TR was scheduled to give
his Nobel Peace Prize Address, the last country on the continent the
family visited was Denmark. They traveled to Copenhagen by way of
Kiel, where the German battle fleet honored the Colonel by manning
the rails in salute. The Danish King Frederick VIII was absent in
Southern Europe so that Crown Prince Christian and Crown Princess
Alexandra of Mecklenberg-Schwerin, played host to them. When
their train arrived at the Copenhagen station TR, preoccupied by the
apparent loss of their baggage, emerged from the wrong car. The waiting Crown Prince, one of the tallest men in Europe, with the longest
legs, loped down the platform to meet him, with the rest of the official
party strewn behind. Maurice Egan, the American Minister, recalled
that Roosevelt, dressed in an army coat and ancient sombrero, seemed
"pleased beyond words to see us all." After he was formally introduced
to a bemused Prince Christian, TR declared, "Now I have lost my
baggage. Let's go look for it!"[45]

Theodore and Edith caused something of a diplomatic uproar
when they were assigned the chamber in the Christian VII Palace that
the Czar had occupied the previous summer. As Roosevelt was "not

even an Excellency" in the United States, the Russian Ambassador protested this unheard of state of affairs. However, the palace officials were duly impressed when Edith, their luggage delayed, agreed that she and her husband would attend a formal dinner in their gray flannel traveling clothes. The Baron in charge commented, "C'était vraiment royale!"[46]

Denmark had a Liberal government with a Social Democratic opposition and over the previous decades had instituted an impressive number of reforms including old age pensions and homes, health insurance, aide for small farmers to buy their leaseholds and government promotion of cooperative farming. Roosevelt was particularly interested in the old age homes and cooperative farming, both of which he was able at least to catch a glimpse of during his visit. But he was "rather puzzled" that this growth of the "wise and democratic use of the power of State toward helping raise the individual standard of social and economic well-being had not made the people more contented." In Copenhagen, as at Rome, the Colonel found himself seated next to a Jewish Socialist Mayor at a municipal dinner. He was rather surprised to find that the man was a banker, who told him bluntly that "as long as individualism persisted" he would be foolish not to be, but that he "hoped for the advent of Socialism in such a form as to destroy the very kind of individualistic business in which he was engaged."[47]

The last destination in Denmark was Elsinore Castle, redolent of TR's re-reading of Shakespeare in Africa. This visit afforded one clever cartoonist the opportunity to picture him as Hamlet, holding a scroll marked "1912" and followed by an anxious ghost ascribed "Third Term Taboo." By this time, Roosevelt had come to a more clear-eyed view of the political situation at home, where he told Lodge, Taft, Aldrich, Cannon and others had "totally misestimated the character of the movement which we now have to face in American life." Since Taft's election, the Colonel had not allowed himself to "think ill" of anything he did, but he finally had to admit that Taft had "gone wrong on certain points." Now TR also had to admit to himself that "deep down underneath" he had known all along his successor was wrong, but that he had "tried to deceive myself, by loudly proclaiming to myself, that he was right." He intended no longer to continue the self-deception.[48] After Elsinore, Roosevelt and his family left for Norway to begin the next, pacific, leg of his journey.

Chapter 7

Peace Emissary

On May 4, 1910, Theodore, Edith, Ethel, and Kermit arrived at Christiana (the future Oslo), and were greeted by King Haakon VII and Queen Maud. Once again they stayed at the Royal Palace. TR reported to Lodge his continuing puzzlement about the "extraordinary" receptions he received in Norway and elsewhere. The royals vied with each other to entertain them and the popular displays were even more remarkable. In his opinion this was largely because to them he represented the American Republic, which stood to the average European as a "queer, attractive dream," sometimes as a "golden utopia partially realized" and on others as a "field for wild adventure of a by no means necessarily moral type—in fact a kind of mixture of Bacon's Utopia and Raleigh's Spanish Main." In addition, the former president appealed personally to their imaginations as a "leader whom they suppose to represent democracy, liberty, honesty and justice." The combination of enormous popular demonstrations, and their being asked to stay in the royal palaces, left the diplomats he met "perfectly paralyzed." It was all very interesting and amusing, but also fatiguing and irksome. As much as he dreaded getting back into the "confusion" of American politics, he longed "inexpressibly to be back at Sagamore Hill, in my own house, with my own books, and among my own friends."[1]

Haakon, a son of King Frederick VIII of Denmark, had been elected King of Norway only five years before, after a treaty of separation was reached with Sweden. It was as if Vermont, TR remarked, should try the "offhand experiment of having a king." Norwegians he had talked to at home had been in favor of the creation of a constitutional kingdom, rather than a republic, but one in which the king would not interfere with the people's complete self-government while at the same time lend an element of stability and credibility to the government, which would be respected by her monarchical neighbors.[2] As president, Roosevelt had granted the new state official recognition and dispatched the first U.S. ambassador.

Though he thought the system curious, Theodore and Edith found the royal family delightful. He commented that if Norway ever did decide to become a republic, they both would love to have them come live near Sagamore Hill. Roosevelt described the King as a "trump, privately and publicly" who took a keen and intelligent interest in every question affecting his people, and "treated them and was treated by them with a curiously simple democracy of attitude." Queen Maud, the youngest daughter of Edward VII, was "dear; shy, good, kind, very much in love with her husband, devoted to her boy, anxious to do anything the people expected from her." The marriage was a love match, unusual among European royals. The antics of their seven-year-old son Olav, who had been born in England, recalled TR to early days at the White House romping with his own small children. On the first afternoon, in the drawing room of the very informal palace, he gave Olav "various bits of bloodcurdling information about lions and elephants" and before long Ethel, Kermit and their father all joined the "dear little boy" in spirited play. Since Olav had no experience of such behavior with anyone else save his parents he "loudly bewailed" their departure.[3]

The one serious duty Roosevelt was obliged to perform at Christiana was to deliver his Nobel Peace Prize Address. This he gave before the Nobel Committee, "at a huge 'Banquet' of the canonical—and unspeakably awful type." Peace, the Colonel told his audience, was "generally good in itself," but it was "never the highest good" unless it came as the "hand maiden of righteousness"; and it became a "very evil thing" if it served "merely as a mask for cowardice and sloth, or as an instrument to further the ends of despotism or anarchy." Nevertheless, he believed great advances could be made in the cause of international peace along several lines.

First, there should be treaties of arbitration between the "really civilized communities." The establishment of a sufficient number of these, Roosevelt argued, would go a long way towards "creating a world opinion which would finally find expression" in the provision of still needed methods to forbid or punish transgressors. A second line of advance could be made in the further development of The Hague Tribunal, particularly of the work of the conference and courts of The Hague. TR agreed with those who said that the first Hague Conference a decade before had framed a Magna Carta for the nations. The Second Conference in 1907 had made further progress and he thought the Third projected for 1914 should do more. The American government had more than once tentatively suggested methods for completing the Court of Arbitral Justice and the statesmen of the world would do well to use the U.S. Supreme Court as a model. In the third place, something should be done to check the growth of armaments, especially naval, by international agreement. In his opinion, granted sincerity of purpose, the Great Powers should find no insurmountable obstacle in reaching an agreement to end the present costly expenditures. Finally, it would be a master stroke if those same Great Powers honestly bent on international amity would form a League of Peace, not only to keep the peace among themselves, but to prevent by force if necessary, its being broken by others.

The "supreme difficulty" with developing the peace work of The Hague, TR went on, lay in the lack of any executive power. Until some form of international police power to enforce the decrees of the court was developed each nation must keep well prepared to defend itself. As things now stood, "such power to command peace throughout the world" could best be assured by some combination between those great nations which sincerely desired peace and had "not thought themselves of committing aggressions." At first this might only secure peace in certain definite limits and conditions; "but the ruler or statesman who should bring about such a combination would have earned his place in history for all time and his title to the gratitude of all mankind."[4]

This speech constituted the strongest appeal for peace made by Roosevelt in Europe and the final sentiment represented an obvious plea to the German Kaiser—the man seen by Andrew Carnegie as the greatest hope for peace, and by many others as its greatest menace. Carnegie's pursuit of Wilhelm had begun by correspondence many years before and the plutocrat peace advocate first met the German Emperor in June 1907 at the Kiel regatta. He explained to Dr. David Jayne Hill, one of the American delegates to the Second Hague Conference, also meeting that month, that at Kiel he hoped to "get my say, which is that I think he is the man responsible for war on earth."[5] He also hoped in his talks with the Kaiser to further "real progress" towards peace at the Hague Conference including the creation of a world council to enforce international arbitration.

To be effective, Carnegie's world council required a linked international police force and he suggested to Roosevelt that its creation should be another aim of the Hague Conference. He hoped the German Emperor would "rise to his destiny and stand with you favoring this" instead of wasting his time "chasing rainbows" in the form of a colonial empire which "he cannot get, and which would do Germany no good if he did."[6] Carnegie told Charlemagne Tower, the American ambassador at Berlin, that Wilhelm had it "in his power to do the world the greatest service ever rendered by man." If he were to propose an international police, Britain, America, France, and the other powers would follow. Carnegie concluded that the Kaiser and Roosevelt "would make a team if they were only hitched up in together for the great cause of peace."[7]

When Carnegie repeated this sentiment to the Kaiser six months later at Kiel aboard the royal yacht *Hohenzollern*, Wilhelm accused his guest of wanting "to drive us. Roosevelt will be in front and I behind." Carnegie, who employed all his considerable gifts of good humor and salesmanship in their talks, replied that he knew better than to "drive such wild colts tandem." No, he would "like to have you both in the shafts, holding you abreast." The two men had three interviews in which the plutocrat was captivated by the Kaiser, who when he wished could be the epitome of charm itself. Carnegie also met with Chancellor von Bülow, who expressed sympathy for his desire to reduce the tensions between Germany and England by agreement on naval building.[8]

Unfortunately for those interested in seeing real progress on arms limitations or arbitration, the 1907 Hague Conference turned out to be an almost complete failure. At the first Hague Conference in 1899 the czar had called for arms limitations, but after the Russo-Japanese War Nicholas II aimed to rebuild his country's devastated and demoralized forces and took disarmament off the table. Meanwhile, Germany successfully opposed the idea of a compulsory court of arbitration, which left the matter to the discretion of the individual governments. Carnegie was deeply disappointed but continued doggedly to put his faith in the duo of the Kaiser and Roosevelt as the world's best hopes for peace. The president, however, disillusioned by the Hague fiasco, and worried about the Japanese threat in the Far East, felt he had to go forward, in the two years that remained to him in office, with a building program for the U.S. fleet to match the other powers. On the other hand, over that same time, Elihu Root, as Secretary of State, negotiated more than twenty arbitration treaties with individual nations. With Germany and Russia, however, Root was able to make no progress.

Though Germany balked at binding agreements, Wilhelm nevertheless attempted more personal approaches to Britain that proved, despite his misplaced good intentions, either heavy handed or inflammatory. The German emperor had an obsessive love/hate relationship with England, where he had spent much time as a child since his mother was Queen Victoria's eldest daughter. He had been showered with British honors, including the most prestigious—a Garter knighthood. Unfortunately, Wilhelm's high regard for his grandmother did not extend to his uncle Edward, whom he looked down upon as a weak womanizer. He saw himself as a much fitter heir to the moral leadership of Europe, if not, in his heart if hearts, the Crown of England itself. After Edward VII succeeded his mother in 1901, his "intrigues" with the French and Russians infuriated Wilhelm, whose own efforts to better relations were slighted, he believed, by his condescending uncle who refused to treat him with proper respect.

Early in 1908 Wilhelm yet again proclaimed his friendship for England in an ill-advised correspondence directly with Lord Tweedmouth, the First Lord of the British Admiralty. This intemperate breech of protocol was hushed up, unlike an "interview" put together later that year by friends of the Emperor in Britain and approved by him. This was meant to ameliorate Anglo-German relations but when it was published in the London *Daily Telegraph* on 27 October, the rather tame article unfortunately had quite the opposite effect intended. Wilhelm declared his love for Britain, but revealed that his people did not share his sentiments, hardly a reassuring message in the charged atmosphere of late 1908. He also revealed the advice he had offered during the Boer War and appeared to take credit for directing the military hero Lord Roberts toward a winning strategy, which affronted many in Britain. The dumbfounded Emperor faced even more harsh criticism at home and, after he was admonished by the Reichstag, promised more discretion in future.[9] Noting this humiliation, Roosevelt told his military aide Archie Butt that the Kaiser had "been riding for a fall for some time." This did not make it "any the less pathetic" and TR feared it was "going to have a serious effect on monarchical Germany."[10]

Not long before the *Daily Telegraph* interview was published, Roosevelt had insisted that the *New York Times* suppress a much more incendiary interview with Wilhelm by Dr. William Bayard Hale, an American journalist who was also a clergymen, and to whom consequently the Kaiser had spoken in confidence. Like TR, Wilhelm was sometimes prone to shockingly frank and childlike outbursts, but his statements often went much further—across the line into paranoia and delusion. The Emperor's three-hour talk with Hale was so unadulterated that the American felt it would be dangerous to repeat it. Wilhelm paced the room, was full of energy and "his eyes snapped when he spoke of England his bitterness was so intense." The Kaiser claimed that Great Britain looked on Germany as her enemy because she was the dominant force on the continent and it had always been England's way to attack the strongest power. Wilhelm appeared very bitter against his Uncle Edward and accused him of trying to set the other powers against Germany. His country was ready for war at any moment and, in the view of the Kaiser, the sooner it came, the better. He was aching for a fight, not for the sake of war, but as something that was unpleasant and inevitable and over the sooner the better.[11]

Because of the degeneration of Great Britain and the "march of progress," Wilhelm claimed to be friendly towards the United States and foresaw America and Germany as the two future dominant world forces. He also revealed to Hale a supposed deal between himself and Roosevelt "to divide the East against itself by becoming the recognized friends of China." Within a few months, he said, a high-ranking Chinese official would visit both the United States and Germany to strike a bargain by which they would guarantee China's integrity and the Open Door. Wilhelm also declared that the invitation that TR's Great White Fleet had accepted to visit Australia and New Zealand was meant to serve notice on Britain that "those colonies were with the white man and not with a renegade mother country." He in addition prophesied that within ten years Japan and the United States would be at war.

Before leaving Germany, Hale shared the interview with the new U.S. ambassador at Berlin, David Jayne Hill, and with German Foreign Office officials who "nearly went though the roof." After Hale brought the interview to the *Times*, its managing editor dispatched his

Washington correspondent, Oscar King Davis, to share its contents with Roosevelt. After hardly more than a glance at the document, TR declared, "You must not print this!" Besides the fact that it would "jeopardize the peace of the world," he also argued that if the paper published the interview the Kaiser would simply disavow it and everyone would think it was a fake. Davis reassured the president that his paper had no intention to do so, but only brought it to him because they thought it important.[12]

After his initial shock that Wilhelm had talked so frankly for publication, TR declared the interview "the funniest thing I have ever known. That Jack of an Emperor talks as if what he happens to want is already an accomplished fact." He freely admitted that the Kaiser had been at him for a year to come to a Chinese agreement, but he had explained in return that any treaty would have to be agreed to by the Senate. In any event the promised Chinese emissary had never appeared. Roosevelt also admitted that the American fleet had been sent to show Britain, he would not call her a "renegade mother country," that Australia and New Zealand were white men's countries. Concerning Japan, as long as the United States kept up its fleet he saw no danger of war.[13]

It was well known, TR told Davis, that the Kaiser was "very jumpy and nervous," but people said that about himself, whereas he never acted without careful deliberation. People also said he and Wilhelm were alike and "have great admiration for each other on that account." Roosevelt admitted that both he and the Emperor seemed to be "particularly susceptible to being misinterpreted or misunderstood" and that he admired Wilhelm, but only as he would "a grizzly bear." He swore Davis to secrecy concerning the bulk of his remarks about the Kaiser.[14]

In light of the Hale interview, TR drafted a letter of warning to his British friend Arthur Lee, who had for some time been worried about what he considered the German menace and as a Conservative MP was much concerned with defense matters. Roosevelt had been persistently telling his English correspondents that he believed they exaggerated the threat and it was unnecessary to arm against it; however, the Hale revelations gave him pause. He told Lee that he felt it "incumbent upon me now to say that I am by no means as confident as I was in this position." In many away he had a real regard for Wilhelm's "ability, his activity" and what TR believed was "his sincere purpose to do all he can for the greatness of his country." However, the German Emperor had shown himself to be "very jumpy"; and more than once in the last seven years Roosevelt had had to "watch him hard and speak to him, with politeness, but with equal decision, in order to prevent his doing things I thought against the best interests of his country." TR now told Lee that he believed it "barely possible" that some time Wilhelm would be "indiscreet enough to act on impulse in a way that would jeopardize the peace." He asked his friend to show his letter only to Sir Edward Grey, the British Foreign Secretary, and Arthur Balfour, the opposition leader.[15]

Andrew Carnegie was not privy to the Hale interview, but a month after TR and Elihu Root had both left office, the former Secretary of State sent Carnegie an even grimmer letter of warning. Based upon his repeated personal experiences, Root told Carnegie, "no well informed person" could doubt that Germany, "under her present Government," was "the great disturber of peace in the world." Whether on arbitration, disarmament, the prevention of war, or any attempts to "lessen the suspicion and alarm of nations toward each other," Germany stood against all progress. Root went on that the truth was that Germany "does not in the least agree as to the views of international duty and right conduct which have inspired the Hague Conferences." To the contrary, she looked "with real contempt and loathing upon the whole system of arbitration" and considered "all talk about it to be mere hypocrisy. She believes in taking what she wants with a strong hand and with her, friendship among nations is merely the application of the wise policy which prohibits having too many enemies at one time."[16] This was a prescient view which Carnegie failed to heed.

In Norway a year later, King Haakon and Queen Maud "frankly commiserated" with Theodore and Edith when they found they were to stay at the palace in Berlin. They looked back with a "lively horror" to the way Wilhelm had "drilled" them when they stayed there. Maud told them she was "so frightened that I finally grew afraid to speak to any of them; and when I tried to speak to the servants I found they were just as much afraid of me!" The day Roosevelt left for Sweden, the last stop before Berlin, the news came of Edward VII's death. Maud had told them much about her close family relations and was heartbroken. Her father had been very pleased that she had fallen in love with Haakon, or Prince Carl of Denmark as he was then, and insisted that he would not force any of his daughters into loveless matches simply for considerations of state.[17]

TR and Edward had both been looking forward to meeting the other when he reached England.[18] The King had voiced his disappointment that Roosevelt had stooped to becoming a "penny a liner" journalist with the *Scribner's* series but sincerely admired his bravery in the Spanish-American War. Spring Rice wrote to TR that the King had wanted to "get into personal relations with you" as the two had "certain aims in common." Edward desired to send Roosevelt something from his personal collection and Spring Rice suggested a miniature of John Hampden, who he knew to be one of Roosevelt's heroes. The picture was of great historical value, but because it was of a man who had led a successful rebellion against the English crown, it was "not at all the sort of thing" a King of England might be expected to give to an American president. That, however, was the reason Edward "jumped at the idea at once." His librarian and others objected strongly, but he insisted. Spring Rice was very sorry Roosevelt would not now meet the King but hoped he would not "forget what I tell you now—quite privately for yourself."[19]

So it was with real sadness on several counts that the Colonel and his family departed on May 7 for Stockholm which Roosevelt nevertheless considered a "delightful" city and the Swedes fine people. As in Hungary and France, the reception given him was not merely one of general friendliness, but, in his opinion, it came from people who felt they were "jeopardized alike by the apostles of reaction, and by the preachers of license under the guise of liberty, and who clutched at any leadership which could be regarded as genuinely popular and yet genuinely sane." He toured several museums and was very interested in the battlefield relics from the era of Gustavus Adolphus to Charles XII, Sweden's seventeenth-century era of martial glory. However, in the present TR was saddened to see how socialism had grown among the people in a "very ugly form" which included an appeal to stop having children. Roosevelt could not comprehend anyone "so bitter in their class hatred as to welcome race destruction as a means of slaking it." And in view of what the Russians were doing in neighboring Finland, he felt it "came pretty near being a crime against all progress and civilization." Since Sweden had not only free but almost democratic institutions he could not understand the extreme bitterness of the socialist attitude.[20]

The Swedish monarch, Gustavus V, was absent and the family stayed at the palace with the Crown Prince Gustavus Adolphus and his wife Margaret, a daughter of the Duke of Connaught and a niece of Edward VII. The Swedish royal family, in concert with the others across Europe, was in mourning for the King of England, so that court entertainment was suspended. The travelers dined only with the members of the family, a state of affairs Roosevelt greeted with great relief. He appraised the Crown Prince as a "thoroughly good fellow, very serious and honest, of fair ability." The kind of man, he told his British friend Sir George Otto Trevleyan, who would have made, if he were in England, a "good but not brilliant, rather radical, Liberal Member of Parliament." His wife was "physically, mentally and morally a thoroughly healthy and charming woman," and their three little children were as "attractive, busy, vigorous, small souls as one could wish to see."[21]

From Sweden the family crossed to Germany. The death of Edward VII gave Roosevelt the opportunity to send word to the Kaiser that, under the circumstances, perhaps it would be more appropriate for the family to stay at the U.S. Embassy rather than the palace. The offer was gratefully accepted. Almost all the plans that had been made, including the Emperor's intention to greet Roosevelt personally at the rail station, were canceled or altered. The state of mourning for Wilhelm's uncle aside, in Germany Roosevelt noted a different attitude across society than in any other European country. He was treated with the proper civility, and the authorities showed him every courtesy, but he encountered no boisterous popular receptions, no decorated and overcrowded streets or cascades of applause at theatres that had become the norm elsewhere. In Sweden tens of thousands had gathered on every occasion, in Germany a few hundred curious citizens might be at a train station or other event.

Roosevelt's chief interest was in Wilhelm II, whom he considered "an able and powerful man."[22] Besides sharing these attributes, the two were similar in several other ways. They were only three months apart in age, TR being the older. Both had overcome childhood disabilities, Roosevelt asthma and eyesight which had given him a mole-like perspective on the world until corrected with glasses—the Emperor a withered left arm which he hid in splendid uniforms. As adults they were similarly burly and active men who dominated their surroundings physically and conversationally. Both were moralists who nevertheless had curious and wide-ranging intellects, the Kaiser's being somewhat limited in scope by his inward-looking Prussian military upbringing.

Given this last factor it is somewhat surprising that Wilhelm shared TR's passion for building up his country's fleet, which both men saw as amongst their greatest national legacies. The Kaiser also considered Roosevelt to be one of the few figures on the world stage with stature great enough to be treated as an equal. After a luncheon on the first day, a special train took the party, which included the German Chancellor, Theobald von Bethmann Hollweg, to Potsdam where the Kaiser proudly showed the family the Sans Souci palace. Wilhelm took the Colonel aside for very rare private talk lasting an hour in which, Roosevelt told Arthur Lee, the Emperor surpassed "even his wildest expectations and treated him with a fulsome familiarity which was as horrifying to the entourage of the 'All-Highest' as it was distasteful to T.R. himself."[23]

The Colonel was able to spend two other afternoons in conversation with the Emperor, the first on horseback for five hours while reviewing army maneuvers at Döberitz. Wilhelm was resplendent in a Hussar General's uniform and helmet, while Roosevelt wore a simple khaki riding suit and black slouch hat, which he from time to time raised to acknowledge the troops. The Kaiser honored TR before his officers by making a point of addressing him as "*mein Freund*" and asked him to remember that he was the only private citizen who had ever reviewed German troops.[24] The Colonel found Wilhelm very interested to know how he was viewed abroad and in reply to a question about American opinion replied, "I don't know whether you will understand our political terminology; but in America we think that if you lived on our side of the water you would carry your ward and turn up at the convention with your delegates behind you—and I cannot say as much for most of your fellow sovereigns!" After some explanation, Wilhelm was "immensely pleased and amused" at the answer.[25]

To Roosevelt's surprise, the Kaiser spoke perfect English and displayed a real sense of humor about the things he knew, such as Germany's industrial and military conditions. Wilhelm's mischievous nature was also displayed in writing on the backs of several photos of themselves on horseback that he gave TR to commemorate the military review. On one depicting them talking seriously the Kaiser wrote, "the Colonel of the Rough Riders instructing the German Emperor in field tactics." On another he inscribed, perhaps more seriously, "When we shake hands we shake the world." The German Foreign Office, afraid of yet another royal indiscretion becoming public, asked for the photos to be returned. TR refused and had them framed in glass so that both sides could be seen.[26]

The two men agreed on fundamental points of domestic and religious morality, but there was a "good deal of dogmatic theology" which meant much to Wilhelm that to Roosevelt was "entirely meaningless." They also completely disagreed on many points of international morality, which TR found understandable given that Wilhelm was brought up in the school of Frederick the Great and Bismarck, while his own heroes were champions of freedom such as Timoleon, John Hampden, Washington and Lincoln. They did concur, however, in a cordial dislike of "shams and pretense" and therefore of the "kind of washy movement for international peace" with which Carnegie's name had become so closely associated. On a photo he sent Roosevelt of the sham battle staged for them, the Kaiser wrote that such exertions would take care of that old "peace bore" Carnegie.[27]

Such an attitude on the part of Wilhelm, coupled with the death of Edward VII, doomed any small chance their meeting might have had of furthering Carnegie's dreams of peace. However, the newspaper revelations that he planned to speak to the Kaiser about universal peace and disarmament did give Roosevelt an opening to broach the subject. The Austrian ambassador in Berlin "nearly choked trying to invent some appropriate remark in response" when TR informed him that sending the conversation in Vienna with von Bienerth to the German Foreign Office had given him the "chance to say what I had to say" and "otherwise probably would not have had." Roosevelt told Wilhelm "he was by no means a peace-at-any-price man" but he felt that the "subject was of such importance as to warrant consideration as to whether or not it was feasible to do something practical toward limiting expense and putting difficulties in the way of war." The Emperor was very courteous, and said he really had no control over the matter, which was "something which effected the German people," who would "never consent to Germany's failing to keep herself able to enforce her rights either on land or at sea."[28]

Roosevelt had especially desired to talk with Wilhelm about the alarming naval rivalry between Germany and England, and raised the possibility of limiting the ever-increasing battleship expenditures of the two nations. The Kaiser responded there was no real use in discussing the matter, as the element he represented in Germany was determined to be powerful on the ocean. The Colonel then confessed that if he were an Englishman he would feel that "naval supremacy was a vital matter" and that under no circumstances would he "permit the fleet to sink to such a position that its mastership of the ocean" could be threatened. He was surprised that Wilhelm agreed and said that, were he an Englishman, he would feel the same way.

Since his mother was Queen Victoria's oldest daughter, Wilhelm had been brought up partly in England and thought of himself as partly English. He claimed, next to Germany, that he cared for England more than any other country and added with "intense emphasis, I ADORE ENGLAND." He did not object to England's keeping up her fleet relatively to all other powers, but he did complain because English statesmen, including the former Conservative Prime Minister Arthur Balfour, who ought to know better, continually held up Germany as the nation against whom they specially needed to prepare. Wilhelm then earnestly asked TR to tell any British leaders he had the chance to meet all he had said and in particular that he was not hostile to England and "on the contrary admired England and did not for a minute believe there would be war between England and Germany." Such a war, both men agreed, would be an "unspeakable calamity."[29]

This did not mean, however, that the Emperor's attitude was entirely without menace. TR reported to his friend Trevelyan that Germany had "the arrogance of a very strong power, as yet almost untouched by that feeble aspiration towards international equity" which the United States and England had at least begun to feel. Germany wanted a navy so strong that she could treat England as she had France over Morocco. This had shown how far Germany was willing to go in doing what she believed her own interests and destiny demanded, in total "disregard of her own engagements and of the equities of other people." If Germany had a navy as strong as England, Roosevelt did not believe "she would intend to use it for the destruction of England," but he did believe that "incidents would be very likely to occur which might make her so use it."[30]

Personally, Roosevelt was fascinated to see in Wilhelm what he already had noticed traces of in other royals, namely "a kind of curious dual consciousness of events" in relation to himself and his fellow monarchs. The Kaiser knew perfectly well he did not have absolute power. At present whenever Germany made up her mind to go in a given direction, he could only "stay at the head of affairs by scampering to take the lead in going in that direction." Down at bottom Wilhelm knew this, but he also knew that as Kaiser in the German system he had still a "genuine power not shared by the great majority of his fellow sovereigns." Taking into account the "curious combination of power, energy, egotism, and restless desire to do, and to seem to do, things" which Wilhelm's character showed, TR could not help but wonder how he would have fared had he been an absolute monarch or Roman Emperor. Unlike several of the other sovereigns he met, Roosevelt did not regard Wilhelm, or Germany, as pleasant prospective neighbors.[31]

While he was in Berlin the Colonel was pleased to be able to talk to the architect of the modern German Navy, Admiral Alfred von Tirpitz, whom he considered an exceedingly able man. One night at dinner the Admiral told Edith that he had always heard the Emperor and her husband were alike, and now he saw the resemblance. But of course Roosevelt had had to take responsibilities and make his own way, and do things for himself, "which naturally made a difference" between them. Von Tirpitz was particularly interested in the voyage of the Great White Fleet round the world and told Roosevelt frankly that he had not believed it could be done successfully and that the British Admiralty and Foreign Office had felt the same way. TR responded that he had been aware of this which made the Fleet's success all the more satisfying.[32]

The Admiral had expected Japan to attack the American fleet while it was on its journey and asked if Roosevelt had feared the same. TR replied that he had not expected such an attack but thought it possible. His view was that if the Japanese attacked it would have been a sign that they meant to strike at the first favorable moment. He had been doing his best to be polite with Japan but had become aware of a "slight undertone of veiled truculence" in regard to affairs on the Pacific slope, and that the Japanese thought him afraid of them. Roosevelt had found out through various sources that Japan's war party believed themselves superior and that they could win. It seemed to him that the British thought the same, so that the time was ripe for a "showdown." He had great confidence in the U.S. Navy, and felt that, in any event, if the fleet was not able to get to the Pacific in first class shape they had better find out. He told von Tirpitz that, once the fleet started, it meant the United States had gained three months and it was doing what it would have to do in case of war. In TR's view, if the Japanese did attack, it would be proof positive that he had followed exactly the right course, and if they became peaceful, the same was true. As it fell out, "every particle of trouble" with the Japanese Government and press "stopped like magic as soon as they found out our fleet had actually sailed and was obviously in good trim." It was a good thing, he told von Tirpitz, that the Japanese should know that there were "fleets of the white races which were totally different" from that of the poor Russian Admiral Rojestvensky annihilated in the Russo-Japanese War.[33]

Before leaving the United States, Roosevelt had agreed to make a German academic address, which he delivered at the University of Berlin on May 12, after he received an honorary doctorate. The scene was noteworthy for the picturesque combination of military uniforms, academic gowns and what Lawrence Abbott considered the "somewhat bizarre dress" of the undergraduate student corps. The ceremony began with fine renditions of *Hail Columbia* and the *Star Spangled Banner* by the student chorus, "harmonized as only the Germans can harmonize choral music."[34] Though suffering from an attack of bronchitis, Roosevelt nevertheless persevered through his subject, "The World Movement," which traced the history of civilization from ancient times to the present. In his view the modern movement towards a world civilization had begun its march four hundred years before with the discovery of printing and the "bold sea ventures" which culminated with the discovery of America. This was followed in Europe by a "tremendous religious ferment" which set off a "moral uprising" matched by a revolution in science. Since then, century by century, the changes had "increased in rapidity and complexity."[35]

Instead of being directed by one or two dominant peoples as in the past, the new movement was shared by many nations and had been from every standpoint of "infinitely greater moment than anything hitherto seen." This was reflected in an extraordinary growth in wealth, in population, in power of organization and in mastery of mechanical activity and natural resources "accompanied and signalized" by an immense outburst of energy and restless initiative. The result of this in the first place has been the conquest of space, to spread into all the practically vacant continents, and the development of "un-heard-of military superiority as compared with their former rivals." In Roosevelt's view, these two factors created for the first time "really something that approaches a world civilization, a world movement." The net outcome of what had occurred over the past four centuries was that civilization of the European type now exercised a "more or less profound effect over practically the entire world." This reflected something "wholly different from what has ever hitherto been seen." The world was bound together as never before. The bonds, he admitted, were "sometimes those of hatred rather than love," but were bonds nevertheless.[36]

In this new world movement the influence of European governmental principles was strikingly illustrated by the fact that admiration for them had even "broken down the iron barriers of Moslem conservatism," so that their introduction had become burning questions in Turkey and in Persia. At the same time, the unrest in Egypt, India and the Philippines, took the form of demanding a government closer in form to the United States or Britain. From new discoveries in science to new methods of combating or applying socialism, there was no movement of note which could take place in any part of the globe "without powerfully affecting masses of people" on every continent. "For weal or for woe," the peoples of mankind were "knit together far closer than ever before."[37]

Unfortunately, Roosevelt saw in this world movement "signs of much that bodes ill." The machinery was "so highly geared," the tension and strain so great that he feared ruin could follow "any great accident, from any breakdown" or the mere wearing out of the machine itself. He saw many "forces and tendencies" at work in the present that had brought down previous civilizations such as Rome. These included "knowledge, luxury, and refinement, wide material conquests, territorial administration on a vast scale, an increase in the mastery of mechanical appliances and in applied sciences."[38]

Personally, however, Roosevelt did not believe the new world civilization would fall. He asserted that on the whole "we have grown better and not worse" and the future "holds more for us than even the great past has held." But it was up to mankind, "high of heart and strong of hand," to make the dreams of the future come true "by our own mighty deeds." TR concluded by expressing his hope that the world movement "which is now felt throbbing in every corner of the globe" would bind the nations of the world together and at the same time leave "unimpaired that love of country in the individual citizen" which in the present stage of the world's progress was "essential to the world's well-being." In his view, the good citizen, must be a good citizen of his own country before he could "with advantage be a citizen of the world at large."[39]

The Emperor, Empress and several other members of the royal family attended the address, and spoke of it approvingly. Nevertheless, unlike elsewhere in Europe, and ominously for the future, TR noted that, though they behaved entirely correctly, the "Germans did not like me, and did not like my country." The "stiff, domineering and formal" upper classes, with the organized army, bureaucracy and industry of their "great, highly civilized and admirably administered country behind them" regarded America with a dislike "all the greater because they could not make it merely contempt." Since they saw America as entirely unorganized, in their view "we had no business to be formidable rivals at all" and they were exasperated to feel that "our great territory, great natural resources, and strength of individual initiative" enabled the United States to be "formidable industrial rivals" and, "more incredible still, that thanks to our Navy and ocean-protected position, we were in a military sense wholly independent and slightly defiant."[40]

Moreover, Roosevelt personally "typified the nation they disliked." The German upper classes did not like the social type he represented. The lower classes were socialists to whom he was "really an enemy rather than a friend" and his ideals were just as alien. The middle classes looked upon him as typifying a middle class country which was their business rival, "whose manners of life and ways of thought they regarded with profound dislike, and whose business rivalry was irritating and obnoxious."[41] It was with little regret, therefore, that the family left Berlin for London.

Traveling through Germany in a royal rail carriage, every attention was shown them, and at the stations a few score or hundred polite and mildly curious people might be on hand. But when they crossed into Holland at the first stop a "wildly enthusiastic" crowd of ten thousand awaited the party. While the Colonel had been in Germany, Taft had wired a request that he act as America's special ambassador to the funeral of Edward VII. In Washington Archie Butt commented that with the Kaiser and TR present, it would be "a wonder if the poor corpse gets a passing thought."[42] It was with his new post foremost in mind that TR arrived in London on May 16, 1910.

Chapter 8

Last Rites: England

The state funeral of Edward VII brought together the grandees of Europe for a final time before World War I swept away most of these human remnants of the old regime. Until the funeral was done, and with it his official capacity as special ambassador, TR stayed at Dorchester House, the cavernous Park Lane mansion that the U.S. ambassador Whitelaw Reid had taken on lease from Earl Morley.[1] With him were Edith, Kermit, Ethel, and a new arrival, his oldest daughter "Princess Alice," or Mrs. Nicholas Longworth as she was since her White House marriage four years before. Alice brought with her black mourning attire from a recent family funeral, while Edith and Ethel, who had been warned in Germany by Mrs. Reid that the London shops had been emptied, bought proper clothing in Berlin. Alice also brought the latest political gossip from Washington and stayed up very late sharing it with her father, who told her of his disappointment in their mutual friend Taft's administration and that he thought it would be impossible for him to speak for it in the fall elections.

A royal carriage of state was put at the Colonel's disposal, complete with a guard of six grave grenadiers in bearskins, who lined up and saluted while a bugler sounded off whenever he left or entered Dorchester House. The British Crown also assigned two special aides, Lord Cochrane and Captain Cunninghame R. N., as guides through the intricacies of the many formal calls TR made on the luminaries gathered in London, including King Frederick VIII of Denmark, King Haakon of Norway, King George I of Greece, and the German emperor, with whom he had another brief interview. Roosevelt commented that not only "all the Kings I had met, but the two or three I had not previously met, were more than courteous and the Kaiser made a point of showing his intimacy with me and of discriminating in my favor over all his fellow sovereigns."[2]

The day they arrived, Roosevelt and his family visited the catafalque of Edward VII at Buckingham Palace and afterwards, he and Ambassador Reid were received by George V and Queen Mary at Marlborough House. The new King was forty-five years old and a younger son who had been trained as a naval officer. But the death in 1892 of his brother, the Duke of Clarence, had thrust him forward. He was something of an unknown quantity and not particularly highly regarded.[3] An avid hunter, though with no big game experience, the King was eager to hear from TR about the safari and conditions in general in his African possessions, all of which Roosevelt gladly supplied. Their hour-long discussion on May 16 soon turned from big game when the King congratulated TR on his speeches at Cairo and Khartoum, adding that he wished something along those lines, "but stronger," could be openly stated at home. Roosevelt responded that he was considering just such a message for the Guildhall address he had already agreed to; however, not wanting to give offence, he intended first to consult with figures from both political parties, particularly Lord Cromer, still considered the British authority on Egypt, and Sir Edward Grey, the Liberal foreign secretary responsible for Egyptian affairs.[4]

At a meeting arranged by Reid, TR found Cromer strongly supportive of a speech about Egypt, while warning him that he should be "rabidly attacked for making it." The former Egyptian Proconsul told Roosevelt that in his view the Liberal government, abetted by his successor Gorst, were reaping the whirlwind from foolishly sharing too much power too soon. This conciliatory policy had only made the Egyptians hungry for more: hence the burgeoning agitation for self-government. Cromer went on that he felt it "almost imperative that England should be told the truth by someone to whom England would listen." The public had already heard what imperialists such as himself had to say, while the "people of the other way of thinking simply refused to listen to the facts."[5] Many of these, in Cromer's estimation, were in the Liberal Government.

During a breakfast with Grey, Roosevelt found him "obviously uneasy" at the course his Liberal party was taking about Egypt. He was surprised that the foreign secretary also was "very anxious" for him to speak out, although both men knew that the Prime Minister, Henry Asquith, would disapprove. According to TR, Grey was in the "unpleasant position of finding his party associates tending as a whole to refuse to allow him to do what was necessary: and he wanted his hand forced." The Colonel offered a vow of secrecy concerning their meeting which Grey declined, telling him that if a question arose in the House of Commons he would not only admit talking the matter over, but that he approved and that TR was "rendering a real service to Great Britain by saying it, and that I was strengthening his hands."[6] Roosevelt appraised Grey as "one of the finest fellows I have ever met" and agreed with him on "both internal and external politics." He also was very much in sympathy with the Radical domestic views of Grey's Cabinet fellows David Lloyd George, the Chancellor of the Exchequer, and John Burns, president of the Local Government Board, and "took a real fancy to both." Burns struck him as having "a saner judgment," while Lloyd George, being a Welshman, was more emotional, but at the same time "the most powerful statesman I met in England, in fact *the* man of power."[7]

The odd man out among the Liberal leaders, in TR's estimation, was Winston Churchill, whom he refused to see. As noted earlier, the two had first met a decade before in New York when the newly elected Member of Parliament was on a speaking tour in support of the British cause in the Boer War. Three years later, Churchill turned his party coat from Conservative to Liberal over the tariff reform/free trade fiscal controversy that still divided the country in 1910. Crossing the aisle in the Commons had gained Churchill office, lately the Presidency of the Board of Trade in the Asquith Government, but he was branded the second most hated man in politics after Joseph Chamberlain, the tariff reform champion. Ironically, in two years' time TR would follow an even more maverick political course and garner a similar reputation.

Another speaker scheduled for the Guildhall that month, on a slightly different subject, world peace, was Andrew Carnegie, who had arrived in England a few days before TR. When asked by the press whether Roosevelt's reelection would further the cause of international peace, he commented that he had "a fine peace record, but we all know there's a bit of the barbarian in him." On the other hand, he declared that the Kaiser was a "true peacemaker" and "peace-lover" who would close his career "unstained by the shedding of human blood."[8] Carnegie sent TR a message of greetings on May 13 from his resort hotel in Torqay, "Welcome Colonel Commanding to London." He warned him to take care of his still ailing throat for which England had a "dangerous climate in May," and he thought it "very fine" that he was to be America's representative at Edward's funeral. He planned to come to London afterwards to try and see Roosevelt's "cronie" [sic] the Kaiser. He went on "If you and he don't make a team that can drag the cart behind I am a disappointed man."[9]

Carnegie did not receive Roosevelt's report on the failure of his Berlin mission until the next day when he wrote again in light of that, and the indefinite postponement of the Wrest Park summit in England. He told TR that he had not seen the Berlin papers and had not known that all had not "past [sic] off well." However, the ever-sanguine Carnegie was sure at least that "you and the Emperor now being friends may some day count for much." He went on that the Wrest Park conference was only a way to give TR "a chance to become known to the leaders here and they to know you. It may make all the difference some day that you are friends." In his usual over the top style, Carnegie continued, "Your future is, recent events excepted, likely to excel your past since you are a born leader of men with the sublime audacity to perform wonders."[10]

Regardless of Roosevelt's lack of success in Berlin, Whitelaw Reid also hoped to salvage the conference at his Oxfordshire house. About the eminent guest list he had worked so hard to build, he told TR, "I am sure that the presence of three prime ministers at one table, filled out with others of such distinction" as John Morley, the Secretary of State for India, and Lord Lansdowne, a former Conservative foreign secretary, "would constitute an occasion not lightly to be lost."[11] Unfortunately for the hopes of Carnegie and Reid, though Roosevelt did visit Wrest Park, the death of Edward VII scrambled all arrangements and there would be no gathering of eagles. TR instead saw Carnegie in London and many other of the notables on the proposed guest list at other occasions.

The night before Edward's funeral, Roosevelt attended a formal dinner at Buckingham Palace for the special envoys that surprised him by turning into, in his words, "a veritable wake—I hardly know what else to call it." TR and Stéphen Pichon, the French Minister of Foreign Affairs, were the only non-royals in the company of seventy. But even Pichon's clothes were "stiff with gold lace and he wore sashes and orders," while Roosevelt was the only one present in plain evening dress. After perfunctory words of condolence to the King, it was "on with the revel! It was not possible to keep up an artificial pretense of grief any longer, and nobody tried."[12]

At dinner George V sat in the middle of one side of the immense table with his cousin Wilhelm II across from him and everyone else arranged by order of precedence. TR had Prince Heinrich of Prussia, the German Emperor's younger brother and commander of the High Seas Fleet, on his right hand. On his left, he found a "tall, shambling young man in a light blue uniform," whose place card proclaimed him Prince Ernest of Cumberland. In reply to TR's remark that the young man's title was English, but he seemed German, he answered, "with a melancholy glance at the very vivacious Emperor" opposite them, that he "ought to be Prince of Brunswick and King of Hanover and would be 'if not for him,'" with a nod to Wilhelm. TR considered suggesting that the young man "relieve his feelings by throwing a carafe at the usurper."[13]

That evening, Roosevelt found himself engaged in conversation by the Bulgarian ruler, Ferdinand I, who had angered his fellow sovereigns by taking the title Czar, which was thought "bumptious." He was also involved in a row with the Austrian Archduke Franz Ferdinand over precedence. The Archduke did not like the Czar or Bulgaria and thought that as heir to "a real and big empire" he should have priority. On the express train to London, the Archduke had succeeded in having his car inserted in front of the Czar's who then refused to let the Austrian walk back through it to the dining car. Instead he was forced to get off and on the train at two stations. All in all, TR considered the royal spat delightfully amusing and as "utterly childish" as similar "nursery quarrels" he had refereed, much to his distaste, in official Washington. Such matters, however, were of import to Europe's rulers, and the Kaiser sided with his Austrian ally in the affair. While the Colonel and Czar Ferdinand chatted, Wilhelm stalked over to introduce Alfonso XIII, the King of Spain, and with a "ferocious" look over his shoulder at the Czar, said of Alfonso, "he is worth talking to."[14]

For the state funeral the next morning, Theodore planned to wear his Rough Rider Colonel's uniform; however, Edith insisted on plain evening dress, which meant that he stood out all the more, a penguin amongst the glorious uniformed plumage of the assembled international nobility. In the procession through London to Paddington

Station, where a royal train for Windsor waited, nine kings riding three abreast followed Edward's coffin, immediately behind which trotted Edward's little white terrier, Caesar. The affronted Kaiser commented that he had "done many things in his life, but he had never before been obliged to yield precedence to a dog."[15] This contretemps aside, Wilhelm put aside his previous animosity and proved, for all appearances at any rate, the "most genuine mourner" present of Edward VII, whose disappearance from the scene he believed would allow him to take his proper place at the head of European affairs.[16]

Further back in the procession, TR shared a coach with the incensed French envoy, Pichon. The night before, he had complained to Roosevelt of the plain black coats of their coachmen, while red was worn for royalty. This he considered "an outrage, a slight upon the two great Republics." At Buckingham Palace the following morning TR found Pichon, whom he described as "a queer looking creature at best" whose anger "made him look like a gargoyle," even more agitated than the night before. Now he was infuriated that the two were to ride in what Roosevelt considered a gorgeous coach. Pichon explained that this was another outrage as the royals all had glass coaches. Since TR "had never heard of a glass coach except in connection with Cinderella," he was "less impressed by the omission."[17]

The Frenchman was also angry at their relative position, eighth in line, behind "toutes ces petites royautés" even "le roi du Portugal" and "ces Chenois," the Chinese ambassador. To make matters worse, "ce Perse," a Persian prince of royal blood, had been put in with them. Pichon insisted that Roosevelt take the place of honor by riding in the right-hand rear seat. The "unfortunate Persian followed," TR noted, "looking about as unaggressive as a rabbit in a cage with two boa constrictors." He was able to mollify Pichon, at least temporarily, by pointing out that the most important thing would be their respective places at the lunch to follow the interment at Windsor Castle. Luckily, Pichon was placed at the Queen's table, while Roosevelt was at the King's and another Gallic "explosion" thereby avoided.[18] Unaware of the melodrama unfolding inside, in his description of the funeral procession for the *Daily Mail*, Sir Arthur Conan Doyle commented on "the strong profile of the great American, set like granite as he leans back in his carriage."[19]

A few days after the funeral, Theodore and Edith had lunch with George V and Queen Mary at Marlborough House. Roosevelt thoroughly liked the King, who asked his advice about accusations brought against him that he had a secret, previous, wife and drank excessively. He responded that it was always a mistake to refute private slander with a public statement and unless the accusations were made in public he would take no notice, but if any public accusation was made it needed to be promptly and effectively met. TR appraised George as a strong man who would keep within the constitutional limitations, but was going to make himself felt, not only in England, but the world. He did not think the King had the tact, from what he had heard, of Edward VII, though that might come. George struck the Colonel as "one who had a thorough hold on himself and thorough knowledge of the people he is to rule."[20]

With his official duties at an end, Roosevelt and the family relocated from the marble halls and gold-plated extravagance of Dorchester House to the still substantial London residence of Arthur Lee, TR's old friend of Rough Rider days, at 10 Chesterfield Street. Lee had married an American heiress and settled into life as a wealthy and well-connected Conservative MP. The move allowed TR the freedom to see whom he liked although the house remained in a "state of siege" while he was in residence. Having nabbed the "prime lion of the season" the endless stream of people at Chesterfield Street included various big game hunters, the headmaster of Eton, where Edith visited with Spring Rice, and the Japanese ambassador. None of these visitors knew the house's mistress, Lee's wife Ruth, and on one occasion an old lady said to her angrily, "if I wasn't TR's daughter, who was I?" Another visitor was Seth Bullock, to whom the Colonel had sent an invitation in Deadwood. TR recalled, "by that time I felt I just had to meet my own people, who spoke my neighborhood dialect."[21] The tall, sinewy westerner, with his long flowing black mustache, black frock coat, string tie, and broad-brimmed black slouch hat, cut quite a figure strolling through the Zoological Gardens or in Mayfair with Roosevelt, who proudly introduced him to all and sundry, including several royals. The marshal was so happy to see TR, he told Kermit, he felt like hanging his hat on the dome of St Paul's and shooting it off. An admiring Arthur Lee called Bullock "one of nature's aristocrats if ever there was one."[22]

Lee was able to arrange a delightful weekend at Chequers Court, the red brick Elizabethan house in the Chiltern Hills, an hour from London, that he had only recently acquired. Roosevelt's visit was meant to be its "house-warming" party. A decade later, Arthur and his wife Ruth gave the residence to the nation to serve as the country home of Britain's prime ministers. Lee gathered a variety of interesting figures, many of whom Roosevelt had requested to meet. Theodore and Edith were on their own as Kermit and Ethel had "decided to bolt off to Scotland," telling their mother that they had had "quite enough of father" and that they wished he would not talk so much about himself or sign his name so large in all the guest books.[23]

At Chequers the Colonel found several of the Conservative Party's leading lights, Arthur Balfour, Alfred Lyttelton and F. S. Oliver, particularly charming. Balfour, the languid and elegant former Prime Minister, was one of the few who was TR's intellectual equal and, after Roosevelt remarked that he had "never demanded of knowledge anything except that it should be valueless," their talk ranged across a wide spectrum.[24] Lee recorded that TR's "conquest" of Balfour was "immediate and complete." Upon his consciousness the Colonel "burst like a meteorite from another planet." He was so entirely different from anything Balfour had "either experienced or imagined" that their two minds "fizzled chemically when brought into contact for the first time." Both men were "at the top of their form" in an "almost ceaseless play of coruscating talk which illumined the weekend like summer lightening."[25]

Another who was present, TR's old friend Cecil Spring Rice, commented, perhaps not without bias, that Roosevelt had "turned us all upside down" while enjoying himself hugely. Springy had to say that, "by the side of our statesman," TR looked a "little bit taller, bigger and stronger."[26] Lee himself thanked TR for the way he "played up" at Chequers. He told his friend, "Personality is a thing which can only explain itself and I am so glad I no longer have any need to attempt (vainly) to explain yours."[27] Roosevelt in turn later told his friend David Gray that Chequers Court was a "delightful place" and that he was almost as fond of Lee as of Spring Rice, and equally fond of both their wives.[28]

The only man the Colonel met at Chequers that he, and Edith, did not like was the one destined the next year to follow Sir Eldon Gorst as Consul-General in Egypt, Lord Kitchener of Khartoum, the hero of Omdurman. TR found him a "strong man, but exceedingly bumptious, and everlastingly posing as a strong man." In contrast, he considered the other military icon on hand, Lord Roberts of Kandahar, whose memoir *Forty-one Years in India* he had read, to be a "particularly gentle, modest and considerate little fellow" whom he treated with a "deference and almost boyish hero-worship" which touched Roberts. At Chequers, Kitchener confronted TR over the Panama Canal, proclaiming loudly that it had been a huge mistake not to make it a sea-level canal. When the Colonel responded reasonably that the engineers on the ground recommended against this on good evidence, Kitchener blustered on that he "never paid heed to protests like that" and would have ordered a sea-level canal be dug nevertheless. In the end Roosevelt told Kitchener that he considered his chief engineer in Panama, Colonel George Goethals, the very best man in the world for the job and took his advice. He added that "Goethals had never seen the Sudan, just as he Kitchener, had never seen Panama," and that he would trust Goethals' opinion rather than Kitchener's as to Goethals' job, just as he would "trust the opinion of Kitchener rather than Goethals if Goethals should criticize Kitchener's job in the Sudan."[29]

A week after Edward's funeral, Edith and Alice accompanied TR to Cambridge, where he was awarded an honorary L. L. D. He had lunch with Arthur Balfour's sister Eleanor Sidgwick, the principal of Cambridge's Newnham College. He also paid informal visits to several other of the colleges, including Trinity, King's and Emmanuel, the college of John Harvard, who had gone on to found Roosevelt's own university at Cambridge, Massachusetts. The Colonel was enchanted with the original Cambridge, which he thought one of the most beautiful places he visited.

At the Student Union, where to prolonged cheers he was made an honorary member, TR participated in a good-natured round of verbal give and take with the undergraduates, whose mental quickness reminded him of those at Harvard. He was subjected to student pranks when a stuffed teddy bear, its paws outstretched, was placed in his path on arrival at the Union, and another lowered on him during his remarks. This followed an old university tradition, which had seen a stuffed monkey dropped on Darwin and a Mahdi replica on Kitchener.

In his extemporaneous remarks TR advised the students that to succeed in life did not need "any remarkable skill, all you need is to possess ordinary qualities, but to develop them to more than an ordinary degree." In public life it was not genius, it was not "extraordinary subtlety, or acuteness of intellect," that was important. The things that were important were "rather commonplace, the rather humdrum virtues that in their sum are designated as character." If a nation had men of common sense, not geniuses, but "men of good abilities, with character, if you possess such men, the Government will go on very well." He confided that he didn't think any president or ex-president "ever enjoyed himself any more than I did" and added that he had enjoyed his life and work because he believed that "success—the real success—does not depend upon the position you hold, but upon how you carry yourself in that position." He concluded that there was "no man there to-day who has not the chance so to shape his life after he leaves this university that he shall have the right to feel, when his life ends, that he has made a real success of it." And his making a real success "does not in the least depend upon the prominence of the position he holds."[30]

Five days later, before a much more serious-minded assembly of almost a thousand notables at the historic Guildhall, TR was given the freedom of the City of London and made his much-anticipated speech on British rule in Africa, thus keeping a pledge to the men and women on the ground who felt themselves misunderstood, neglected and without proper support at home.[31] The company included many of the British statesmen he had met, such as Grey, Balfour, Cromer and Burns, but also Americans such as Whitelaw Reid and the painter John Singer Sargent. "Your men in Africa," Roosevelt declared, were "doing a great work for your Empire" and also "a great work for civilization." His sympathy for and belief in them were his reasons for speaking. In his opinion, "the great fact of world history during the last century" had been "the spread of civilization over the world's waste spaces" and that work was still being carried out by these soldiers, settlers and civic officials who were "entitled to the heartiest respect and the fullest support from their brothers who remain at home."[32]

About British East Africa, Uganda and the Sudan Roosevelt had "nothing to say to you save what is pleasant, as well as true." In the first he had found a land which could be made "a true white Man's country." And for the settlers he had a "peculiar sympathy," because they so strikingly reminded him of his own beloved westerners at home. In his view it was "of high importance" to encourage them in every way. Referring to the ongoing controversy over immigration from India, he exhorted his audience to ensure that no "alien race should be permitted to come into competition with the settlers." He praised the governor, Sir Percy Girouard, as a "man admirably fitted to deal wisely and firmly with all the many problems before him." All that was necessary was to "follow his lead, and to give him cordial support and backing." The principle on which Roosevelt thought it was wise to act in dealing with "far-away possessions," was "choose your man, change him if you become discontented with him, but while you keep him back him up."[33]

Unlike British East Africa, Uganda, because of the large native population and different geography and climate, would never be a "white man's country." There the "prime need" was to "administer the land in the interests of the native races, and to help forward their development." In his view missionary activity in Uganda had resulted in "an extraordinary development of Christianity" and the inhabitants therefore stood "far above most races in the Dark Continent in their capacity for progress towards civilization." All that was necessary was to "go forward on the paths you have already marked out."[34]

The Sudan was "peculiarly interesting" because it afforded the best possible example of "disregarding the well-meaning but unwise sentimentalists who object to the spread of civilization at the expense of savagery." The English "restored order, kept the peace, and gave to each individual a liberty" previously enjoyed only by the "blood-stained tyrant who at the moment was ruler." In his view, the governor-general, Sir Reginald Wingate, and his lieutenants, had in their reconstruction efforts in administration, education and police work, "performed to perfection a task equally important and difficult" and had "a claim upon all civilized mankind which should be heartily admitted." Not to go on with the work in the Sudan would be a crime and it was the "duty of England to stay there."[35]

Turning last to Egypt, Roosevelt declared that as a "sincere well-wisher of the British Empire," he felt "impelled to speak" mainly because of his "deep concern in the welfare of mankind and in the future of civilization." In Egypt, he saw Britain as "not only the guardians of your own interests" but also of civilization. The present condition of affairs, in TR's opinion, was a "grave menace to both your Empire and the entire civilized world." Britain had given Egypt the best Government in two thousand years, particularly for the fellahin "tiller of the soil," yet recent events, such as the assassination of Boutros Ghali, had shown that "in certain vital points you have erred." It was up to the British to correct this error, which had sprung from "the effort to do too much and not too little in the interests of the Egyptians themselves." Showing weakness, timidity and sentimentality might cause "even more far-reaching harm than violence and injustice."[36]

Treating all religions with fairness and impartiality, Roosevelt continued, had only resulted in a "noisy section of the native population" taking advantage to bring about an "anti-foreign movement" in which "murder on a large or small scale is expected to play a leading part." Boutros was assassinated "simply and solely" because he was the "best and most competent Egyptian official, a steadfast upholder of English rule, and an earnest worker for the welfare of his countrymen." The attitude of the Egyptian Nationalist party in response to this outrage had shown that they were "neither desirous nor capable of guaranteeing even that primary justice the failure to supply which makes self-government not merely an empty, but a noxious farce."[37]

Britain's first duty, TR asserted, was to keep order, and above all to punish murder and bring justice to all who committed or condoned it. When a people treated "assassination as a corner-stone of self-government," it forfeited "all rights to be treated as worthy of self-government." The British had saved the Egyptians from ruin in 1882 by coming in, and at the present moment if they were not ruled from outside they would "again sink into a welter of chaos." Some nation must govern Egypt and he believed that "you will decide that it is your duty to be that nation." Roosevelt went on, "Now, either you have the right to be in Egypt or you have not; either it is or is not your duty to establish and keep order. If you feel that you have not the right to be in Egypt, if you do not wish to establish and keep order there, why then, by all means get out." However, if as he hoped, "you feel that your duty to civilized mankind and your fealty to your own great traditions alike bid you to stay, then make the fact and the name agree and show that you are ready to meet...the responsibility which is yours."[38]

During the speech, Sir Edward Grey had whispered to Arthur Lee, "this will cause the devil of a row—although I hope a good one."[39] As he had promised he would, the foreign secretary defended the address against attacks in the House of Commons, but another member of the British Cabinet, John Morley, was less supportive. Morley told his peace ally Carnegie that the speech was a "grievous mistake, in spite of Grey being an accomplice." It only gave "powder and shot to our war men, and heaven knows they have plenty of ammunitions already."[40] In the Liberal press, the London *Daily News* questioned the propriety of TR lecturing the British on their own problems and asked what he would have thought if during the Philippine or Japanese crises a former British prime minister had opined in a similar fashion in the United States. It also doubted whether the former president fully appreciated the "complexity of the problems which he resolved yesterday in characteristically vigorous style." The Colonel claimed to speak from "first hand knowledge" of affairs in British East Africa, but after his relatively brief visit the *Daily News* questioned his assertion that "no alien race" should be allowed to come into competition with whites or his advice to "follow blindly the man on the spot." These views came from the "quality of his own mind" and he would have held them even if he had never shot big game in the protectorate. About Egypt, the paper decried TR's "crude" way of handling a complex problem which would not be helped by labeling Muslims as "fanatical" or "uncivilized" because of a single murder or labeling the nationalists "anti-foreign." Such a "Big Stick" approach would not work and the British should not abandon their Liberal principles, even on the advice of Theodore Roosevelt.[41]

British imperialists on the other hand were ecstatic. Balfour and Cromer "made no secret of their delight" with the speech and among the many letters of congratulations, one was addressed to "His Excellency 'Govern-or-go' Roosevelt."[42] In the *Spectator*, TR's friend St. Loe Strachey noted that because he had the courage to speak out "timid, fussy and pedantic people had charged Mr. Roosevelt with all sorts of crimes." Some had even accused him of "unfriendliness to this country." Happily the British people as a whole were not so foolish. He had told them "something useful and practical and has not lost himself in abstraction and platitude." The paper thanked TR "once again for giving us so useful a reminder of our duty." *The Times*, widely considered the voice of the British establishment, gave verbatim coverage, while remarking that "Mr. Roosevelt has reminded us in the most friendly way of what we are at least in danger of forgetting, and no impatience of outside criticism ought to be allowed to divert us from considering the substantial truth of his words."[43]

Reports of the Guildhall address published in Egypt further stirred nationalist resentment and Sir Eldon Gorst felt that Roosevelt's "mischievous remarks" helped to confirm the opinion of the critics of his policy. Gorst recorded in his diary that TR was "again disporting himself as the bull in the China shop—this time at my expense." His manner of expression was "most unfortunate" and most of his information had come from American missionary authorities, "a worthy but prejudiced and narrow-minded body," subject to the influence of the native Christians.[44] Lord Elgin, the former Colonial Secretary involved in a government review of Egyptian affairs, called the speech "a pity" because it would only raise resentment and because it over-simplified the issues. He did not agree that pro-Egyptian "sentiment" had done mischief in Egypt. In his view that was as rare as the "white rhinoceros (of which I fear Mr. Roosevelt killed too many)." The mischief instead had come from "intellectual indolence, which misapplies political maxims in countries like Egypt by treating them as if they were fundamental truths."[45] Whatever the truth of the matter, Roosevelt's speech was another nail in the coffin of Gorst's experiment in liberalization and he would soon be replaced by the strong man Kitchener who would with some success return to a sterner and more Cromer-like administration.

The day after the Guildhall address, TR left for Worplesdon, Surrey to spend a night with Frederick Selous at his house, Heatherside. There he inspected the impressive private museum of hunting trophies Selous had accumulated over four decades. Leaving Surrey, Roosevelt and family visited their old friend Sir George Otto Trevleyan, whom TR and Edith had first met on their honeymoon trip in 1886, at his house, Welcombe, in lovely country a mile from Stratford-on-Avon. This allowed Theodore to complete his rehabilitation in Shakespeare by visiting the Bard's birthplace. Their host's son George Macaulay Trevelyan, who had already written studies of Garibaldi and would go on to be a noted historian, reported to Cecil Spring Rice on the visit of the "Playboy of the Western World," who he liked very much, as did the whole family. Roosevelt displayed a considerable sense of humor and told delightful stories about kings and potentates quarreling with each other. "Needless to say," he told Spring Rice, "the vigour of his conversation" was "in the highest degree abnormal," but Trevleyan did not find it "ever wearying."

TR's talk on history was as good as any the younger Trevelyan had ever heard and his knowledge of both the American and European past immense. The Colonel's frankness on some matters was such that Trevelyan was unwilling to put them even in a private letter but he promised to fill in Spring Rice when they met on such topics as the systems of the Pope in Rome and the Russian Czar. He did reveal that TR thought the "greatest misfortune in modern history" was that the three Scandinavian peoples never could form a political union or even an entente. If they had done so in the fifteenth or sixteenth centuries they might have made the Baltic a Scandinavian lake and "prevented the planting of a 'sodden barbarism' on its eastern shore." TR also revealed himself to be a "terrific Radical" and Trevelyan confided that if he had said at the Guildhall what he thought about English Budgets, the House of Lords, Home Rule for Ireland, and other things he would "not have been applauded by the papers that most loudly cheered him."[46]

Roosevelt's final public address in England, given in a packed Sheldonian Theatre at Oxford on June 7, 1910, was the Romanes lecture, named in honor of George John Romanes, a celebrated naturalist and Fullerian Professor of Physiology at the Royal Institute. TR gave the scholarly speech, "Biological Analogies in History," in a scarlet gown donned to accept the honorary Doctorate of Civil Law he was awarded beforehand by the Chancellor, Lord Curzon, who had given the Romanes Lecture himself three years before. In his introduction of Roosevelt, Dr. Henry Goudy, the Regius Professor of Civil Law, declaimed, "His onslaughts on the wild beasts of the desert have been not less fierce nor less successful than over the many-headed hydra of corruption in his own land. Now, like another Ulysses, on his homeward way he has come to us . . . after visiting many cities and discoursing on many themes . . . it will be our privilege to listen to him discoursing on a lofty theme."[47]

The address, though rather dry and academic in nature, afforded Roosevelt one last European opportunity to praise the "homely, commonplace virtues," most importantly national character. His jeremiad warned that if this vanished in "graceful self-indulgence, if the virile qualities atrophy," then the nation had lost "what no material prosperity can offset." Comparing the "national growth and decay" of new and old nations, Roosevelt found commonalities and differences, both for good and evil. Rome had fallen "because the ills within her own borders had grown incurable" and at present he saw a similar "national danger patent" to all civilized peoples from the "growth of soft luxury" out of which the average women ceased to "become the mother of a family of healthy children" and the average man lost the "will and the power to work up to old age and to fight whenever the need arises." To survive the "really high civilizations must themselves supply the antidote to the self-indulgence and love of ease that they tend to produce." Each advanced nation must deal with its own problems, such as the juxtaposition of wealth and poverty, in its own fashion, but he thought the spirit "fundamentally the same." This must be of a "broad humanity, of brotherly kindness, of acceptance of responsibility, one for each and each for all, and at the same time a spirit as remote as the poles from every form of weakness and sentimentality."[48]

Turning to the British and U.S. empires, Roosevelt asserted that in the long run there could be "no justification for one race managing or controlling another unless the management and control are exercised in the interest and for the benefit of that other race." This was what the English speaking peoples had in "the main done and must continue in the future in an even greater degree" in India, Egypt and the Philippines alike. In his view, the laws of morality which governed individuals "in their dealings with one another," were "just as binding concerning nations in their dealings one with another" and he had followed this principle in his foreign relations as president. However, since nations could not depend on the courts for protection, it was the "highest duty of the most advanced and freest peoples to keep themselves in such a state of readiness as to forbid any barbarism or despotism the hope of arresting the progress of the world." The nations that led in that progress would be "foolish indeed to pay heed to the unwise persons who desire disarmament to be begun by the very nations who, among all others, should not be left helpless before any possible foe."[49]

The Archbishop of York commented that in the way of grading they had at Oxford, "we agreed to give the lecture a 'beta minus,' but the lecturer 'alpha plus.'" His Grace went on that "while we felt the lecture was not a very great contribution to science, we were sure the lecturer was a very great man." Roosevelt told the Archbishop that the lecture would have been "a great deal stronger had not one of my scientific friends in America *blue penciled the best part of it.*"[50] While at Oxford, TR attended a meeting of Rhodes Scholars and other American students at the American Club. He was also able to see, as he had requested, several writers of note, including Gilbert Murray, whose books on Ancient Greece he admired, and Charles Oman, author of *The Art of War in the Middle Ages*. After dinner with Sir Thomas Warren at Magdalene College, the Colonel spent the night at Nuneham Park, the country house nearby of the Liberal politician Lewis Harcourt, who would soon be made Colonial Secretary and had a particular interest in African affairs.

Back in London, with his trip almost at an end, Roosevelt attended a joint meeting of the Geographical and Alpine Clubs. In his note of acceptance TR declared, "You do no know how attractive an invitation is from people 'who have done things!' "[51] At a Society for the Preservation of the Fauna of the Empire dinner presided over by Edward North Buxton, TR regaled the three hundred fellow big game hunters and naturalists present with "an unusually vivid description" of African scenes, and particularly the Nandi lion hunt he had witnessed in which the warriors surrounded their prey and closed in with their spears for the kill.[52] Earlier that day he had lunch at the Shikar Club with Buxton, Selous and the other donors of the 450/500 Holland & Holland he had wielded so successfully in Africa and which R. J. Cuninghame brought to the affair. Reid gave the Colonel a farewell dinner at Dorchester House on June 8. The next day, which Roosevelt claimed was the one he enjoyed the most in all his time in Europe, was spent back in nature with Sir Edward Grey.

The foreign secretary and Roosevelt had a common love of birds and TR, anxious to see and hear at first hand the English species he knew so well from his books, gladly accepted an invitation for a final quiet day comparing bird lore while walking Grey's home ground. The two tramped through the rain in the Valley of the Itchen, ate their lunch on a bank, then motored to an inn near the New Forest for tea. Afterwards, they hiked through the New Forest, reaching an inn on the other side that evening, "tired and happy and ready for a warm bath, a hot supper, and bed."[53] Though both the weather and lateness of the season somewhat hampered the experience, Grey made a list of forty-one birds they had seen, twenty-three of which they heard sing.[54]

Grey later recalled that on their trek he was astounded by TR's knowledge of English birds. Roosevelt "not only knew more about American birds than I did about British birds, but he knew more about British birds also." What he had lacked was an opportunity of hearing their songs. On their walk he told Roosevelt the name of birds as they sang and "it was unnecessary to tell him more." He knew the "kind of bird it was, its habits and appearance. He just wanted to complete his knowledge by hearing the song." How Roosevelt had found the time in his busy life to gain such an expertly trained ear Grey could not fathom. Of all the songs, Roosevelt was the most impressed by the blackbird, and he became positively indignant that he had not heard more of its reputation. He theorized that its name hurt its standing in comparison to the more lauded thrush.[55] To be with Roosevelt, wrote Grey, was to be "stimulated in the best sense of the word for the work of life."[56]

The admiration of the two men for each other was mutual. In TR's estimation, Grey was "not a brilliant man like Balfour, or a born leader like Lloyd George," but he was the "kind of high-minded public servant, as straight in all private as in all public relations, whom it is essential for a country to have." He did not remember meeting anyone, except for Leonard Wood, his commanding officer in Cuba, to whom he "took so strong a fancy on such short acquaintance."[57] At the time, however, Arthur Lee thought he noted in TR a certain disillusionment in what he considered Grey's lukewarm support of the Guildhall speech. Roosevelt said of Grey that he had "the profile of an eagle but I cannot help wondering whether his heart may be that of a sparrow-hawk."[58] The Colonel arose at 4 a.m. on June 10 to spend a final few hours listening to bird songs, before Lee took him to the train for Southampton where he joined Edith and Ethel already aboard the liner *Kaiserin Auguste Victoria* for the eight-day voyage home.

While in London, Roosevelt met at the American Embassy with Elihu Root, who spent an hour defending President Taft's record. He urged Roosevelt to stay out of politics for at least sixty days after his return. Taft also sent a letter, his first since the one Archie Butt delivered to TR at Hoboken fifteen months before. The president explained that he had not written "for the reason that he did not wish to invite your comment or judgment on matters at long range" or to commit him on issues he would need to decide on once he returned to the United States. He now congratulated Roosevelt on "a trip exceptional in history and most successful in every detail."

Turning to politics, Taft admitted that he had had a hard time as president, a task made heavier by the illness of his wife. "I do not know that I have had harder luck than other Presidents," he wrote, "but I do know that thus far I have succeeded far less than others." The Pinchot-Ballinger controversy had given him "a great deal of personal pain and suffering," but he was not going to say a word on the subject. TR would have to "look into that wholly for yourself without influence by the parties if you would find the truth." He defended the Payne-Aldrich Tariff as a good one and a real downward revision, "not as radical a change" as he had favored, but "still a change for the better."

Taft claimed that he had been "conscientiously trying to carry out your policies," but his methods of doing so had not worked for several reasons. First, the Republican insurgents had "done all in their power to defeat us." The added hostility of the press, Taft put down to the fact that the tariff did not sufficiently lower the rate on print paper. Outside the newspapers, the general enthusiasm of business had been curbed by the corporation tax about to be tested in court. The president concluded by telling Roosevelt that it would "give me a great deal of personal pleasure if after you get settled at Oyster Bay, you could come over to Washington and spend a few days at the White House."[59]

In reply to this *cri de coeur*, TR commiserated with Taft over his wife's illness which had "added immeasurably to your burden." He told his old friend that, even though he was "much concerned about some of the things I see and am told," what he felt it was best to do was "say absolutely nothing—and indeed to keep my mind as open as I keep mouth shut!" This would prove difficult in the short term and impossible afterwards. Finally, and ominously for their future relations, TR asked Taft "to let me defer my answer" to his "more than kind invitation" to visit the White House "until I reach Oyster Bay, and find out something about what work is in store for me."[60]

In a P.S to his letter, Taft had mentioned that a great reception was being prepared for Roosevelt in New York, which would be "non-partisan and the sincere expression of all the people of their joy at your return." This insured that there would be no quiet return to a "Promised Land" of quiet retirement at Sagamore Hill, as Edith had hoped, but only the beginning of another quest for her husband, this time sadly against an old friend.

Chapter 9

The Old Lion Is Dead: Epilogue and Dramatis Personae

Theodore Roosevelt died unexpectedly in January 1919, at only sixty years of age, before he could snatch back one last time the presidency he had walked away from ten years before. Carl Akeley, whose story of lions had helped send TR to Africa, and who counted the quiet talk he had with Roosevelt under the shade of an acacia tree on the Uasin Gushu plateau in 1909 one as of the great experiences of his life, was among the many shaken by the death. Since their meeting on safari TR had more than once reminded Akeley of his promised book on Africa and volunteered to contribute a foreword and a chapter. However, it was not until ten years later that Akeley sat down to write that he meant at last to start the work. He had finished only two words, "Dear Colonel," when the phone rang and he was given the news of Roosevelt's death. For Akeley, the "bottom dropped out of everything" and until he returned from the funeral he did nothing.

To escape his depression Akeley began to sculpt a model of a lion. He meant to make it "symbolic of Roosevelt, of his strength, courage, fearlessness—of his kingly qualities in the old-fashioned sense." This modeling offered him great comfort and one day Archie Roosevelt came by his studio and he showed him the still unfinished lion. TR's son told Akeley that none of the family wanted "to see statues of father. They can't make father." But as he put his arms around the pedestal of the lion, he said "this is father. Of course, you do not know it, but among ourselves we boys always called him the 'Old Lion' and when he died I cabled the others in France, 'the Old Lion is dead.' "[1]

Taken as a whole, Roosevelt's last decade makes a rather sad coda to an otherwise remarkable career. The feud with Taft which, as we have seen, was well developed before the Colonel returned to America in June 1910, culminated two years later in the Bull Moose Progressive campaign. This bitter division in the Republican ranks delivered the presidency into the hands of the Democratic candidate, Woodrow Wilson, and placed a political mark of Cain on TR. He never fully recovered from illnesses and injuries suffered on a perilous expedition down the Amazon, which in the shadow of the electoral defeat afforded him "one last chance to be a boy."[2]

After the Great War began in 1914, Roosevelt's last years were marred by virulent outbursts aimed at what he considered Wilson's foolhardy and cowardly policy which kept America out of the war until 1917 and in the bargain frustrated the Colonel's long-stated hope to lead troops again as he had in Cuba. It is tantalizing to wonder how Wilhelm II and Germany's course might have been deflected had TR been president in 1914, something which must have weighed on Roosevelt's active mind as well. In 1918, much of his joy, and perhaps also his indomitable will to live, were drained away by news of the death of his youngest son Quentin in aerial combat over France. TR's own death less than a year later forestalled any possibility of the third term prophesied more than once on the journey a decade earlier. At any rate, though he might have garnered the Republican nomination in 1920, and possibly been elected, the old warrior was rather out of step with the temper of a nation tired of moralists and crusaders like both Wilson and himself.

The fifteen-month 1909–1910 odyssey, however, marks a shining example of TR still living and preaching the righteous, strenuous life to friend and foe alike and represents a high point of his post-presidential career. Though today soiled by its bloodiness, the African safari greatly increased scientific understanding of little known and even previously unknown fauna and flora, some recorded in *Life-Histories of African Game Animals* (1914), the scholarly work TR co-authored with Edmund Heller. Henry Fairfield Osborn described the volumes as "replete from cover to cover with accurate, original information—in fact a real contribution."[3] Researchers continue actively to consult the thousands of specimens brought back from

Africa, whose value has increased over the last few decades in which animals are no longer shot. The practice of taking family groups, rather than simply record trophies, has provided an invaluable variety of specimens for study a century on and as benchmarks for modern DNA research.

Roosevelt's *African Game Trails: An Account of the Wanderings of an American Hunter-Naturalist*, which has sold more than a million copies in numerous editions, is still considered one of the finest and most valuable safari records ever published.[4] In his review of the book, Sir Harry Johnston applauded the gain to science from the expedition. In this TR was "quite as anxious" to obtain the white-billed stork, the pygmy mouse, the green-backed day flying bat, the elephant shrew, as he was the white rhino or Abyssinian buffalo or giant eland. No notable bird or animal "died in vain." Their remains would enrich the great natural history museums of America and be of "ever-growing interest to millions of men, women and children who will thus be able to realize the marvels of the African fauna."[5]

The announcement in 1913 of a dedicated hall at the National Museum to display the mounted African specimens led also to renewed condemnation of the safari. William Hornaday, of the New York Zoological Garden, eloquently defended the expedition and Roosevelt from the critics, of which there continues to be no shortage down to today. He first praised TR, and the safari's benefactors, for building at their own expense a collection of which the nation could be proud but that Congress, historically, had been unwilling to fund. Turning to those who questioned the ethics of the safari, Hornaday declared that "Ethically the world has decreed that whenever it does not spell extermination it is right to kill enough of the mammals, birds, reptiles and fishes of the world to stock the world's museums with a satisfactory supply." Otherwise, species would be exterminated without any permanent evidence of their existence being left behind. Death was the "ultimate portion of every living creature, and the collectors for museums are no more cruel or wasteful of life than are the forces of nature herself." Those who thought the killing of animals wrong would no doubt condemn the Roosevelt expedition. But to do so was to condemn "the museum idea so far as it relates to zoological forms." Some killing was necessary and, in his opinion, if it was wrong to kill wild animals for museums, it was also wrong to kill domestic animals, poultry, and fish for the table.

Hornaday wished that the public could see, as he had, the entire lot of specimens and "trophies" that TR had taken for himself. He had the right to retain a great many, but the number he kept were so few and "so trifling in value that they made, when placed on exhibition, a showing that was pitifully meager." Literally, everything fine was given over to the National Museum in Washington except the two white rhinoceros heads that went to New York, one to his own institution and the other to the American Museum of Natural History. He regarded it as "particularly fine" that Roosevelt did not keep even one white rhino head for his own collection. In the end, Hornaday believed, when the splendid groups were finally mounted and put on exhibition in the new space, then the ethics of the Roosevelt collecting expedition to Africa would be "as firmly fixed as the foundations of the Rocky Mountains."[6] Sadly, all save one of the specimens that were displayed for decades in beautifully painted dioramas in what became the National Museum of Natural History in Washington have been dismantled. The only significant specimen shot by Roosevelt in Africa still on display is a single white rhino.

The European leg of TR's journey had much less tangible and lasting results. Nevertheless, until Woodrow Wilson's triumphant postwar visit in 1919 no American would touch the imagination of Europe to a greater degree. Across the Continent the Colonel raised the "consciousness that every country" needed a "Roosevelt of its own."[7] Lord Curzon, his host at Oxford, wrote TR soon after he departed that "the echoes of your great tour still survive & here we all think that the English was not the least successful part of it." He could not recall "any man who has left a similar impression."[8] Roosevelt in return liked and respected almost all the aristocrats and royals he met. They struck him as "serious persons, devoted to their people and anxious to justify their own positions by the way they did their duty." On the other hand, he did not find "the average among them very high as regards intellect and force." Further, he could not imagine a "more appallingly dreary life for a man of ambition and power."[9] Almost all of these European notables, who assumed their distinguished guest would again be president, would either be swept away by the cataclysm of World War I or find their powers and prestige greatly reduced in its aftermath.

It is unfortunate that, however much he might have disagreed with Andrew Carnegie's schemes, TR was unable to further the cause of peace before 1914, as he had done to garner the Nobel Prize in 1906.

His belated Nobel Address shows that, at least in 1910, he stood for many of the aims Woodrow Wilson would list in his Fourteen Points program for peace eight years later, including arms control and a League of Nations. The failure to form an international police force, which Roosevelt called for a century ago to enforce peace, has proven the Achilles heel, first of the League of Nations, and then of the United Nations today, to the world's detriment.

In London at the end, Roosevelt's private conversations and Guildhall address in support of the aims of Britain's African colonists and governors, and to urge a stiffer policy in Egypt, gave at least a brief fillip to Britain's imperialists. In the long run, however, the dream of a "White Man's Country" in British East Africa, which Roosevelt supported, proved as illusory as the overall imperial idea. Whatever its shortcomings, however, TR's post-presidential odyssey represents a luminous example of a man at the height of his powers enjoying his life immensely, and still attempting to shape the world in his own image.

* * *

For three decades after her husband's death, Edith Roosevelt defended his record and name. She traveled widely, and in 1932 campaigned vigorously for Herbert Hoover against Theodore's fifth cousin Franklin's first bid for the presidency. She died in 1948 at Sagamore Hill, aged eighty-seven. Five years earlier, Edith's favorite child Kermit, who had accompanied his father down the Amazon as he had done to Africa, succumbed to the Roosevelt family's predilection to alcoholism and depression. He committed suicide while serving in the army in Alaska during World War II. His mother was told he suffered a heart attack.

TR's obedient and upright daughter Ethel married a surgeon friend of Kermit's, Richard Derby, in 1913. They had two children, Richard and Edith. The last in particular became a favorite of grandfather Theodore in visits to Sagamore Hill. On her father's death, Ethel commented "The whole country mourns him and I mourn for the country. There's no one now to say what we want said."[10] She went on to lead a successful fight to make Sagamore Hill an historic site, opened to the public in 1953. Ethel died in December 1977, outlived only by her brother Archie, and by "Princess" Alice, who kept her place as a feared and revered leader of Washington society for decades. Dubbed "the <u>other</u> Washington monument," she called herself "Washington's only perambulatory monument."[11] Alice died in February 1980, only days after her ninety-sixth birthday.

After the failure of TR's peace mission to Germany, Andrew Carnegie did not give up his crusade, or the hope that the German Emperor might yet be brought to his side in the struggle. At home Carnegie put his faith in President Taft and with his blessing at the end of 1910 the plutocrat's efforts took a new course when he used $10,000,000 in United States Steel bonds to fund the Carnegie Endowment for Peace still at work today.[12] Elihu Root became the endowment's first president and held the position for the next fifteen formative years. In 1912, for his labors in the vineyards of international arbitration, Root joined Roosevelt as a recipient of the Nobel Peace Prize. That same year their friendship ended when Root supported Taft's nomination over TR.

The next year Carnegie led a delegation to Germany for the celebration of the twenty-fifth anniversary of Wilhelm's reign. When they met the boisterous Kaiser, wagging his index finger, exclaimed, "Remember Carnegie! Twenty-five years!—and twenty-five years of peace! If I am Emperor for another twenty-five years not a shot shall be fired in Europe!"[13] The following year, German troops invaded Belgium, which Carnegie had passed through in 1913, noting its beauty, and that it could never be attacked, because Germany, France, and England guaranteed its neutrality. When the last entered World War I, ostensibly on account of her pledge to Belgium, Carnegie's friend John Morley was one of the two men in the British Cabinet who resigned rather than support the decision. The foremost proponent of intervention in the Cabinet was Sir Edward Grey, who lived up to Roosevelt's hopes for him in this matter at least.

The sacrifices Britain and her colonies made in the Great War only increased TR's admiration for the British Empire. Among the million British casualties was Sir Frederick Selous, who enlisted at age sixty-four and was killed in action in 1917, fighting the German foe in East Africa, and gaining the heroic death the old Rough Rider felt cheated of by Woodrow Wilson. Before the end of the war Theodore and Edith's friend Sir Cecil Spring Rice also died, but in less gallant circumstances. In poor health for several years, he was forced out as ambassador to the United States in late 1917 and passed away a few months later. Another close English friend, Arthur Lee, like Theodore unable to serve in arms, accepted various government posts during the war and was First Lord of the Admiralty by the end of the Lloyd George coalition government that won it. Of TR and the Welshman, Lee commented that "in drive and sense of humour they were almost equally matched and...they both possessed that higher genius for leadership which enabled men to serve under their banner and to follow them 'over the top' with a sense of exhilaration and without counting the cost."[14] An avid and talented collector of art, Lee co-founded the Courtauld Institute in London and died in 1947.

Though dispirited by the ghastly world cataclysm of 1914–1918, Andrew Carnegie continued to call for a League of Peace. He died in August 1919, while Woodrow Wilson was in the midst of his losing postwar battle to have the United States join his brainchild League of Nations. TR's old friend Henry Cabot Lodge was instrumental in the Senate defeat of the Versailles Treaty, and with it American membership in Wilson's League. Lodge and Roosevelt also fell out in 1912 over the Bull Moose rebellion, and he certainly would not have understood or forgiven Lodge's support of the belated 1920s payment of $25,000,000 to Colombia by the United States for TR's "theft" of the Panama Canal.

Roosevelt, however, was able to come to a rapprochement with another old friend, Will Taft, who in his heart of hearts had never really wanted or enjoyed the presidency, and soon got over the humiliation of coming in third in the 1912 election behind Wilson and TR. Despite the fears of Roosevelt and Gifford Pinchot, the Taft administration left behind a quite respectable record in conservation, about which Taft and Ballinger had differed with their predecessors more in style and speed, than in the final goal. After spending a quiet eight years as a professor of Law at his beloved Yale, Taft was appointed chief justice of the Supreme Court by the next Republican president, Warren G. Harding, giving the former president the position he had always wanted most of all. He proved a sound choice for the conservative times and happily stayed on the court until his death in 1930.

Pinchot, whose battle with Richard Ballinger was so instrumental in pulling Roosevelt back into the political fray against Taft in 1910, carried on the struggle for his brand of conservation policy for the rest of his long life. He also embarked on a political career, winning the first of two terms as governor of Pennsylvania in 1922. His memoir *Breaking New Ground* constituted a defense of his and TR's conservation policies. Roosevelt's death in 1919, he feared, might result in "such control by the reactionaries" as to put "the policies they had fought for "back many years." In Pinchot's estimation, TR's life had been one lived "at its warmest, and fullest and truest, at its utmost in vigor, at its sanest in purpose, and its clearest of clearest—life tremendous in volume, unbounded in scope, yet controlled and guided with a disciplined power that made him, as few men have even been, the captain of his soul."[15] Another man who had served both Roosevelt and Taft, their military aide Archie Butt, tragically went down with the *Titanic* in 1912.

Among the royals Roosevelt came to know in 1910, the little King Victor Emmanuel III, who so impressed him, defied parliamentary majorities in 1915 to bring Italy into World War I on the side of the Allies. Less wisely seven years later, to avoid civil war, he offered Benito Mussolini the premiership, opening the door for the Fascist regime. In 1936 Mussolini added the title Emperor of Abyssinia to his titles and Victor Emmanuel supported Il Duce until his fall. In June 1944, on the occupation of Rome by the Allies, the King retired from public life. Two years later he abdicated and was followed, for a month, by his son Umberto II, who himself abdicated when a national referendum voted for a republic.

Kaiser Wilhelm II led Germany into World War I confident that his glorious army and modern navy would win great victories. However, during the four bloody years of total war, he was for the most part relegated to the role of figurehead by the generals, who wielded true power. Wilhelm was forced to abdicate in November 1918, clearing the way for the Armistice which ended the war. Despite postwar cries of "Hang the Kaiser," he was allowed to live quietly in exile in Holland until his death in 1941. To his credit he refused to be used for propaganda purposes by Hitler and the Nazi regime. The Kaiser's cousin, George V, was a dutiful king in war and peace for twenty-five years until his death in 1935, and was followed, briefly, by his son Edward VIII, who abdicated rather than abandon his American lover, Wallis Simpson. This left the throne to George VI, the father of the present monarch, Elizabeth II.

Finally, the energetic little Prince Olav of Norway, who so charmed TR in 1910, lived a long and strenuous life himself. He grew into a handsome youth, noted as a sportsman and Olympic yachtsman. Olav was educated at Balliol College, Oxford, a famous training ground of British statesmen. He stayed in Norway when it was invaded by Germany in 1940 and was very briefly head of the country's over-matched armed forces. Olav escaped to England with his father and returned in 1945. He succeeded to the throne in 1957 as Olav V and reigned until his death in 1991, the last surviving grandchild of Edward VII. All in all a "bully" life of which TR would have been proud.

Notes

Preface and Acknowledgments

1. Many safari books were published at the time in an attempt to take advantage of the TR frenzy at home. Most were generic and made no mention of Roosevelt, but several sensational titles interspersed accounts of TR with general information on Africa.
2. For two notable exceptions, see Douglas Brinkley, *The Wilderness Warrior: Theodore Roosevelt and the Crusade for America* (New York: HarperCollins, 2009) and Paul Cutwright, *Theodore Roosevelt: The Making of a Conservationist* (Urbana: University of Illinois Press, 1985).
3. For Wilhelm, see Lamar Cecil, *Wilhelm II*, 2 vols. (Chapel Hill: University of North Carolina Press, 1996).

Prologue

1. Ziegfield to TR, June 19, 1910, Series 1, Reel 91, Theodore Roosevelt Papers, Library of Congress, hereafter TRP; Archibald Butt, *Taft and Roosevelt: The Intimate Letters of Archie Butt, Military Aide*, 2 vols. (New York: Doubleday, Doran & Company, 1930), 2: 400–401.
2. TR commented that the poem was, "Rather poor poetry," but that it made "good sense from the expansionist standpoint." David Gilmour, *The Long Recessional: The Imperial Life of Rudyard Kipling* (London: John Murray, 2002), 128.
3. Carnegie to TR, June 30, 1910, Series 1, Reel 92, TRP.
4. Pinchot to TR, July 6, 1910, Pinchot Papers, Library of Congress.

1 The Old Lion Departs

1. For a list of the thirty-one men, see Lawrence Abbott, ed., *The Letters of Archie Butt: Personal Aide to President Roosevelt* (New York: Doubleday, Page & Company, 1924), 366.

2. Undated "Notes From Tennis Cabinet Address," Series 6, Reel 428, TRP. Archie Butt described the Frenchman as a "bearded little fellow, full of enthusiasm and vim and a great chum of the President, playing tennis with him and quite his equal in the walking contests." October 10, 1908, in Abbott, *Letters of Archie Butt*, 118–19. For a recent comment on TR, Jusserand, and the Moroccan crisis, see Serge Ricard, "Foreign Policy Making in the White House: Rooseveltian-Style Personal Diplomacy." In William N. Tilchin and Charles E. Neu, eds., *Artists of Power: Theodore Roosevelt, Woodrow Wilson, and Their Enduring Impact on U.S. Foreign Policy* (London: Praeger, 2006), 17–22.

3. March 1, 1909, in Abbott, *Letters of Archie Butt*, 365–70.

4. July 27, 1908, in Abbott, *Letters of Archie Butt*, 84–85.

5. Carl Akeley, "Roosevelt in Africa," in Theodore Roosevelt, *African Game Trails: An Account of the African Wanderings of an American Hunter-Naturalist* (New York: Charles Scribner's Sons, 1926), x–xi. Congressman Mann is probably best known as the author of the "anti-white slavery" Mann Act of 1910, which prohibited the transportation of women across state lines for purposes of prostitution.

6. For Edith, see Sylvia Morris, *Edith Kermit Roosevelt: Portrait of a First Lady* (New York: Coward, McCann & Geoghegan, 1980) and Tom Lansford, *A "Bully" First Lady: Edith Kermit Roosevelt* (Huntington, NY: Nova History Publications, 2001).

7. Quoted in David H. Burton, "Theodore Roosevelt and His English Correspondents: A Special Relationship of Friends," *Transactions of the American Philosophical Society*, New Series, Volume 63, Part 2 (Philadelphia, 1973), 9. For Spring Rice, see David H. Burton, *Cecil Spring Rice: A Diplomat's Life* (Madison, NJ; Fairleigh Dickinson University Press, 1990).

8. Kermit Roosevelt, *The Happy Hunting-Grounds* (New York: Charles Scribner's Sons, 1920), 14–15. Besides his interest in Africa, TR believed the safari would build up Kermit, who had been a frail child. The other children had various disqualifications. Theodore Jr. had embarked on a business career and Quentin and Archie were too young. Alice had married and the idea of the prim Ethel on safari was preposterous.

9. David Wallace, "Sagamore Hill: An Interior History." In Natalie Naylor, Douglas Brinkley, John Allen Gable, eds. *Theodore Roosevelt; Many-Sided American* (Interlaken, NY: Heart of Lakes Publishing, 1992), 531.

10. Henry Fairfield Osborn, *Impressions of Great Naturalists* (New York: Charles Scribner's Sons, 1928), 260.

11. For Selous, see Stephen Taylor, *The Mighty Nimrod: A Life of Frederick Courteney Selous African Hunter and Adventurer 1851–1917* (London: Collins, 1989).

12. Gerald Monsman, *H. Rider Haggard and the Imperial Frontier* (Greensboro, NC: ELT Press, 2006), 233.

13. Theodore Roosevelt, "Foreword" to Frederick Courtenay Selous, *African Nature Notes and Reminiscences* (London: Macmillan, 1908), xi–xiii.

14. TR to Selous, March 20, 1908, Series 2, Reel 348, TRP.

15. TR to Kermit Roosevelt, April 11, 1908, Series 2, Reel 349, TRP.

16. For Roosevelt, hunting and conservation, see Douglas Brinkley, *The Wilderness Warrior: Theodore Roosevelt and the Crusade for America* (New York: HarperCollins, 2009); Daniel Justin Herman, *Hunting and the American Imagination* (Washington, DC: Smithsonian Institution Press, 2001); William Beinart and Peter Coates, *Environment and History: The Taming of Nature in the USA and South Africa* (London: Routledge, 1995); Paul Schullery, "Theodore Roosevelt: The Scandal of the Hunter as Nature Lover," in Naylor et al., *Theodore Roosevelt: Many-Sided American*; Cutwright, *Making of a Conservationist*; John F. Reiger, *American Sportsmen and the Origins of Conservation* (New York: Winchester Press, 1975); and Kate Stewart, "Theodore Roosevelt: Hunter-Naturalist on Safari," *Quarterly Journal of the Library of Congress* 27, 3 (July, 1970).

17. Cutwright, *Making of a Conservationist*, 171.

18. For Burroughs' recollections of their friendship in nature, see *Camping and Tramping with Roosevelt* (New York: Charles Scribner's Sons, 1907). For Muir and Roosevelt, see Stephen Fox, *John Muir and His Legacy: The American Conservation Movement* (Boston: Little, Brown, 1981).

19. Many of these, and others collected over the years by TR, are still available for study at the National Museum of Natural History's Bird Division.

20. For TR's attack on Long, see his article "Nature Fakers" in the September 19, 1907 *Everybody's* magazine. For this subject also see Chapter 9, "The Nature Fakers & Roosevelt," in Edward J. Renehan, Jr. *John Burroughs: An American Naturalist* (Post Mills, VT: Chelsea Green Publishing, 1992). For the charges of "game butchery" aimed at Roosevelt, see Gerald Carson, "TR and the 'Nature Fakers,'" *American Heritage Magazine* 22, 2 (February 1971).

21. TR to Kermit Roosevelt, May 10, 1908, Series 2, Reel 349, TRP. For Burroughs's recollection of this episode, see "Theodore Roosevelt," *Natural History* 19, 1 (January 1919), 5.

22. Burroughs to TR, February 20, 1909, Series 1, Reel 88, TRP.

23. Cutwright, *Making of a Conservationist*, 229.

24. TR to Kermit Roosevelt, May 17, 1908, Series 2, Reel 349, TRP.

25. TR to Trevelyan, June 20, 1908, Box 113, Elihu Root Papers, Library of Congress.

26. For Pinchot, see Char Miller, *Gifford Pinchot and the Making of Modern Environmentalism* (Washington, DC: Island Press, 2001).

27. Char Miller, "Keeper of His Conscience? Pinchot, Roosevelt, and the Politics of Conservation," in Naylor et al., *Theodore Roosevelt: Many-Sided American*, 241.

28. Cutwright, *Making of a Conservationist*, 201.

29. Gifford Pinchot, *Breaking New Ground* (New York: Harcourt Brace, 1947), 382.

30. TR to Pinchot, March 1, 1909, Series 2, Reel 354, TRP.

31. TR to Buxton, June 25, 1908, Series 3A, Reel 363, TRP.

32. John M. Mackenzie, *The Empire of Nature: Hunting, Conservation and British Imperialism* (Manchester: Manchester University Press, 1982), 211. This organization, which later was instrumental in setting aside several national parks in Africa, continues today as Fauna and Flora International. For its origins, see David K. Prendergast, "Colonial Wildlife Conservation and the Origins of the Society for the Preservation of the Wild Fauna of the Empire (1903–1914)," *Oryx* 37, 2 (April 2003). For a history to 1978, see Richard Fitter and Sir Peter Scott, *The Penitent Butchers: The Fauna Preservation Society 1903–1978* (London: Collins, 1978).

33. TR to Buxton, June 25, 1908, Series 3A, Reel 363, TRP.

34. TR to Walcott, June 20, 1908, RU 45, Box 48, Office of the Secretary Records, Smithsonian Archive. The present National Museum of Natural History was formally established only in 1968.

35. Walcott to TR, June 27, 1908, RU 45, Box 48, Office of the Secretary Records, Smithsonian Archive.

36. TR to Selous, June 25, 1908, Series 3A, Reel 363, TRP.

37. Walcott to TR, June 27, 1908, RU 45, Box 48, Office of the Secretary Records, Smithsonian Archive. For the subscribers, see Elting Morison, ed., *The Letters of Theodore Roosevelt*, vol. VII (Cambridge, MA: Harvard University Press., 1954), n. 1, 13.

38. The only names TR knew at the time were Andrew Carnegie, Oscar Straus and Leigh Hunt. None were released to the public until 1913. In the end the total cost of the safari was close to $75,000, of which TR paid $20,000.

39. December 10, 1908, in Abbott, *Letters of Archie Butt*, 232.

40. David Patterson, *Towards a Warless World: The Travail of the American Peace Movement 1887–1914* (London: Routledge, 1976), 35, 146.

41. Carnegie to Morley, June 20, 1908, Volume 167, Carnegie Papers, Library of Congress.

42. TR to Strachey, November 28, 1908, STR/28/3/21, Strachey Papers, Parliamentary Archives.

43. For this see William Tilchin, *Theodore Roosevelt and the British Empire* (New York: St. Martin's Press, 1997) and David H. Burton, "Theodore Roosevelt and the 'Special Relationship' with Britain," *History Today* 23, 8 (1973), 527–35. For a few other representative examples concerning the "Special Relationship," which has attracted a considerable literature, see Bernard Porter, *Empire and Superempire: Britain, America and the World* (London: Yale University Press, 2006); Andrew Roberts, *A History of the English-Speaking Peoples Since 1900* (London: HarperCollins, 2006); Christopher Hitchens, *Blood, Class and Empire: The Enduring Anglo-American Relationship* (New York: Nation Books, 2004); Max Beloff, "The Special Relationship: An Anglo-American Myth," in Martin Gilbert, ed., *A Century of Conflict 1850–1950: Essays for A. J. P. Taylor* (London: Collins, 1966), 151–71.

44. Only three years before that, during the 1895–96 Venezuela crisis with British Guiana, TR had called for war with Britain, despite the disparity in naval power. He confided to one of his imperialist brethren, Henry Cabot Lodge, "Let the fight come if it must; I don't care whether our seacoast cities are bombarded or not; we would take Canada." Tilchin, *Roosevelt and the British Empire*, 17.

45. Ibid., 17–19.

46. TR to Reid, July 20, 1908, Series 3A, Reel 363, TRP.

47. TR to Buxton, July 21, 1908, Series 3A, Reel 363, TRP.

48. TR to Churchill, January 6, 1909, Series 2, Reel 353, TRP. Churchill appears to have made a bad impression across the entire Roosevelt clan, even so far as TR's young fifth cousin Franklin in the Democratic branch.

49. TR to Pease, July 25, 1908, Series 3A, Reel 363; September 5, 1908, Series 2, Reel 351; December 12, 1908, Series 2, Reel 353, TRP.

50. November 26, 1908, in Abbott, *Letters of Archie Butt*, 203.

51. TR to Stone, December 2, 1908, Series 2, Reel 352, TRP. For TR and the media, see George Juergens, *News from the White House: The Presidential-Press Relationship in the Progressive Era* (Chicago: University of Chicago Press, 1981) and Stephen Ponder, *Managing the Press: Origins of the Media Presidency, 1897–1933* (New York: St. Martin's Press, 1999).

52. November 26, 1908, in Abbott, *Letters of Archie Butt*, 203.

53. November 5, 1908, in Abbott, *Letters of Archie Butt*, 156.

54. TR to Sullivan, October 30, 1908, Series 2, Reel 352, TRP.

55. Corinne Robinson to TR, February 19, 1909, Series 1, Reel 88, TRP. For her recollections of the gift, see Corinne Roosevelt Robinson, *My Brother Theodore Roosevelt* (New York: Charles Scribner's Sons, 1921), 251–53.

56. July 27, 1908, in Abbott, *Letters of Archie Butt*, 86. For Roosevelt's comments on the library, the remnants of which are in the Roosevelt Collection at Harvard, see "The Pigskin Library," in Theodore Roosevelt, *Literary Essays* (New York: Charles Scribner's Sons, 1926), 337–46.

57. TR to Buxton, August 1, 1908, Series 3A, Reel 363, TRP.

58. TR to Spring Rice, August 1, 1908, Series 4A, Reel 416, TRP.

59. July 26, 1908, in Abbott, *Letters of Archie Butt*, 72–73.

60. June 19, 1908, in Abbott, *Letters of Archie Butt*, 42.

61. Edith Roosevelt to Spring Rice, August 9, 1908, CASR 9/1, Spring Rice Papers, Churchill College Archive, Cambridge.

62. TR to Mearns, January 12, 1909, RU 45, Box 48, Office of the Secretary, Records, Smithsonian Archive.

63. Quoted in Wilson, *Theodore Roosevelt Outdoorsman*, 177. Several books on the geography and the fauna of Africa by Sir Harry Johnston were on the long list TR consulted for the safari and the former British Commissioner in South Central Africa visited the White House at Roosevelt's invitation for a more personal exchange of ideas. In 1901 Johnston had prepared a report on East Africa for the British government that became the first to draw attention to the possibility of the highlands as an area of settlement for white men on the lines of Australia and New Zealand. For Johnson, see Roland Oliver, *Sir Harry Johnston and the Scramble for Africa* (London: Chatto & Windus, 1957).

64. TR to Kermit Roosevelt, October 27, 1908, Series 2, Reel 352, TRP.

65. TR to Buxton, August 20, 1908, Series 3A, Reel 363, TRP.

66. TR to Lodge, August 8, 1908, in Elting Morison, ed., *The Letters of Theodore Roosevelt*, vol. VI (Cambridge, MA: Harvard University Press, 1952), 1161–62. Lodge had boosted TR's career at several pivotal points, in particular promoting him for assistant secretary of the Navy and the vice-presidency.

67. Dr. Mearns brought along several cases of champagne, also for medicinal purposes, which proved effective in treating fevers during the expedition.

68. TR to Buxton, Series 3A, Reel 363, TRP.

69. October 21, 1908, in Abbott, *Letters of Archie Butt*, 143–44.

70. TR to Curzon, September 12, 1908, Series 2, Reel 351, TRP.

71. Osborn, *Impressions of Great Naturalists*, 263. For more recent comment on Osborn and Roosevelt, see Ronald Rainger, *An Agenda for Antiquity: Henry Fairfield Osborn & Vertebrate Paleontology at the American Museum of Natural History* (Tuscaloosa: University of Alabama Press, 1991).

72. TR to White, September 10, 1908, Box 28, White Papers, Library of Congress.

73. Wilhelm II to Roosevelt, November 12, 1908, Series 1B, Reel 309, TRP. For comment on the Willy-Teddy relationship see, Ragnhild Fiebig-von Hase, "The Uses of 'Friendship': The 'Personal Regime' of Wilhelm II and Theodore Roosevelt, 1901–1909." In Annika Mombauer and Wilhelm Diest, eds., *The Kaiser: New Research on Wilhelm II's Role in Imperial Germany* (Cambridge: Cambridge University Press, 2003), 143–75.

74. For example, in 1904 TR commented about the troubled Dominican Republic, over which he would promulgate his Roosevelt Corollary to the Monroe Doctrine, that he had "about the same desire to annex it as a gorged boa-constrictor might have to swallow a porcupine end-to." Porter, *Empire and Superempire*, 71.

75. TR to Taft, November 3, 10, 1908, Series 2, Reel 352, TRP.

76. Taft to TR, November 7, 1908, quoted in Lewis Gould, *Four Hats in the Ring: The 1912 Election and the Birth of Modern American Politics* (Lawrence, Kansas: University of Kansas Press, 2008), 3.

77. Taft to TR, February 1, 1909, Series 1, Reel 88, TRP.

78. November 5, 1908, in Abbott, *Letters of Archie Butt*, 156.

79. Cutwright, *Making of a Conservationist*, 231.

80. For the voyage, see Kenneth Wimmel, *Theodore Roosevelt and the Great White Fleet: American Sea Power Comes of Age* (Washington, DC: Brassey's, 1998); James R. Reckner, *Teddy Roosevelt's Great White Fleet* (Annapolis, Maryland: Naval Institute Press, 1988).

81. February 24, 1909, in Abbott, *Letters of Archie Butt*, 354–55.

82. TR to Lee, December 20, 1908, Series 2, Reel 353, TRP.

83. Butt, *Taft and Roosevelt*, I, 202.

84. TR to Reid, Series 3A, Reel 363, TRP.

85. TR to Taft, March 3, 1909, Series 2, Reel 354, TRP.

86. February 24, 1909, in Abbott, *Letters of Archie Butt*, 358.

87. March 22, 1909, in Butt, *Taft and Roosevelt*, 1: 27.

88. Muir to TR, March 11, 1909, Series 1, Reel 88, TRP.

89. Burroughs to TR, February 20, 1909, Series 1, Reel 88, TRP.

90. Morris, *Edith Kermit Roosevelt*, 347–48.

91. March 24, 1909, in Butt, *Taft and Roosevelt*, 1: 29.

92. February 1, 1909, in Abbott, *Letters of Archie Butt*, 323.

2   The Great Adventure Begins

1. Butt, *Taft and Roosevelt*, 1: 25–26.

2. Taft to TR, March 21, 1909, Series 1, Reel 88, TRP.

3. TR to Taft, March 23, 1910, in Morison, *Letters of Theodore Roosevelt*, 7: 3–4.

4. TR to Anna Roosevelt Cowles, April 13, 1909, bmsAm 1834, Theodore Roosevelt Collection, Houghton Library, Harvard University, hereafter TRC. Also in Anna Roosevelt Cowles, *Letters from Theodore Roosevelt to Anna Roosevelt Cowles 1870–1918* (New York: Charles Scribner's Sons, 1924), 277–78.

5. TR to Heller, October 24, 1908, Series 2, Reel 352, TRP.

6. Mearns to Mrs. Mearns, April 1, 1909, RU 7083, Box 1, Mearns Papers, Smithsonian Archive.

7. TR to Anna Roosevelt Cowles, April 13, 1909, bmsAm 1834, TRC.

8. Robinson, *My Brother Theodore Roosevelt*, 255.

9. Francis Warrington Dawson, *Opportunity and Theodore Roosevelt* (New York: Honest Truth Publishing Company, 1923), 52–53.

10. For Dawson's recollections, see Dawson, *Opportunity and Theodore Roosevelt*.

11. TR to Anna Roosevelt Cowles, April 13, 1909, bmsAm 1834, TRC.

12. Ethel Roosevelt to Kermit Roosevelt, nd, Box 4, Kermit Roosevelt Papers, Library of Congress; Patricia O'Toole, *When Trumpet's Call: Theodore Roosevelt After the White House* (New York: Simon & Schuster, 2005), 40.

13. TR to Corinne Roosevelt Robinson, April 14, 1909, bmsAm1540, TRC.

14. Mearns to Mrs. Mearns, April 21, 1909, RU 7083, Box 1, Mearns Papers, Smithsonian Archive.

15. Theodore Roosevelt, *African Game Trails: An Account of the African Wanderings of an American Hunter-Naturalist* (New York: Charles Scribner's Sons, 1910), 15.

16. For a list of the donors, see Roosevelt, *African Game Trails*, 20–21. For this weapon and the others he took to Africa, see Wilson, *Theodore Roosevelt Outdoorsman*.

17. TR to Robert Ferguson, January 17, 1909, Series 2, Reel 353, TRP.

18. TR to Buxton, January 27, 1909, Series 2, Reel 353, TRP.

19. Buxton to TR, February 10, 1910, Series 1, Reel 88.

20. Francis Warrington Dawson, "Hunting with Roosevelt in East Africa," *Hampton's Magazine* 23, 5 (November 1909), 595.

21. Roosevelt, *African Game Trails*, 86. In his review of *African Game Trails*, Sir Harry Johnston corrected TR's Swahili. According to Johnston, Kermit's nickname should have been spelled Malidadi, meaning a smart young man rather than simply a dandy. TR's Makumba meant tombs and should have been Mkubwa. "The Roosevelts in Africa," *The Outlook*, December 17, 1910, 864.

22. Roosevelt, *African Game Trails*, 23, 45.
23. Ibid., 23–26.
24. Roosevelt's 1909 Diary is in the Theodore Roosevelt Collection, Houghton Library, Harvard.
25. Roosevelt, *African Game Trails*, 27.
26. O'Toole, *When Trumpet's Call*, 50–51.
27. Roosevelt, *African Game Trails*, 27–29.
28. Ibid., 62.
29. Ibid., 78, 80.
30. Alex Johnston, *The Life and Letters of Sir Harry Johnston* (New York: Jonathan Cape, 1929), 266.
31. Corinne Roosevelt Robinson, "Foreword," in Edward H. Cotton, *The Ideals of Theodore Roosevelt* (New York: D. Appleton & Company, 1923), xi–xii.
32. Roosevelt, *African Game Trails*, 91–92, 104–5.
33. Mearns to Mrs. Mearns, May 21, 1909, RU 7083, Box 1, Mearns Papers, Smithsonian Archive.
34. TR to Lodge, May 15, 1909, in Morison, *Letters of Theodore Roosevelt*, 7: 10.
35. Lodge to TR, nd, in Henry Cabot Lodge, *Selections from the Correspondence of Theodore Roosevelt and Henry Cabot Lodge*, 2 vols. (New York: Charles Scribner's Sons, 1925), 2: 330.
36. Roosevelt, *African Game Trails*, 93–95.
37. Ibid., 100–102.
38. TR to Corinne Roosevelt Robinson, June 21, 1909, bmsAm1540, TRC.
39. TR to Foran, May 21, 1909, Series 4A, Reel 416, TRP.
40. Heller to Miller, June 3, 1909, RU 208, Box 52, Division of Mammals Records, National Museum of Natural History, Smithsonian Archive.
41. Roosevelt, *African Game Trails*, 123.
42. Ibid., 8.
43. For Churchill at the Colonial Office and his and the Liberal government's view of British East Africa, see Ronald Hyam, *Elgin and Churchill at the Colonial Office 1905–1908: The Watershed of the Empire-Commonwealth* (London: Macmillan, 1968).
44. TR to Trevelyan, October 1, 1911, Series 4A, Reel 416, TRP. When TR had visited England in 1910 he greatly amused the Trevelyan clan with his travel stories and promised to put them in a letter "for the eyes of only you and your family." His account, from Khartoum to London, also included asides such as this one concerning Churchill. For Sir George Otto, and this interesting family in general, see Laura Trevelyan, *A Very*

British Family: The Trevelyans and Their World (London: I. B. Tauris, 2006).

45. Winston Churchill, *My African Journey* (London: Hodder & Stoughton, 1908, Reprint: Holland Press, 1962), 31–41.

46. Roosevelt, *African Game Trails*, 131–32, 143.

47. Ibid., 132–33.

48. Ibid., 136.

49. Ibid., 146.

50. TR to Ethel Roosevelt, June 24, 1909, bmsAm1541.2, TRC.

51. TR to Anna Roosevelt Cowles, June 21, 1909, bmsAm 1834, TRC.

52. TR to Corinne Roosevelt Robinson, July 27, 1909, bmsAm1540, TRC.

53. Unfortunately, Edith destroyed almost all of her correspondence with her husband.

54. Frederick S. Wood, *Roosevelt As We Knew Him* (Philadelphia: John C. Winston Company, 1927), 213. TR replied to Lodge that there was bound to be dissatisfaction with any tariff bill and hoped this would die down in a few months, provided the bill was "fundamentally sound" and there was a "return of prosperity when once the tariffs are out of the way." TR to Lodge, May 15, 1909, in Morison, *Letters of Theodore Roosevelt*, 7: 9.

55. Thomas Gore of Oklahoma, on July 8, 1909, in Kenneth W. Heckler, *Insurgency: Personalities and Politics of the Taft Era* (New York: Russell & Russell Inc, 1964), 131.

56. Edith Roosevelt to Taft, June 25, 1909, Series 4A, Reel 322, Taft Papers.

57. TR to Root, May 17, 1909, Box 163, Elihu Root Papers, Library of Congress.

58. Roosevelt, *African Game Trails*, 184–85.

59. TR to White, July 21 1909, White Papers, Box 28, Library of Congress.

60. Jusserand to TR, July 24, 1909, Series 1, Reel 89, TRP.

61. "Long Attacks Roosevelt," *New York Times*, May 27, 1909.

62. TR to Bridges, July 17, 1909, in Morison, *Letters of Theodore Roosevelt*, 7: 20. Many safari books were published at the time in an attempt to take advantage of the TR frenzy at home. Most were generic and made no mention of Roosevelt, but several sensational titles interspersed accounts of TR with general information on Africa. These included John J. Mowbray, *Roosevelt's Marvelous Exploits in the Wilds of Africa* (New York: George W. Bertron, 1909); Frederick Seymour, *Roosevelt in Africa* (New York: D. B. McCurdy, 1909); and Marshall Everett, *Roosevelt's Thrilling Experiences in the Wilds of Africa Hunting Big Game* (New York: J. T. Moss, 1910). At least one book of satirical cartoons

joined the parade, Fletcher C. Ransom's *My Policies in Jungleland* (New York: Barse and Hopkins, 1910).

63. Roosevelt, *African Game Trails*, 186–87.
64. Dawson, *Opportunity and Theodore Roosevelt*, 108–9.
65. TR to Foran, July 15, 1909, Series 4A, Reel 416, TRP.
66. TR to Anna Roosevelt Cowles, July 27, 1909, bmsAm 1834, TRC.
67. Lodge to TR, June 21, 1909, in Lodge, *Correspondence of Theodore Roosevelt and Henry Cabot Lodge*, 2: 337.
68. TR to Lodge, July 26, 1909, in Morison, *Letters of Theodore Roosevelt*, 7: 22.
69. TR to Spring Rice, October 6, 1909, Series 4A, Reel 416, TRP.

3   A Lion Roars in East Africa

1. August 3, 1909, in Butt, *Taft and Roosevelt*, 1: 168; O'Toole, *When Trumpets Call*, 60.
2. bmsAm 1541.2, TRC.
3. TR to Ethel Roosevelt, September 26, 1909, bmsAm 1541.2, TRC.
4. Edith Roosevelt to Spring Rice, September 11, 1909, CASR 9/1, Spring Rice Papers, Churchill College Archive, Cambridge University.
5. Morris, *Edith Kermit Roosevelt*, 349–51; Edith Roosevelt to Spring Rice, December 17, 1909, CASR 9/1, Spring Rice Papers, Churchill College Archive, Cambridge University.
6. TR to Edith Roosevelt, bmsAm 1541.2, TRC.
7. *The Leader of British East Africa*, August 3, 1909.
8. September 10, 1909, in Morison, *Letters of Theodore Roosevelt*, 7: 31. The better known American novelist forced the Englishman, who badly needed the publishing cash, to add an S (for Spencer) to his name for literary purposes.
9. TR to Lodge, August 2, 1909, in Lodge, *Selections from the Correspondence of Theodore Roosevelt and Henry Cabot Lodge*, 2: 345.
10. August 17, 1909, in Butt, *Taft and Roosevelt*, 1: 178–79.
11. Roosevelt, *African Game Trails*, 203–4. Roosevelt's friends in the Society for the Preservation of the Wild Fauna of the Empire had been instrumental in this preservation effort.
12. Roosevelt, *African Game Trails*, 199.
13. Ibid., 197.
14. Ibid., 207–11.
15. Ibid., 212.
16. Ibid., 225.
17. Ibid., 266. For Burroughs's recollection of the gallop among the elk, see "Camping with President Roosevelt," *Atlantic* (May 1906).

18. Roosevelt, *African Game Trails*, 228–30.
19. Ibid., 231.
20. Ibid., 213–16.
21. TR to Lodge, September 10, 1909, in Lodge, *Correspondence of Theodore Roosevelt and Henry Cabot Lodge*, 2: 347.
22. Theodore Roosevelt, "Introduction" to Robert E. Peary, *The North Pole* (London: John Murray, 1910); TR to Peary, November 7, 1908, Series 2, Reel 352, TRP.
23. TR to Foran, September 12, 1909, Series 4A, Reel 416, TRP.
24. Roosevelt, *African Game Trails*, 249–51.
25. Ibid., 254–63.
26. October 17, 1909, in Morison, *Letters of Theodore Roosevelt*, 7: 37–38.
27. Roosevelt, *African Game Trails*, 283–87.
28. Mearns to Miller, November 5, 1909, RU 208, Box 52, National Museum of Natural History, Division of Mammals Records, Smithsonian Archive.
29. Carl Akeley, *In Brightest Africa* (New York: Garden City Publishing Company, 1920), 161.
30. Ibid., 162.
31. November 22, 1909, in Morison, *Letters of Theodore Roosevelt*, 7: 39.
32. Roosevelt, *African Game Trails*, 291.
33. Akeley, *In Brightest Africa*, 163.
34. Roosevelt, *African Game Trails*, 294–95.
35. Ibid., 296–97.
36. For this see James Penick, Jr., *Progressive Politics and Conservation: The Ballinger-Pinchot Affair* (Chicago: University of Chicago Press, 1968).
37. Thomas Ross, *Jonathan Prentiss Dolliver: A Study in Political Integrity and Independence* (Iowa City: State Historical Society of Iowa, 1958), 264.
38. Bacon to TR, September 3, 1909, Series 1, Reel 89, TRP.
39. TR to Pinchot, March 1, 1909, Series 2, Reel 354, TRP.
40. Ross, *Dolliver*, 267.
41. Taft to Helen Taft, October 18, 1909, Series 2, Reel 26, Taft Papers.
42. Ross, *Dolliver*, 266.
43. One read simply: "Taft is burning your soup. You had better come home." J. E. Forbes to TR, October 28, 1909, Series 1, Reel 89, TRP.
44. Butt, *Taft and Roosevelt*, 1: 269–70.
45. December 17, 1909, bmsAm 1834, TRC.
46. November 28, 1909, in Morris, *Edith Kermit Roosevelt*, 352. Some complained that the "Back from Elba" slogan was illogical as Napoleon had been almost immediately defeated and at least one newspaper letter

writer asserted that "Back From Egypt" would therefore be more accurate. However, as it turned out, "Back from Elba" was quite appropriate.

47. Worthington Ford, ed., *Letters of Henry Adams*, 2 vols. (New York: Charles Scribner's Sons, 1938), 2: 531.

48. Roosevelt, *African Game Trails*, 299–300.

49. For this see Elspeth Huxley, *White Man's Country: Lord Delamere and the Making of Kenya* (New York: Praeger, 1967) and more recently Kathryn Tidrick, *Empire and the English Character* (London: I. B. Tauris, 1990).

50. Roosevelt, *African Game Trails*, 300.

51. TR to Walcott, December 15, 1909, Box 52, RU 208, National Museum of Natural History Division of Mammals Records, Smithsonian Archive.

52. Excerpt from Girouad Papers, courtesy of Michael Smith, TRC subject files.

53. TR to Girouad, July 21, 1910, Series 3A, Reel 363, TRP. For Girouard, see Errol Trzebinski, *The Kenya Pioneers* (New York: W. W. Norton & Company, 1985). For a glowing appraisal of TR by Girouard, see Lawrence F. Abbott, *Impressions of Theodore Roosevelt* (Garden City, NY: Doubleday, Page & Company, 1919), 263.

54. October 6, 1909, in Morison, *Letters of Theodore Roosevelt*, 7: 32.

55. Delamere to TR, April 11, 1910, Series 1, Reel 90, TRP.

56. Huxley, *White Man's Country*, 251.

4   White Rhino and Giant Eland

1. Mearns to Mrs. Mearns, December 20, 1910, Box 1, RU7083, Mearns Papers, Smithsonian Archive; Roosevelt, *African Game Trails*, 309–10.

2. Roosevelt, *African Game Trails*, 315.

3. TR to Ethel Roosevelt, December 23, 1909, in Joan Paterson Kerr, *A Bully Father: Theodore Roosevelt's Letters to His Children* (New York: Random House, 1995), 244–45.

4. Roosevelt, *African Game Trails*, 313–14.

5. Ibid., 311–12.

6. Ibid.

7. TR to Lodge, January 1, 1910, in Lodge, *Selections from the Correspondence of Theodore Roosevelt and Henry Cabot Lodge*, 2: 355–56.

8. Roosevelt, *African Game Trails*, 335. The white rhino was also sometimes called the "square lipped" rhino.

9. Ibid., 336–37.

10. Ibid., 337–38.

11. Mark Sullivan. *Our Times*, 6 vols. (New York: Charles Scribner's Sons, 1939), 4: 394.
12. Morris, *Edith Kermit Roosevelt*, 356.
13. TR to Pinchot, January 17, 1910, in Morison, *Letters of Theodore Roosevelt*, 7: 45–46.
14. TR to Lodge, January 17, 1910, in Morison, *Letters of Theodore Roosevelt*, 7: 46.
15. Roosevelt, *African Game Trails*, 342–52.
16. TR to Anna Roosevelt Cowles, January 21, 1910, bmsAm 1834, TRC.
17. TR to Lodge, February 5, 1910, in Morison, *Letters of Theodore Roosevelt*, 7: 47.
18. Box 1, RU 7083, Mearns Papers, Smithsonian Archive.
19. Pinchot to TR, December 31, 1909, Series 1, Pinchot Papers, Library of Congress.
20. TR to Pinchot, March 1, 1910, in Morison, *Letters of Theodore Roosevelt*, 7: 50–51.
21. Swift to TR, March 4, 1910, Series 1, Reel 89, TRP.
22. TR to Lodge, January 8, 1910, in Lodge, *Correspondence of Theodore Roosevelt and Henry Cabot Lodge*, 2: 356.
23. Root to TR, February 11, 1910, Series 1, Reel 89, TRP.
24. The scientific value of the specimens was first revealed in papers written by Mearns, Heller and others published between 1910 and 1914 in the *Smithsonian Miscellaneous Collections*, 54, 56, 60, and 61. For further initial analysis, see also Ned Hollister, *East African Mammals in the United States National Museum* (Washington, DC: Smithsonian Institution Press, 1918–24).
25. For a list of the game shot by rifle, see Roosevelt, *African Game Trails*, 389–90. Also see TR's preliminary report to Walcott dated March 15, 1910 listing all the specimens, published in the 1910 *Annual Report of the Board of Regents of the Smithsonian Institution* (Washington, DC, 1911), 10.
26. Selous to TR, March 6, 1910, Series 1, Reel 90, TRP.
27. TR to Corinne Roosevelt Robinson, January 21, 1910, bmsAm 1540, TRC.
28. TR to Wingate, July 29, November 27, 1908, Series 3A, Reel 363, TRP. For Wingate's regime, see Gabriel Warburg, *The Sudan under Wingate: Administration in the Anglo-Egyptian Sudan 1899–1916* (London: Frank Cass, 1971).
29. TR to Sir George Otto Trevelyan, October 1, 1911, Series 3A, Reel 369, TRP.
30. "British Rule in Africa," Address Delivered at the Guildhall, London, May 31, 1910, in Theodore Roosevelt, *African and European Addresses* (New York: Charles Scribner's Sons, 1910), 163–66.

31. "Peace and Justice in the Sudan," in Roosevelt, *African and European Addresses*, 3–4.

32. TR to Lodge, January 15, 1910, in Lodge, *Correspondence of Theodore Roosevelt and Henry Cabot Lodge*, 2: 357.

5 Down the Nile: Khartoum to Cairo

1. John Callan O'Laughlin, *From the Jungle through Europe with Roosevelt* (Boston: Chapple Publishing Company, 1910), 29–31.

2. Jusserand to TR, March 22, 1910, Series 1, Reel 90, TRP.

3. The book's publication in 1895 helped swing British public opinion behind reoccupying the Sudan and a measured campaign for the purpose began the year after it appeared. *Fire and Sword* also gained Slatin the favor of Queen Victoria, who bestowed a rare knighthood on the foreigner, while the Khedive, the titular ruler of Egypt by leave of the Ottoman Sultan, made him a Pasha. For Slatin see Gordon Brook-Shepherd, *Between Two Flags: the Life of Baron Sir Rudolph von Slatin Pasha* (London, 1978) and for Wingate, see M. W. Daly, *The Sirdar: Sir Reginald Wingate and the British Empire in the Middle East* (Philadelphia: G. P. Putnam's Sons, 1997).

4. Morris, *Edith Kermit Roosevelt*, 353.

5. TR to Walcott, March 15, 1910, Box 49, RU 45, Records of the Office of the Secretary, National Museum of Natural History, Smithsonian Archive. Heller was appointed to undertake the final report.

6. TR to Tarlton, July 12, 1910, Series 3A, Reel 363, TRP.

7. TR to Walcott, March 15, 1910, Box 49, RU 45, Records of the Office of the Secretary, National Museum of Natural History, Smithsonian Archive.

8. Roosevelt, *African Game Trails*, 118, 388.

9. Theodore confided to his sister Anna that he was "simply driven to death now and would literally be unable to do anything at all" if the two had not signed on. He continued that it would mean "such an infinity of trouble and labor to them that if I were not quite shameless I should refuse to let them act." TR to Anna Roosevelt Cowles, March 19, 1910, bmsAm 1834, TRC.

10. Both men published records of their experiences. See O'Laughlin, *From the Jungle through Europe with Roosevelt* and Abbott, *Impressions of Theodore Roosevelt*. Abbot also wrote an introduction for and edited Roosevelt's *African and European Addresses*.

11. Roosevelt, *African Game Trails*, xxiv–xxv.

12. Abbot, *Impressions of Theodore Roosevelt*, 154–55.

13. TR to George Otto Trevelyan, October 1, 1911, Series 3A, Reel 369, TRP.
14. Cutwright, *Theodore Roosevelt: The Making of a Conservationist*, 42–50.
15. O'Laughlin, *From the Jungle through Europe with Roosevelt*, 49–54.
16. *The Times* (London), March 24, 1910.
17. O'Laughlin, *From the Jungle through Europe with Roosevelt*, 58–60.
18. Ibid., 61–63.
19. "Mr. Roosevelt In Egypt," *Outlook* 94 (April 30, 1910), 981.
20. Wingate to TR, March 30, 1910, Series 1, Reel 90, TRP.
21. For Gorst, see Peter Mellini, *Sir Eldon Gorst: The Overshadowed Proconsul* (Stanford: Hoover Institution Press, 1977).
22. The Earl of Cromer, *Modern Egypt*, 2 vols. (London: John Murray, 1908), 1: 5.
23. TR to Wingate, July 29, 1908, Series 3, Reel 363, TRP.
24. Roosevelt to White, April 2, 1910, Box 28, White Papers, Library of Congress.
25. TR to George Otto Trevelyan, October 1, 1911, Series 3A, Reel 369, TRP.
26. Ibid.
27. TR to Spring Rice, September 17, 1908, Series 4A, Reel 416, TRP.
28. TR to George Otto Trevelyan, October 1, 1911, Series 3A, Reel 369, TRP.
29. "Law and Order in Egypt," March 28, 1910, in Roosevelt, *African and European Addresses*, 15–16.
30. Ibid., 20–23.
31. Ibid., 24–26.
32. Ibid., 26–29.
33. *New York Times*, March 29, 1910.
34. Sheikh Ali Youssuf, "Egypt's Reply to Colonel Roosevelt," *North American Review* 191 (June 1910), 729–35.
35. Ibid., 735–37.
36. TR to George Otto Trevelyan, October 1, 1911, Series 3A, Reel 369, TRP.
37. Gorst to TR, March 26, 1910, Series 1, Reel 90, TRP.
38. Roosevelt to White, April 2, 1910, Box 28, White Papers, Library of Congress.
39. Gorst to Arthur Hardinge, April 1, 1910, in Mellini, *Gorst*, 214.
40. Wingate to Gilbert Clayton, March 29, 1910, in Mellini, *Gorst*, 214.
41. Roosevelt to Reid, March 24, 1910, Series 1, Reel 90, TRP.
42. Taft to Carnegie, December 25, 1909, Volume 172, Carnegie Papers, Library of Congress.
43. TR to Carnegie, February 18, 1910, Volume 174, Carnegie Papers, Library of Congress.

44. TR to Carnegie, October 16, 1909, Volume 170, Carnegie Papers, Library of Congress.
45. TR to Carnegie, December 14, 1909, Volume 172, Carnegie Papers, Library of Congress.
46. Root to TR, February 11, 1910, Series 1, Reel 89, TRP.
47. Ibid.
48. Ibid.
49. TR to Carnegie, March 14, 1910, Volume 175, Carnegie Papers, Library of Congress.
50. Roosevelt to Lodge, April 6, 1910, Series 1, Reel 90, TRP.

6 European Whirl

1. Quoted in Arnaldo Testi, "The Gender of Reform Politics: Theodore Roosevelt and the Culture of Masculinity," *The Journal of American History* 81, 4 (March 1995), 1513.
2. TR to George Otto Trevelyan, October 1, 1911, Series 3A, Reel 369, TRP.
3. Ibid.
4. Ibid. For O'Laughlin's lengthy account of the affair, see *From the Jungle through Europe with Roosevelt*, 72–94.
5. For this see Abbott, *Impressions of Theodore Roosevelt*, 216–17.
6. TR to Lee, April 5, 1910, Series 3A, Reel 363, TRP.
7. TR to George Otto Trevelyan, October 1, 1911, Series 3A, Reel 369, TRP.
8. Leishman to TR, March 15, 1910, Series 1, Reel 89, TRP.
9. Quoted in Testi, "The Gender of Reform Politics," 1513–14.
10. TR to George Otto Trevelyan, October 1, 1911, Series 3A, Reel 369, TRP.
11. Ibid.
12. *Washington Post*, March 23, 1910.
13. Roosevelt to Lodge, April 6, 1910, in Morrison, *Letters of Theodore Roosevelt*, 7: 67–68.
14. O'Laughlin, *From the Jungle through Europe with Roosevelt*, 97–98.
15. *New York Evening Post*, March 22, 1910.
16. Gifford Pinchot, *Breaking New Ground* (New York, 1947; Reprint 1972), 502.
17. Pinchot to Garfield, April 27, 1910, Pinchot Papers, Library of Congress.
18. For example, see Beveridge to Pinchot, March 24, 1910, Series 1, Reel 90, TRP.

19. Ross, *Dolliver*, 272–73.
20. *New York Times*, April 12, 1910.
21. Roosevelt to Lodge, April 11, 1910, in Morrison, *Letters of Theodore Roosevelt*, 7: 73; Morris, *Edith Kermit Roosevelt*, 356.
22. Quoted in O'Laughlin, *From the Jungle through Europe with Roosevelt*, 101.
23. TR to David Gray, October 5, 1911, Series 3A, Reel 369, TRP.
24. TR to George Otto Trevelyan, October 1, 1911, Series 3A, Reel 369, TRP.
25. Ibid.
26. Ibid.
27. O'Laughlin, *From the Jungle through Europe with Roosevelt*, 110–15. In TR's estimation, Apponyi was a "really fine fellow" who Roosevelt had met in Washington six years before when he had been one of the Inter-Parliamentary Peace Conference delegates.
28. Roosevelt to Bacon, April 5, 1910, Series 3A, Reel 363, TRP.
29. Jusserand to TR, May 10, 1910, Series 1, Reel 91, TRP.
30. TR to George Otto Trevelyan, October 1, 1911, Series 3A, Reel 369, TRP.
31. Jusserand to TR, December 25, 1909, Series 1, Reel 89, TRP.
32. Roosevelt to Bacon, April 5, 1910, Series 3A, Reel 363, TRP.
33. "Citizenship in a Republic," An Address Delivered at the Sorbonne, Paris, April 23, 1910, in Theodore Roosevelt, *African and European Addresses*, 31–41.
34. Ibid., 42–44.
35. Ibid., 55–60.
36. TR to George Otto Trevelyan, October 1, 1911, Series 3A, Reel 369, TRP.
37. Jusserand to TR, May 10, 1910, Series 1, Reel 91, TRP.
38. TR to George Otto Trevelyan, October 1, 1911, Series 3A, Reel 369, TRP.
39. TR to Carnegie, April 22, 1910, Volume 176, Carnegie Papers, Library of Congress.
40. TR to George Otto Trevelyan, October 1, 1911, Series 3A, Reel 369, TRP.
41. Lodge to TR, July 26, 1908, in Lodge, *Selections from the Correspondence of Henry Cabot Lodge and Theodore Roosevelt*, 309.
42. TR to George Otto Trevelyan, October 1, 1911, Series 3A, Reel 369, TRP.
43. Viscount Lee of Fareham, *"A Good Innings and a Great Partnership: Being the Life Story of Arthur and Ruth Lee,"* 3 vols. (Privately Printed, 1939), 1: 418.

44. *Algemeen Hardlsblad*, April 30, 1910, quoted in *Sayings of Social Wisdom by Theodore Roosevelt* (The Hague, 1910), 7.

45. Abbott, *Impressions of Theodore Roosevelt*, 239.

46. TR to George Otto Trevelyan, October 1, 1911, Series 3A, Reel 369, TRP.

47. Ibid.

48. Roosevelt to Lodge, May 5, 1910, in Morrison, *Letters of Theodore Roosevelt*, 7: 80.

7   Peace Emissary

1. Roosevelt to Lodge, May 5, 1910, in Morison, *Letters of Theodore Roosevelt*, 7: 81.

2. TR to George Otto Trevelyan, October 1, 1911, Series 3A, Reel 369, TRP.

3. Ibid.

4. Roosevelt, *African and European Addresses*, 78–83.

5. Carnegie to Hill, June 12, 1907, in Burton J. Hendrick, *The Life of Andrew Carnegie*, 2 vols. (New York: Doubleday, Doran & Company, 1932), 2: 299.

6. Carnegie to TR, February 14, 1907, in Hendrick, *Andrew Carnegie*, 2: 310.

7. Carnegie to Tower, January 23, 1907, in Hendrick, *Andrew Carnegie*, 2: 311.

8. Hendrick, *Andrew Carnegie*, 2: 314–15.

9. Cecil, *Wilhelm II*, 1: 137.

10. November 19, 1908, in Abbott, *Letters of Archie Butt*, 184.

11. August 26, 1908, Transcript of Hale Interview, Northcliffe Add. Ms 62299, British Library.

12. TR to Lee, October 17, 1908, Series 2, Reel 351, TRP; Oscar King Davis, *Released for Publication: Some Inside Political History of Theodore Roosevelt and His Times* (Boston: Houghton, Mifflin, 1925), 81; B. L. Raymond Esthus, *Theodore Roosevelt and the International Rivalries* (Waltham, MA: Ginn Blaisdell, 1970), 126–30.

13. Davis, *Released for Publication*, 82.

14. Ibid., 83–85, Though TR helped keep it out of the *Times*, an excerpt was printed in the November 22, 1908, *New York World*.

15. TR to Lee, October 17, 1908, Series 2, Reel 351, TRP.

16. Root to Carnegie, April 3, 1909, Volume 164, Carnegie Papers, Library of Congress.

17. TR to George Otto Trevelyan, October 1, 1911, Series 3A, Reel 369, TRP.

18. For the latest judgment on their relations, see David Fromkin, *The King and the Cowboy: Theodore Roosevelt and Edward the Seventh, Secret Partners* (New York: Penguin, 2008).

19. Spring Rice to TR, CASR 9/1, Spring Rice Papers, Churchill College Archive, Cambridge.

20. TR to George Otto Trevelyan, October 1, 1911, Series 3A, Reel 369, TRP.

21. Ibid.

22. For comment on the Willy-Teddy relationship which includes the 1910 trip see, Ragnhild Fiebig-von Hase, "The Uses of 'Friendship': The 'Personal Regime' of Wilhelm II and Theodore Roosevelt, 1901–1909," in Annika Mombauer and Wilhelm Diest, eds., *The Kaiser: New Research on Wilhelm II's role Imperial Germany* (Cambridge: Cambridge University Press, 2003), 143–75.

23. Viscount Lee of Fareham, *"A Good Innings,"* 1: 418.

24. Abbott, *Impressions of Theodore Roosevelt*, 248–51.

25. TR to George Otto Trevelyan, October 1, 1911, Series 3A, Reel 369, TRP.

26. Henry Pringle, *Theodore Roosevelt: A Biography* (New York: Harcourt, Brace & World, 1931), 365.

27. TR to George Otto Trevelyan, October 1, 1911, Series 3A, Reel 369, TRP.

28. Ibid.

29. Ibid.

30. Ibid.

31. Ibid.

32. Ibid.

33. Ibid.

34. Roosevelt, *African and European Addresses*, xxviii–xxix.

35. Roosevelt, *Literary Essays*, 61–70.

36. Ibid., 70–71.

37. Ibid., 71–72.

38. Ibid., 72–81.

39. Ibid., 81–84.

40. TR to George Otto Trevelyan, October 1, 1911, Series 3A, Reel 369, TRP.

41. Ibid.

42. Butt, *Taft and Roosevelt*, 1: 348.

8   Last Rites: England

1. The Park Lane house was pulled down in the 1920s to make way for the Dorchester Hotel.

2. TR to David Gray, October 5, 1911, Series 3A, Reel 369, TRP. This long account of the English visit was composed, TR wrote Gray, "to meet the request you so solemnly made 'In the name of the Gods of Mirth and Truth.'" Gray was a New York lawyer and journalist whom TR had known for some time. Roosevelt said of him, "I always find something companionable in a man who cares both for the outside of a horse and the inside of a book." TR to Kermit Roosevelt, Series 2, Reel 349, TRP.

3. Robert Wynne to TR, May 6, 1910, Series 1, Reel 91, TRP.

4. TR to David Gray, October 5, 1911, Series 3A, Reel 369, TRP.

5. Ibid. TR described Cromer as "the most wonderful personality he had ever met." Allan Nevins, *Henry White: Thirty Years of American Diplomacy* (New York: Harper & Brothers, 1930), 302.

6. TR to David Gray, October 5, 1911, Series 3A, Reel 369, TRP.

7. Ibid. Arthur Lee, who served in Lloyd George's Cabinet during World War I, arranged a meeting and recalled that TR said of the Welshman, "That man is by far the most interesting, and I should say the most dangerous, of all your politicians. He is an incalculable force for the future." *"A Good Innings,"* 1: 427–8.

8. *Daily News*, May 13, 1910.

9. Carnegie to TR, May 13, 1910, Series 1, Reel 91, TRP.

10. Carnegie to TR, May 14, 1910, Series 1, Reel 91, TRP.

11. Reid to TR, May 10, 1910, Series 1, Reel 91, TRP.

12. TR to David Gray, October 5, 1911, Series 3A, Reel 369, TRP.

13. Ibid. The young man in question was the grandson of George V, King of Hanover, who was dethroned in 1866 when Prussia took control of the state. From the arrival of George I until 1837, when Queen Victoria took the British throne, the Kings of England had also ruled Hanover. Its Salic Law, however, did not allow a woman to inherit and Hanover was divided from the English crown. Thirty-three years later it became part of the new German Empire.

14. TR to David Gray, October 5, 1911, Series 3A, Reel 369, TRP.

15. Kenneth Rose, *King George V* (London: Frank Cass, 1984), 76–7.

16. May 25, 1910 Diary, ESHR 2/12, Esher Papers, Churchill College Archive, Cambridge. The royal insider Lord Esher also recorded that, three days after the funeral, at Wilhelm's request, the two had spent forty minutes "clambering over the Queen's memorial" in front of Buckingham Palace, in very TR-like fashion.

17. TR to David Gray, October 5, 1911, Series 3A, Reel 369, TRP.

18. Ibid.

19. Pringle, *Theodore Roosevelt*, 370.

20. Butt, *Taft and Roosevelt*, 1: 428–29.

21. Lee, *"A Good Innings,"* 1: 421.
22. Lee to TR, July 7, 1910, Series 1, Reel 92, TRP.
23. Lee, *"A Good Innings,"* 1: 421.
24. TR to David Gray, October 5, 1911, Series 3A, Reel 369, TRP. For the latest judgment on Balfour, see R. J. Q. Adams, *Balfour: The Last Grandee* (London: John Murray, 2007). The sportsman Lyttelton, considered one of the most handsome men of his generation, had been colonial secretary under Balfour and was equally sympathetic with TR's view of Britain's imperial responsibilities. The same was true of the witty and charming Fred Oliver, the "gentleman draper" and noted biographer of Alexander Hamilton who used the fortune he made at Debenham and Freebody in support of imperial causes.
25. Lee, *"A Good Innings,"* 1: 422.
26. Morris, *Edith Kermit Roosevelt*, 360.
27. Lee to TR, July 7, 1910, Series 1, Reel 92, TRP.
28. TR to David Gray, October 5, 1911, Series 3A, Reel 369, TRP.
29. Ibid.
30. "Conditions of Success," An Address at the Cambridge Union, May 26, 1910, in Roosevelt, *African and European Addresses*, 143–54.
31. To aid his preparation, Whitelaw Reid had sent TR previous addresses by Wilhelm II and President Grant.
32. "British Rule in Africa," Address Delivered at the Guildhall, London, May 31, 1910, in Roosevelt, *African and European Addresses*, 157–60.
33. Ibid., 160–63.
34. Ibid., 163.
35. Ibid., 163–66.
36. Ibid., 167–69.
37. Ibid., 169–70.
38. Ibid., 171–72.
39. Lee, *"A Good Innings,"* 1: 425–26. Ruth Lee recorded in her diary that "T. R. moved and spoke with great dignity and with astonishing courage and reality. He looked so young too, and so tousle-headed in spite of the fact that Arthur had brushed his hair most carefully for him before starting from Chesterfield Street."
40. Morley to Carnegie, June 19, 1910, Volume 177, Carnegie Papers, Library of Congress.
41. *Daily News*, June 1, 1910.
42. Whitelaw Reid reported to the U.S. secretary of state, Philander Knox, that he knew confidentially that Grey was equally pleased, but "under more necessity to conceal it" and was sure to take up the same line in the House of Commons when the subject came up. In fact he thought Grey would have been happy to have had the opportunity to "say the

same thing first"; but since he didn't Reid believed he was glad "to have such a powerful impression made in advance on the public mind by way of preparation for the Government's approaching change of attitude." Quoted in Royal Cortissoz, *The Life of Whitelaw Reid*, 2 vols. (New York: Charles Scribner's Sons, 1921), 2: 417–18.

43. Quoted in Abbott, *Impressions of Roosevelt*, 159–60.
44. Mellini, *Gorst*, n. 73, 292.
45. Mellini, *Gorst*, 215–16.
46. G. M. Trevelyan to Spring Rice, CASR 1/22, Spring Rice Papers, Churchill College Archive, Cambridge.
47. Quoted in O'Laughlin, *From the Jungle through Europe with Roosevelt*, 170.
48. "Biological Analogies in History," in Roosevelt, *Literary Essays*, 55–56.
49. Ibid., 57–59.
50. Osborn, *Impressions of Great Naturalists*, 265.
51. TR to Sir Martin Conway, November 6, 1908, Series 2, Reel 352, TRP.
52. Reid to Mrs. Taft, June 10, 1910, in David R. Contosta and Jessica R. Hawthorne, eds., *Rise to World Power: Selected Letters of Whitelaw Reid 1895–1912* (Philadelphia: American Philosophical Society, 1986), 147.
53. TR to David Gray, October 5, 1911, Series 3A, Reel 369, TRP.
54. These are listed in TR's published account, "English Song Birds," *The Outlook*, July 23, 1910.
55. Address at Harvard University, 8 December 1919.
56. Morris, *Edith Kermit Roosevelt*, 360.
57. TR to David Gray, October 5, 1911, Series 3A, Reel 369, TRP.
58. Lee, *"A Good Innings,"* 1939), 1: 428.
59. Taft to TR, May 26, 1910, Series 1, Reel 91, TRP.
60. TR to Taft, June 8, 1910, in Morison, *Letters of Theodore Roosevelt*, 7: 88–89.

9   The Old Lion Is Dead: Epilogue and Dramatis Personae

1. Abbott, *Letters of Archie Butt*, 374–75.
2. For this, see Candice Millard, *River of Doubt: Theodore Roosevelt's Darkest Journey* (New York: Doubleday, 2005).
3. Osborn, *Impressions of Great Naturalists*, 269. The scientific value of the specimens is also revealed in papers written by Mearns, Heller and others published between 1910 and 1914 in the *Smithsonian Miscellaneous Collections*, 54, 56, 60 and 61. For further analysis, see also Ned Hollister, *East African Mammals in the United States National Museum* (Washington, DC: Smithsonian Institution Press, 1918–24).

4. The latest edition was published in 2001 by the Cooper Square Press with an introduction by the TR biographer H. W. Brands.

5. "The Roosevelts in Africa," *The Outlook*, December 17, 1910, 865.

6. *New York Times*, February 7, 1913.

7. Sydney Brooks, "What Europe Thinks of Roosevelt," *McClure's Magazine* 35, 5 (July 1910), 271–72.

8. Curzon to TR, June 28, 1910, Series 1, Reel 92, TRP.

9. TR to David Gray, October 5, 1911, Series 3A, Reel 369, TRP.

10. Betty Boyd Caroli, *The Roosevelt Women* (New York: Basic Books, 1998), 356.

11. Michael Teague, *Mrs. L: Conversations with Alice Roosevelt Longworth* (New York: Doubleday & Company, 1981), 150.

12. For this see Larry L. Fabian, *Andrew Carnegie's Peace Endowment: The Tycoon, The President, and Their Bargain of 1910* (Washington, DC: Carnegie Endowment for Peace, 1985).

13. Peter Krass, *Carnegie* (Hoboken, NJ: John Wiley & Sons, 2002), 514.

14. *"A Good Innings,"* 1: 427–28.

15. Miller, *Gifford Pinchot and the Making of Modern Environmentalism*, 247.

Selected Bibliography

Primary Sources

Manuscript Collections Consulted

Asquith Papers, Bodleian Library, Oxford University
Balfour Papers, British Library, London
Campbell-Bannerman Papers, British Library, London
Carnegie Papers, Library of Congress
Churchill Papers, Churchill College Archive, Cambridge
Cromer Papers, National Archive and Private Collection, London
Curzon Papers, British Library, Asia, Pacific and Africa Collections, London
James R. Garfield Papers, Library of Congress
Harcourt Papers, Bodleian Library, Oxford
Heller Papers, Smithsonian Archive
Kitchener Papers, National Archive, Kew
Lloyd George Papers, Parliamentary Record Office, London
Lord Lee of Fareham Papers, Courtauld Institute, London
Loring Papers, Smithsonian Archive
Mearns Papers, Smithsonian Archive
Morley Papers, British Library, Asia, Pacific and Africa Collections, London
National Museum of Natural History, Division of Mammals Papers, Smithsonian Archive
National Zoological Park Papers, Smithsonian Archive
Northcliffe Papers, British Library, London
Office of the Secretary Papers, Smithsonian Institution, Smithsonian Archive
O'Laughlin Papers, Library of Congress
Pinchot Papers, Library of Congress
Riddell Diaries, British Library, London

Roberts Papers, National Army Museum, London
Kermit Roosevelt Papers, Library of Congress
Theodore Roosevelt Papers, Library of Congress, Harvard University, Smithsonian Archive
Root Papers, Library of Congress
Spring Rice Papers, Churchill College Archive, Cambridge University
Strachey Papers, Parliamentary Record Office, London
Oscar Straus Papers, Library of Congress
Taft Papers, Library of Congress
Walcott Papers, Smithsonian Archive
White Papers, Library of Congress
Wister Papers, Library of Congress

Newspapers and Periodicals

Daily Mail (London)
Daily News (London)
Evening News (London)
The Globe (London)
The Gownsman (Cambridge)
The Leader of British East Africa (Nairobi)
The National Review (London)
The New York Evening Post
The New York Times
The New York World
The North American Review
The Spectator (London)
The Times (London)
The Washington Post

Collections of Printed Primary Documents

Abbott, Lawrence, ed. *The Letters of Archie Butt: Personal Aide to President Roosevelt.* Garden City, NY: Doubleday, Page & Company, 1924.
Brett, Maurice, ed. *Journals and Letters of Reginald Viscount Esher.* London: Ivor Nicholson & Watson Limited, 1938.
Butt, Archibald. *Taft and Roosevelt: The Intimate Letters of Archie Butt Military Aide.* 2 vols. Garden City, NY: Doubleday, Doran & Company, 1930.
Clark, Alan, ed. *"A Good Innings": The Private Papers of Viscount Lee of Fareham.* London: John Murray, 1974.

Contosta, David, R. and Jessica R. Hawthorne, eds. *Rise to World Power: Selected Letters of Whitelaw Reid 1895–1912*. Philadelphia: American Philosophical Society, 1986.

Cowles, Anna Roosevelt. *Letters from Theodore Roosevelt to Anna Roosevelt Cowles 1870–1918*. New York: Charles Scribner's Sons, 1924.

Ford, Worthington Chauncey, ed. *Letters of Henry Adams*. 2 vols. Boston: Houghton Mifflin, 1930–38.

Kerr, Joan Paterson. *A Bully Father: Theodore Roosevelt's Letters to His Children*. New York: Random House, 1995.

Lodge, Henry Cabot. *Selections from the Correspondence of Theodore Roosevelt and Henry Cabot Lodge*. 2 vols. New York: Charles Scribner's Sons, 1925.

Morison, Elting, ed. *The Letters of Theodore Roosevelt*. Vols. VI and VII. Cambridge, MA: Harvard University Press, 1952, 1954.

Roosevelt, Theodore. *African and European Addresses*. New York: Charles Scribner's Sons, 1910.

———. *Literary Essays*. New York: Charles Scribner's Sons, 1926.

Vincent, John. *The Crawford Papers: The Journals of David Lindsay, Twenty-Seventh Earl of Crawford and Tenth Earl Balcarres 1871–1940 during the Years 1892–1940*. Manchester: Manchester University Press, 1984.

Memoirs and Autobiographies

Abbott, Lawrence F. *Impressions of Theodore Roosevelt*. Garden City, NY: Doubleday, Page & Company, 1919.

Akeley, Carl. *In Brightest Africa*. Garden City, NY: Garden City Publishing, 1920.

Asquith, Herbert Henry. *Memories and Reflections 1852–1927*. Boston: Little, Brown, 1928.

Burroughs, John. *Camping and Tramping with Roosevelt*. New York: Charles Scribner's Sons, 1907.

Buxton, Edward North. *Two African Trips*. London: Edward Stanford, 1902.

Churchill, Winston. *My African Journey*. London: Hodder and Stoughtom, 1908. Reprint: Holland Press, 1962.

Cromer, Lord. *Modern Egypt*. 2 vols. London: John Murray, 1908.

Davis, Oscar King. *Released for Publication: Some Inside Political History of Theodore Roosevelt and His Times*. Boston: Houghton Mifflin, 1925.

Dawson, Francis Warington. *Opportunity and Theodore Roosevelt*. New York: Honest Truth Publishing Company, 1923.

Johnston, Sir Harry. *The Story of My Life*. Indianapolis: Bobs-Merrill Company, 1923.

Lee of Fareham, Viscount. *"A Good Innings and a Great Partnership: Being the Life Story of Arthur and Ruth Lee."* 3 vols. Privately Printed, 1939.

O'Laughlin, John Callan. *From the Jungle through Europe with Roosevelt.* Boston: Chapple Publishing Company, 1910.

Peary, Robert E. *The North Pole.* London: John Murray, 1910.

Pinchot, Gifford. *Breaking New Ground.* New York: Harcourt, Brace, 1947.

Robinson, Corinne Roosevelt. *My Brother Theodore Roosevelt.* New York: Charles Scribner's Sons, 1921.

Roosevelt, Kermit. *The Happy Hunting-Grounds.* New York: Charles Scribner's Sons, 1920.

Roosevelt, Theodore. *African Game Trails: An Account of the African Wanderings of an American Hunter-Naturalist.* New York: Charles Scribner's Sons, 1910.

Selous, Frederick Courtenay. *African Nature Notes and Reminiscences.* London: Macmillan, 1908.

Sullivan, Mark. *Our Times.* 6 vols. New York: Charles Scribner's Sons, 1939.

Wood, Frederick S. *Roosevelt As We Knew Him.* Philadelphia: John C. Winston Company, 1927.

Secondary Works

Books

Adams, R. J. Q. *Balfour: The Last Grandee.* London: John Murray, 2007.

Beinart, William and Peter Coates, *Environment and History: The Taming of Nature in the USA and South Africa.* London: Routledge, 1995.

Brinkley, Douglas. *The Wilderness Warrior: Theodore Roosevelt and the Crusade for America.* New York: HarperCollins, 2009.

Brook-Shepherd, Gordon. *Between Two Flags: The Life of Baron Sir Rudolph von Slatin Pasha.* New York: G. P. Putnam's Sons, 1978.

Burton, David. *Taft, Roosevelt and the Limits of Friendship.* Madison, NJ: Fairleigh Dickinson University Press, 2005.

Caroli, Betty Boyd. *The Roosevelt Women.* New York: Basic Books, 1998.

Cecil, Lamar. *Wilhelm II.* 2 vols. Chapel Hill: University of North Carolina Press, 1996.

Cortissoz, Royal. *The Life of Whitelaw Reid.* 2 vols. New York: Charles Scribner's Sons, 1921.

Cotton, Edward H. *The Ideals of Theodore Roosevelt.* New York: D. Appleton and Company, 1923.

Cutwright, Paul. *Theodore Roosevelt: The Making of a Conservationist.* Urbana: University of Illinois Press, 1985.

Daly, M. W. *The Sirdar: Sir Reginald Wingate and the British Empire in the Middle East.* Philadelphia: American Philosophical Society, 1997.

Dyer, Thomas. *Theodore Roosevelt and the Idea of Race.* Baton Rouge: Louisiana State University Press, 1980.

Esthus, Raymond. *Theodore Roosevelt and the International Rivalries.* Waltham, MA: Ginn-Blaisdell, 1970.

Everett, Marshall. *Roosevelt's Thrilling Experiences in the Wilds of Africa Hunting Big Game.* New York: J. T. Moss, 1909.

Fabian, Larry L. *Andrew Carnegie's Peace Endowment: The Tycoon, the President and Their Bargain of 1910.* Washington, DC: Carnegie Endowment for Peace, 1985.

Fitter, Richard and Sir Peter Scott. *The Penitent Butchers: The Fauna Preservation Society 1903–1978.* London: Collins, 1978.

Fox, Stephen. *John Muir and His Legacy: The American Conservation Movement.* Boston: Little, Brown, 1981.

Fraser, Peter. *Lord Esher: A Political Biography.* London: Hart-Davis, MacGibbon, 1973.

Fromkin, David. *The King and the Cowboy: Theodore Roosevelt and Edward the Seventh, Secret Partners.* New York: Penguin, 2008.

Gardner, Joseph L. *Departing Glory; Theodore Roosevelt as Ex-President.* New York: Charles Scribner's Sons, 1973.

Gilmour, David. *Curzon.* London: John Murray, 1994.

———. *The Long Recessional: The Imperial Life of Rudyard Kipling.* London: John Murray, 2002.

Gould, Lewis. *Four Hats in the Ring: The 1912 Election and the Birth of Modern American Politics.* Lawrence: University of Kansas Press, 2008.

Grigg, John. *Lloyd George: The People's Champion, 1902–1911.* London: Eyre Methuen, 1978.

Hechler, Kenneth W. *Insurgency: Personalities and the Politics of the Taft Era.* New York: Russell & Russell Inc., 1964.

Hendrick, Burton J. *The Life of Andrew Carnegie.* 2 vols. Garden City, NY: Doubleday, Doran and Co., 1932.

Herman, Daniel Justin. *Hunting and the American Imagination.* Washington, DC: Smithsonian Institution Press, 2001.

Herwig, Holger. *Germany's Vision of Empire in Venezuela 1871–1914.* Princeton: Princeton University Press, 1986.

Hoyt, Edwin P. *Teddy Roosevelt in Africa.* New York: Duell, Sloan and Pearce, 1966.

Huxley, Elspeth. *White Man's Country: Lord Delamere and the Making of Kenya.* New York: Praeger, 1967.

Hyam, Ronald. *Elgin and Churchill at the Colonial Office 1905–1908: The Watershed of the Empire-Commonwealth.* London: Macmillan, 1968.

Jackson, Patrick. *Harcourt and Son: A Political Biography of Sir William Harcourt, 1827–1904.* Madison, NJ: Fairleigh Dickinson University Press, 2004.

James, David. *Lord Roberts.* London; Hollis & Carter, 1956.

Johnston, Alex. *The Life and Letters of Sir Harry Johnston.* New York: Jonathan Cape, 1929.

Judd, Denis. *Balfour and the British Empire: A Study in Imperial Evolution.* London: Macmillan, 1968.

Juergens, George. *News from the White House: The Presidential-Press Relationship in the Progressive Era.* Chicago: University of Chicago Press, 1981.

Krass, Peter. *Carnegie.* Hoboken, NJ: John Wiley and Sons, 2002.

Lansford, Tom. *A "Bully" First Lady: Edith Kermit Roosevelt.* Huntington, NY: Nova History Publications, 2001.

Mackenzie, John M. *The Empire of Nature: Hunting, Conservation and British Imperialism.* Manchester: Manchester University Press, 1982.

Matthew, H. C. G. *The Liberal Imperialists: The Ideas and Politics of a Post-Gladstonian Elite.* Oxford: Oxford University Press, 1973.

Mellini, Peter. *Sir Eldon Gorst: The Overshadowed Proconsul.* Stanford: Hoover Institution Press, 1975.

Miller, Char. *Gifford Pinchot and the Making of Modern Environmentalism.* Washington: Island Press, 2001.

Mombauer, Annika and Wilhelm Diest, eds. *The Kaiser: New Research on Wilhelm II's Role in Imperial Germany.* Cambridge: Cambridge University Press, 2003.

Monsman, Gerald. *H. Rider Haggard on the Imperial Frontier.* Greensboro, NC: ELT Press, 2006.

Morris, Edmund. *Theodore Rex.* New York: Random House, 2001.

Morris, Sylvia Jukes. *Edith Kermit Roosevelt: Portrait of a First Lady.* New York: Coward, McCann & Geoghegan, 1980.

Mowbray, John J. *Roosevelt's Marvelous Exploits in the Wilds of Africa.* New York: George W. Bertron, 1909.

Naylor, Natalie, Douglas Brinkley, and John Allen Gable, eds. *Theodore Roosevelt: Many-Sided American.* Interlaken, NY: Heart of Lakes Publishing, 1992.

Nevins, Allan. *Henry White: Thirty Years of American Diplomacy.* New York: Harper & Brothers, 1930.

Oliver, Roland. *Sir Harry Johnston & the Scramble for Africa.* London: Chatto & Windus, 1964.

Osborn, Henry Fairfield. *Impressions of Great Naturalists.* New York: Charles Scribner's Sons, 1928.

O'Toole, Patricia. *When Trumpet's Call: Theodore Roosevelt after the White House.* New York: Simon & Schuster, 2005.

Owen, Roger. *Lord Cromer: Victorian Imperialist, Edwardian Proconsul.* Oxford: Oxford University Press, 2004.

Patterson, David. *Towards a Warless World: The Travail of the American Peace Movement 1887–1914.* London: Routledge, 1976.

Penick, James Jr. *Progressive Politics and Conservation: The Ballinger-Pinchot Affair.* Chicago: University of Chicago Press, 1968.

Ponder, Stephen. *Managing the Press: Origins of the Media Presidency, 1897–1933.* New York: St Martin's Press, 1998.

Porter, Bernard. *Empire and Superempire: Britain, America and the World.* New Haven: Yale University Press, 2006.

Pringle, Henry. *Theodore Roosevelt: A Biography.* New York: Harcourt, Brace and World, 1931.

Rainger, Ronald. *An Agenda for Antiquity: Henry Fairfield Osborn & Vertebrate Paleontology at the American Museum of Natural History.* Tuscaloosa: University of Alabama Press, 1991.

Ransom, Fletcher C. *My Policies in Jungleland.* New York: Barse and Hopkins, 1910.

Reckner, James R. *Teddy Roosevelt's Great White Fleet.* Annapolis, MD: Naval Institute Press, 1988.

Reiger, John F. *American Sportsmen and the Origins of Conservation.* New York: Winchester Press, 1975.

Renehan, Edward J. *John Burroughs: An American Naturalist.* Post Mills, VT: Chelsea Green Publishing, 1992.

Roberts, Andrew. *A History of the English-Speaking Peoples since 1900.* London: HarperCollins, 2006.

Rose, Kenneth. *King George V.* London: Frank Cass, 1984.

Ross, Thomas Richard. *Jonathan Prentiss Dolliver: A Study in Political Integrity and Independence.* Iowa City: State Historical Society of Iowa, 1958.

Seymour, Frederick. *Roosevelt in Africa.* New York: D. B. McCurdy, 1909.

Taylor, Stephen. *The Mighty Nimrod: A Life of Frederick Courteney Selous African Hunter and Adventurer 1851–1917.* London: Collins, 1989.

Teague, Michael. *Mrs. L: Conversations with Alice Roosevelt Longworth.* Garden City, NY: Doubleday & Company, 1981.

Tidrick, Kathryn. *Empire and the English Character.* London: I. B. Tauris, 1990.

Tilchin, William. *Theodore Roosevelt and the British Empire.* New York: St. Martin's Press, 1997.

Trevelyan, Laura. *A Very British Family: The Trevelyans and Their World.* London: I. B. Tauris, 2006.

Trzebinski, Errol. *The Kenya Pioneers.* New York: W. W. Norton & Co., 1985.

Twaddle, Michael. *Imperialism, the State and the Third World.* London: British Academic Press, 1992.

Warburg, Gabriel. *The Sudan under Wingate: Administration in the Anglo-Egyptian Sudan 1899–1916.* London: Frank Cass, 1971.

Wilson, John. *CB: A Life of Sir Henry Campbell-Bannerman.* New York: St Martin's Press, 1974.

Wilson, R. L. *Theodore Roosevelt Outdoorsman.* New York: Winchester Press, 1971.

Wimmel, Kenneth. *Theodore Roosevelt and the Great White Fleet: American Sea Power Comes of Age.* Washington, DC: Brassey's, 1998.

Articles and Book Chapters

Brooks, Sydney, "What Europe Thinks of Roosevelt," *McClures's Magazine* 35, 5 (July 1910).

Burton, David H., "Theodore Roosevelt and His English Correspondents: A Special Relationship of Friends," *Transactions of the American Philosophical Society*, New Series, Volume 63, Part 2 (Philadelphia, 1973).

Burroughs, John, "Theodore Roosevelt," *Natural History* 19, 1 (January 1919).

Carson, Gerald, "TR and the 'Nature Fakers,'" *American Heritage Magazine* 22, 2 (February 1971).

Dawson, Francis Warrington, "Hunting with Roosevelt in East Africa," *Hampton's Magazine* 23, 5 (November 1909).

Fiebig-von Hase, Ragnhild, "The Uses of 'Friendship': The 'Personal Regime' of Wilhelm II and Theodore Roosevelt, 1901–1909," in Annika Mombauer and Wilhelm Diest, eds., *The Kaiser: New Research on Wilhelm II's Role in Imperial Germany.* Cambridge: Cambridge University Press, 2003.

Johnston, Sir Harry, "The Roosevelts in Africa," *The Outlook*, December 17, 1910.

Miller, Char, "Keeper of His Conscience? Pinchot, Roosevelt, and the Politics of Conservation," in Natalie Naylor, Douglas Brinkley, John Allen Gable, eds., *Theodore Roosevelt: Many-Sided American.* Interlaken, NY: Heart of Lakes Publishing, 1992.

Prendergast, David K., "Colonial Wildlife Conservation and the Origins of the Society for the Preservation of the Wild Fauna of the Empire (1903–1914)," *Oryx* 37, 2 (April 2003).

Ricard, Serge, "The Anglo-German Intervention in Venezuela and Theodore Roosevelt's Ultimatum to the Kaiser: Taking a Fresh Look at an Old Enigma," in Serge Ricard and Hélène Cristol, eds., *Anglo-Saxonism in U.S. Foreign Policy: The Diplomacy of Imperialism, 1899–1919.* Aix-en-Provence: Publications de l'Université de Provence, 1991.

———, "Foreign Policy Making in the White House: Rooseveltian-Style Personal Diplomacy," in William Tilchin and Charles E. Neu, eds., *Artists of Power: Theodore Roosevelt, Woodrow Wilson and Their Enduring Impact on U.S. Foreign Policy.* London: Praeger, 2006.

Schullery, Paul, "Theodore Roosevelt: The Scandal of the Hunter as Nature Lover," in Natalie A. Naylor, Douglas Brinkley, and John Allen Gable, eds., *Theodore Roosevelt: Many-Sided American.* Interlaken, NY: Heart of Lakes Publishing, 1992.

Stewart, Kate, "Theodore Roosevelt: Hunter-Naturalist on Safari," *Quarterly Journal of the Library of Congress* 27, 3 (July 1970).

Testi, Arnaldo, "The Gender of Reform Politics: Theodore Roosevelt and the Culture of Masculinity," *The Journal of American History* 81, 4 (March 1995).

Wallace, David, "Sagamore Hill: An Interior History," in Natalie Naylor, Douglas Brinkley, John Allen Gable, eds., *Theodore Roosevelt: Many-Sided American.* Interlaken, NY: Heart of Lakes Publishing, 1992.

Youssuf, Sheikh Ali, "Egypt's Reply to Colonel Roosevelt," *North American Review* 191 (June 1910).

Index